Further Praise for T?

"A fantastic look at the past, present, and _____ .s experienced by a fun-loving Iranian surfer, a ꜰɪᴇʀᴄᴇʟʏ ᴘʀᴏᴜᴅ ꜱᴄʜᴏᴏʟᴛᴇᴀᴄʜᴇʀ in Watts, and dozens of others. . . . Theroux translates these viewpoints into a warm, moving portrait of the people we have been, are, and might become."
—Richard Foss, *LA Reader*

"He is the best sort of guide—smart, curious, and generous—and his observations are enormously sensible."   —Alan Ryan, *USA Today*

"Like a freeway-age update of Philip Marlowe, Raymond Chandler's private-eye-on-wheels, Theroux, in search of knowing, speeds across the endless highways of Los Angeles . . . . The search skillfully notates an unstable, tumultuous human geography that echoes the geological instability of the land itself."   —David Fine, *San Francisco Chronicle*

"Theroux's rendering has a sense of wet ink, of immediacy. His engagement with this fabulous city is warm, lively, and noninvasive. . . . Ultimately, he shows how, in the face of a city that can be unlivable, a rainbow of citizens can come together to create community."   —Sarah Sarai, *Seattle Times*

"From the surreal to the ridiculous, Peter Theroux is our witty and lucid guide to life in La-La Land."   —*Condé Nast Traveler*

"Theroux comports himself with humor, compassion, and yes, insight and irony. . . . A delightfully different point of view."
—Roger Bloom, *Orange County Register*

"Peter Theroux . . . cuts through the smog of banality to make *Translating LA* an apocalyptic tour, full of surreptitious insight."
—Nicholas Wollaston, *London Observer Review*

"[I]ntriguing and fresh. . . . Peter Theroux's book has come closer than any other I have read in discovering the true pulse of Los Angeles."
—Deborah Bosley, *London Literary Review*

"Theroux arrived in LA sometime in the mid-80's, and probably only an outsider like him could see and write so persuasively about Los Angeles as metaphor rather than sociology."   —Steve Erickson

TRANSLATING LA

A Tour of the Rainbow City

PETER THEROUX

W.W. NORTON & COMPANY

NEW YORK / LONDON

The text of this book is composed in Galliard
with the display set in Broadway and Charme.
Composition and manufacturing by the Haddon Craftsmen, Inc.
Book design by Jo Anne Metsch.

Library of Congress Cataloging-in-Publication Data
Theroux, Peter.
Translating LA : a tour of the Rainbow City / Peter Theroux.
        p.   cm.
1. Los Angeles (Calif.)—Tours.   I. Title.   II. Title:
Translating Los Angeles.
F869.L83T47   1994
917.94'940453—dc20   93-34682

ISBN 0-393-31394-8

1 2 3 4 5 6 7 8 9 0

For my parents,
Albert and Anne Theroux

Contents

Map appears on pages 14–15

In the spring of 1923 I believed that I was dying in Palestine. . . . In the black depths of misery, I climbed a hill overlooking Jerusalem. . . . As I looked out over the inhospitable mountains I remembered home in a way which given any other frame of mind would have astonished me. I solemnly cursed every moment I had spent wandering foolishly, and I swore that if I ever saw the Dover Cliffs again I would never leave them. I had by this time made myself too ill to realize that it is this rare stay-at-home sanity which justifies travel. . . . It was the only religious moment I experienced in Jerusalem.

—H. V. Morton, *In Search of England*

Preface

I moved to Los Angeles in 1985, after nearly a decade of living in the Middle East. The Massachusetts Miracle prevented me from resettling in the city of my birth, Boston: rents had doubled, and gentrification was rife, with even the old red-brick high school my brothers had attended converted into luxury condominiums ("The Schoolhouse at Medford"). I was used to hot weather, and the years abroad had erased—as they do for most people—most of my domestic regional prejudices, so I headed west, to LA.

For me, only a few short years in LA contradicted the storied vapidity of the place. This Tinseltown, this ethereally stupid lotus land, would brave the 1992 riots and the 1994 Northridge earthquake with unexampled courage and optimism. Suddenly there was a little of Stalingrad in the citizenry of the supposedly shallow city of broken dreams. Its military economy came apart along with the Berlin Wall. And yet people kept coming, despite the apocalypses.

At first glance, Los Angeles is such a splendid ethnic sprawl, and such a pretentious mess, that newcomers often compare it to the Third World—a sly insult that was immediately given the lie to me, after ten years in the Third World, by the simple fact that practically everyone was coming here instead of leaving. What I did have in common with many newcomers was my shock at the size of the place. I had been born and educated up to age twenty-one within a six-mile radius, unable to conceive of a city where you might easily drive forty miles for lunch. I had never even seen the kind of American city that flight attendants call an "area" ("We wish you a pleasant stay in the Los Angeles area")—metropolises that sprawled over the borders of dozens of cities or at least a couple of counties. "The Boston area" is a weather term, because snow, rain, and nor'easters do not respect city limits. "The Los Angeles area" is an admission that LA is made up of eighty-five cities, and that its most famous attractions—Beverly Hills, Disneyland, the studios where *The Wizard of Oz* and *Gone with the Wind* were made, and many of the beaches and mountains—lie outside its rather arbitrary boundaries.

In another sense, it really was a city. "Beirut," the Lebanese used to brag to me, "is a *village.*" They meant that their capital's population of a million people—or at least the few that counted—were on such cozy terms that everyone knew everyone else. "Cairo is a village," the Cairenes insisted—a far bolder piece of cynicism, suggesting the speed at which gossip traveled through the upper crust of Africa's greatest city, which with fourteen million inhabitants is no village. But the claim to be a village, even in party chatter, is actually a prideful statement of solidarity with one's home city, a rather affectionate scolding of a town that cannot keep a secret. Israel is no different. I had once traveled to Jerusalem from Tel Aviv to visit an author for a single day, and returned for dinner to find that not only my hosts but even some perfect strangers knew the outcome of my business there. I was amazed, but should have expected to be told, as I then was, "This country is a kibbutz!"

This is certainly not true of Los Angeles. It is vaster than the Sahara, a whole flat planet with a Venusian veil of smog. Ninety-two languages are spoken in its school system. It is not easy to know. Novels set there, no less than guidebooks, tend to concentrate on the entertainment industry, movie sites, and celebrity trivia. Very few LA books seem to have been unpremeditated—written by people who lived there never intending to write a book, or who eventually did so with no wish to promote the place or settle a score with it. LA books often seethe with tendentious exhibitions of adoration, bitchery, or gloating pessimism. At a certain point, I had lived in LA for exactly as long as I had lived in the Middle East. Each year of LA's dramatic new troubles, sociopathic and seismic—an endless round of Armageddon and Armageddon-outta-here—made me more determined to stay. At that point I decided to weigh in, not as an accidental tourist, but as something of an accidental resident.

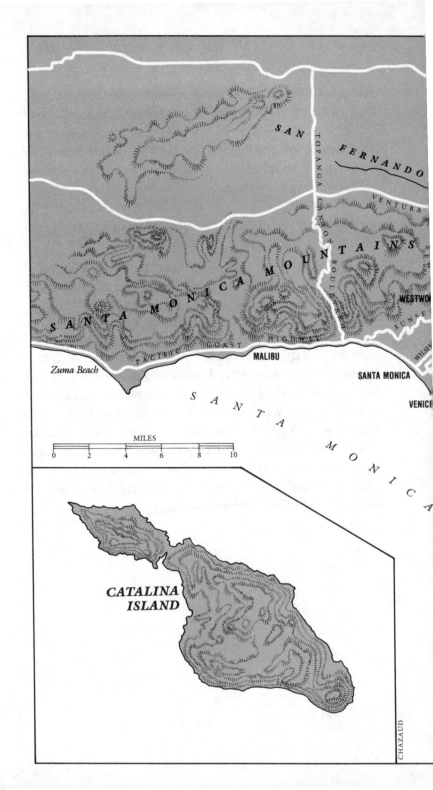

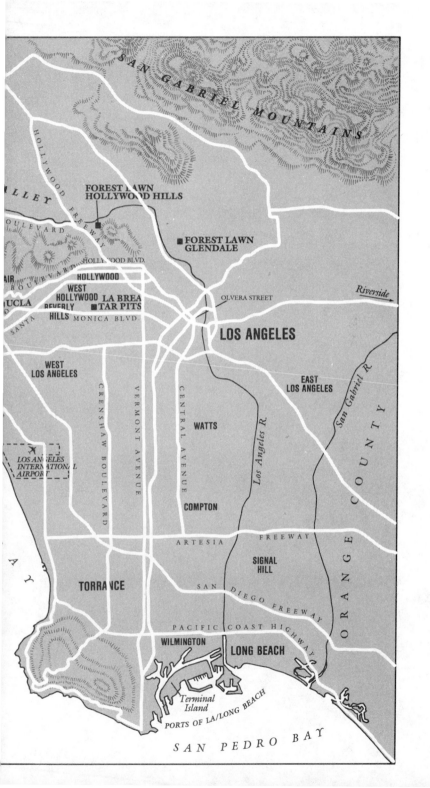

1

Seismic City

As the global capital of illusion, LA is naturally the capital of easy metaphors, too. It is Babylon and Dogpatch and Iowa-by-the-Sea, the boudoir of fantasy on the Boulevard of Broken Dreams and the rest of the mean streets, and the inspiration of quotes, like that of Raymond Dasman in *The Destruction of California*, who sought in vain "any good reason why the city of Los Angeles should have come into existence." Its glamour is coequal with its dark side, with the corpses of Marilyn Monroe and Judy Garland, the Hollywood blacklist, the banning of Chaplin, the Chinese Massacre, the Zoot Suit and Watts riots, and the Manson family. Its multiethnicity is legend—just as famous as the Hollywood sign are all the often-photographed variations of the strip mall sign that proclaims Kosher Enchiladas, Wong's Italian Subs, Saigon Hot Dogs, and three or four other vertical and right-to-left entries in Yiddish, Korean, Persian, all with a Buddhist monk reading *Buzz* in the background. The crossroads-of-the-world mini-mall with its Rosetta Stone signboard is LA's Statue of Liberty, proclaiming that nothing here is lost in translation.

What is less well known is the fact that the fossilized "ancient and modern side by side" cliché is actually yet another in which LA tops the world, beating Cairo, Beijing, and Rome. The proof is conveniently located at the intersection of Wilshire Boulevard and Curson Avenue, where an ancient tar pit, whose waterlogged surface is broken by intermittent methane bubbles, marks the site of the world's biggest mastodon graveyard, right in the shadow of the gleaming Benefit Mutual skyscraper. A life-size (twelve-foot-high) fiberglass family of imperial mammoths stands at the east end; one is pathetically entrapped in the lethal tar, the other two—one colossal, one calf-sized—stand on the bank. According to a nearby plaque, "The mother has become trapped; her mate and offspring watch helplessly." The baby mammoth's trunk is extended straight out as he trumpets his panic, like a cartoon elephant comically blowing its nose.

Of course, you have to have seen the orientation film in the Page Museum, in whose forecourt the tar pit simmers, to know why all the mammoths look so worried: their plight is an invitation for a saber-toothed tiger to attack. The tiger will go for the mother, whose bellowing will attract dire wolf packs, with both predators and prey getting stuck in the tar. Vultures and condors will circle, then swoop down on the feast, and get into a fight, trapping at least one of them, too, until they are all pulled under the gluey black surface and nothing is left of the scene but a few methane bubbles. Thousands of such incidents resulted in the fabulous skeleton deposits and the millions of bones, dyed molasses brown by their ten-thousand-year-long asphalt bath. They are assembled, behind velvet ropes, into truly horrifying saber-toothed tigers with nine-inch fangs, American mastodons with five-foot swerving tusks, cavernous eyeholes, and Bob Hope jaw-lines, and eerie Brea condors. There is a wall of 404 dire wolf skulls set like a symmetrical and rather sadistic modern art installation, on a lighted goldenrod background.

This was the thing I most wanted to see in LA—far more than Hollywood, to which I was a reluctant and belated visitor (it had always cost me a distinct effort to watch movies, even my favorite ones, because of the preset length and pacing, as opposed to reading books, which could be enjoyed anywhere and in any dose). When I finally realized my childhood dream of seeing the fiberglass prehistoric elephants, I had not lived in LA long enough to register the easy metaphor—extinct, two-ton beasts sinking into bituminous death while, twenty feet away, LA's main street was strangulated by two-ton hydrocarbon-fueled metal monsters. One instinctively reaches for a dinosaur metaphor, but all the bone museum's wall plaques remind you that while Los Angeles was the happy habitat of huge mastodon, mammoth, tiger, wolf, condor, and sloth populations forty thousand years ago, it was never a haunt for dinosaurs, not even 150 million years ago. To buck up extinction enthusiasts who have come expecting dinosaurs, the museum has provided a short dinosaur film presentation, an ancient timeline that thoughtfully includes dinosaur days, and there is a lavish gift shop selection of rubber brontosauruses and pterodactyls. These are far better made, actually, than the one-third-life-sized woolly mammoth, mechanized by Dinamation. His eyes click back and forth, he nods in jerks, he emits a roar that unfortunately sounds as if it were coming from a scratchy 78 behind a curtain.

This habitat, the Los Angeles Basin, was formed not only long ago, as it happens, but far away—the building blocks of the San Gabriel Mountains that hang over Los Angeles were actually formed south of the equator and migrated northward. A California Institute of Technology geologist, Leon Silver, once gave the *Los Angeles Times* an account of the chain that made them sound like true loose-footed Californians: "Since [1.7 million years ago], the San Gabriel Mountains have traveled all over the Southwest. We have evidence that they were as far north as Lake Tahoe and as far south as Mexico before reaching their present position north of Los Angeles."

The San Gabriels, he said, used to be one megarange that included the inland San Bernardino range to the northeast, until the San Andreas Fault split them apart five million years ago, heaving the San Gabriels west onto the Pacific plate. This is the plate that hugs the continent as it moves up, thumping along and causing earthquakes—it is not earthquakes that cause plate movements, but the other way around.

At least five dangerous fault lines cross the flat Los Angeles Basin: the Hollywood Fault under the Hollywood Hills north of Sunset Boulevard, the Santa Monica Fault along Santa Monica Boulevard, the Newport-Inglewood Fault running from Newport Beach into Westside Los Angeles, passing through Long Beach (much of which it demolished in 1933), and two new ones discovered only in 1992: the MacArthur Park Fault along Wilshire Boulevard, and the Echo Park Fault running from East LA west to the Hollywood Freeway. The potentially disruptive and murderous fault lines sound like common diseases, with their familiar but ominous place names; their activity tags yet more place-names with violent associations, darkening pleasant words like Redlands, Sylmar, Landers, and Whittier Narrows with the qualifier "quake." The old geology of Los Angeles is one of the inescapable facts of living there today, and it provides another easy metaphor for circumscribing the place. The long beaches, snowy mountains, canyons, rivers, and plains that compose LA's physical setting were formed by the violent convulsions of tectonic plates, toppling mountains, and treacherous slip-strike faults, like the San Andreas, that fine-tune the city's altitude. There is a temptation to look at the human geography of LA, with its rich history of Spanish domination, Yankee connivance, mob-led lynchings, black, Chicano, and white riots, and surging influxes of Asians, as a mirror of the tortured terrestrial evolution. It is easy to see how a demo-geologist might record the eructations of LA's ethnic history:

The Uto-Aztecan or Shoshonean plate was struck and largely submerged by the Impero-Hispanic plate in 1786, which pushed up Catholic fault blocks through the pacifist thrust-faults of the Uto-Aztecan plate. The migrating Yankee plate created strains in the rock whose compressional force pushed up slabs of Iowa granite, eventually resulting in Los Angeles' first Protestant church service in 1850, which in turn jolted the deep Padre Serra Fault. Well into the twentieth century, faraway geotectonic temblors continued to shape the varied structure of the area, notably the Indochinese Cataclysm, the long-dormant but recently active Latino Fault aggravated by the northward movement of the Guatemalo-Salvadoro-Nicaraguan seismic web, and the Khomeini earthquake in Southwest Asia, which spewed plumes of Iranians over the Transverse Range into the San Fernando Valley. So far the Polynesian-Filipino Fault, one of the largest but longest-dormant earthquake faults, has failed to budge, unlike the

Afro-Confederate Fault, whose violent eruptions have dramatically altered the formerly agrarian flatland of South Central Los Angeles.

Without the shifting and thrusting movements of turbulent human masses, and its coastline, Los Angeles would undoubtedly look exactly like its geologic twin neighbor to the north, Death Valley. Actually, its first demographic rumbling began in Asia, with the movement of some clearly very fit Mongolians over the Bering Strait land bridge—this was when the last ice age had frozen up enough precipitation for the water to recede and the bridge to emerge. Thirty thousand years ago, the glaciers ebbed enough for the new North Americans in 6000 B.C. to follow their plentiful animal prey south, and the result, in part, was the founding of villages like Cahuenga, Puvunga, and Yangna in the mountains and basin of LA. The suffix *nga* or *na* meant town or settlement—to the ancients, these were Cahuetown, Puvu Acres, and Yangville.

The Shoshone inhabitants, later named Gabrielinos after the local Spanish mission of San Gabriel, seem to have been the Amish of the native Americans—they did not make war, blankets, or cooking pots; they did not engage in human sacrifices or build pyramids or canals. They ate acorns, berries, fish, and insects, and worshiped a lawgiver god, Chinigchinich, who was born at Puvunga in present-day Long Beach. (In fact, a controversy erupted in 1993 when California State University at Long Beach wanted to build a parking lot on empty land bordering Bellflower Boulevard, because a wooden sign marked, somewhere on the twenty-two acres, Chinigchinich's actual birthplace—making Long Beach not only LA's Brooklyn but its Bethlehem.)

"No doubt these Indians passed a miserable life, ever idle, and more like the brutes, than rational beings," wrote Geronimo Boscana, a Franciscan missionary, of the southern California Indians. "The women were obliged to gather seeds in the fields, prepare them for cooking, and to perform all the meanest offices, as well as the most laborous . . . their lazy husband either at play or sleeping." (The series of missions that the Franciscans eventually established converted the Indians to Christianity and introduced some degree of labor equality, with Indians of both sexes performing the meanest and most "laborous" jobs.) It was all a far cry from the romantic Spanish vision that had given California its name. An imaginative thriller by García Rodríguez Ordóñez de Montalvo, entitled *Las sergas de Esplandian,* published in Madrid in 1510, extolled an all-woman paradise "on the right hand of the Indies."

> . . . there is an island called California, very near the Terrestrial Paradise and inhabited by black women . . . living in the manner of the Amazons. They are robust of body, strong and passionate in heart, and of great valor. . . . Their arms are all of gold. . . . They live in well-excavated caves. They have ships in which they go to raid other places, and the men they capture they carry off with them, later to be killed as will be told. At other times, being at peace with their opponents, they consort with them freely and have carnal relations.

Ur-LA's innocence ended on October 8, 1542, when Portuguese explorer Juan Rodríguez Cabrillo entered either Santa Monica or San Pedro Bay, flying the Spanish flag on two ships. He immediately took note of the smog, probably a mixture of campfires and ocean fog, in christening his discovery Bahía de los Fumos, or Bay of Smokes—even Renaissance LA had an inversion layer. Only 227 years later did Gaspar de Portola, the Spanish governor of the Californias, arrive and name the Shoshoneans' river—*not* their city—after Our Lady the Queen of Angels. The name was later shortened from El Río de Nuestra Señora de los Angeles del Río Porciuncula to the Porciuncula River. The cumbersome name was due to the feast day of September 3, which in the Catholic calendar is dedicated to the Madonna of the chapel in which St. Francis of Assisi had prayed five hundred years before. Still later the waterway became simply the Los Angeles River.

The formal founding of El Pueblo de la Reina de los Angeles took place the next day, on September 4, 1781, when forty-four African, Spanish, and mixed-blood newcomers— mostly the dependents of eleven adult settlers—took up residence. It was during this same month that, back in Virginia, Generals Washington and Rochambeau arrived at Williamsburg to plan the siege of the British army that would end British imperial rule on the East Coast one year later. The West Coast of America was still part of the Spanish Empire, however, and the first families of Los Angeles were there as the designated settlers of the Spanish governor, Felipe de Neve. The queenly pueblo measured only twenty-eight square miles, and a century later would have grown by only one more square mile.

Spain lost Los Angeles in 1821: the town became part of the short-lived Mexican Empire when General Agustín Iturbide made Mexico independent and proclaimed himself Emperor Agustín I in that year. The republic was declared in 1823, but the design of the flag run up the pole in the downtown plaza had little effect on the way life proceeded in Los Angeles. The decentralized mosaic of enormous cattle ranches was run by a ruling class of prosperous *californios*, into which ambitious New England pioneer men married, having first converted to Catholicism. Officially, LA was the capital of the Mexican state of Alta California, having been designated a city, up from *pueblo*, in 1835, but its population was increasingly English-speaking. These new arrivals were the despair of the Mexican governor, Pío Pico, who in 1846 voiced much the same misgivings that must have run through the heads of the natives of Yangna when the Spanish arrived: the strangers were "cultivating farms, establishing vineyards, sawing up lumber, building workshops, and doing a thousand things which seem natural to them, but which Californians neglect or despise. . . . Shall these incursions go unchecked, until we shall become strangers in our own land?"

That most Angeleno of questions was answered two years later, when Alta California was severed from Baja California and the rest of Mexico by America's Mexican War. Mexico's cession of its territories north of the Rio Grande coincided with the discovery of gold in northern California (the state motto is, of course, "Eureka"), which would quickly enrich and populate all the city's commercial centers.

Los Angeles would always be a mad mosaic. According to the county census of 1850—the year Los Angeles was incorporated as an American city—half of the immense county's 8,300 residents were Indians. The city of LA, a landlocked town amid dozens of sprawling ranches, had a population of 3,530, of whom 512 men and women had originated in twenty-nine states (at the time there were thirty-one American states); 699 came from twenty-eight different countries. Immigrants came in response to gold or land rushes, silk, wool, and cattle booms, to escape from the law or from foreign powers. The population of Chinese laborers, Mexican and Indian natives, whites, and blacks was ruthless, profit-seeking, and dangerous. The city was famous for its bull-fights, brothels, gambling, and rough bars. There was a murder every night in the 1870s, moving the more God-fearing Angelenos to put their faith in vigilantism, lynching, horse-whipping, and flight to the suburbs. LA was always mobile and multiethnic, always triumphantly violent, never a gorgeous mosaic. Justice was "not blind but cockeyed," as one new Angeleno wrote in the 1830s, with everyone "bristly, all edge and challenge." The only good old days to look back upon were those before the place existed.

Beautiful weather and the orange, the most photogenic of fruits, came to rescue the murderous Yankee boom town of the mid-1800s. The juicy, thick-skinned Washington navel orange—so called though it was bred in Bahia, Brazil—turned out to be perfect for the southern California climate. They were first sent to the East Coast and Europe in 1877. Exotic as mangoes in the beginning, they found enthusiastic markets, and by 1893 the California orange cooperatives united as Sunkist. Of course, the mass movement of oranges east started an equal and opposite migration west, as citrus appeal brought millions of settlers west. Huge chromographs in Eastern general stores portrayed oranges being fondled by beauty queens, grasped by delighted babies, and brandished by proud Uncle Sams; they were depicted peeking lushly through their dark green foliage, basking in sunshine, and as dazzling rising suns whose orange beams illuminated the plains.

"California for Wealth—Oranges for Health" was one motto that speeded up the shipment of oranges east and East-erners west. Pomona, Pasadena, Uplands, and other towns surrounding Los Angeles became wall-to-wall orange groves;

Riverside was so rapidly populated by settlers from the Northeast that its whole street plan was based on Philadelphia's. In the four to five years that it took orange trees to get started, growers cultivated beans as a cash crop. In addition to the new wave of Yankees, there were waves of Chinese and Japanese fruit pickers around the turn of the century; in the 1920s, Mexicans took over the harvesting jobs, when the Asians moved on to gardening and small retail businesses. Even the orange boom would not last, though. There had always been tension between growers and their poorly paid workers, and in 1936 a pickers' strike was violently suppressed in Orange County, where the police were given shoot-to-kill orders. In the 1940s, a million war workers came to Los Angeles County, and millions of acres of orange groves were leveled to make way for the factories and houses they needed. By 1990, there was not a single orange grove left in Orange County, and a local philanthropist was trying to raise money for a little orange grove to be planted as a shrine for visiting schoolchildren.

The Los Angeles economy rested heavily on defense and entertainment industries instead, though modern times have leached much of both to other states and countries. The high cost of maintaining the sunny but unnatural habitat, the groaning tectonics of accommodating rich and poor, new religions and nationalities, and the fact that the magic of film worked everywhere, not just in Hollywood, sent many golden opportunities elsewhere. It is not inconceivable that the future will bring yellow school buses pulling up outside a miniature Stealth bomber plant to showcase the city's glorious aerospace past. You could speculate on possible field trips to other remnants of LA's venerable history—ranches, Catholic missions, movie studios—if they did not already exist at the Paramount ranch, San Gabriel Mission, and Universal Studios.

LA's shrines do tend to blend the past and the present in such a way as to obliterate the past. Even the sunshine that bathes the fiberglass mastodons in their tar bath is a reminder of the amnesiac, of the pleasant present—the moment is just too overwhelmingly enjoyable in southern California. You hang on to it. This is no easy metaphor—the proof is there. Even the city's great institutions are named after *living* people—the airport's Tom Bradley International Terminal, the Maxine Waters Employment Preparation Center, the Annenberg School of Communications at USC.

Four miles from the heart of the old pueblo of Los Angeles, shoving children are tempted away from the towering mastodon skeletons by a wall where they crowd around the earliest Angeleno whose cause of death is known. The La Brea Woman is also the first to provide historians with a cynical metaphor. Her nine-thousand-year-old remains, adorned with a shell necklace, are the only human bones of the tar-pit era to survive. The skeleton is displayed in a dark and deeply recessed glass case and clothed, every few seconds, with hologrammatic flesh, hair, and loincloth. Her skull was bashed in with a blunt object; this first Angeleno, the wall label tells you, was also LA's first known homicide victim.

1

Translating, LA

Newcomers generally have much better luck than tourists at seeing the best places right away, and it is often by the kind of luck that comes from having free time and local friends. As you settle in and get a job, you have less access to both of these. I had no job yet except for casual translating, which was one reason I was cruising through one of Los Angeles' more scenic canyon roads.

Topanga Canyon Boulevard is one of the byways people move to LA for. Even its name suggests both wilderness and urban sprawl—the city's canyons are steep and overgrown, and its boulevards are like parking lots, half auto museum and half drag race. Topanga Canyon Boulevard is in part a six-lane expressway running south through the San Fernando Valley to the ocean. Through the communities of Chatsworth and Canoga Park, it is flat, bordered by shopping malls and tightly enclosed in the dead, shimmering air of the Valley, which is locked in by mountains on all sides, and sealed on top by the inversion layer of cool air. At Woodland Hills, the boulevard exhibits an inanely beautiful change of temperament, becoming a mountain road weaving toward Malibu, whose Pacific breeze you can almost smell. In an instant you have gone from the most anonymous suburban nonplace to what could be West Virginia, all the time very much within the city limits of Los Angeles. It sometimes seems that LA's flat, congested intersections, streets, parking lots, and general dead paved space serve as the spatial equivalents of the Styrofoam peanuts that protect packed valuables—inside which lurk the stupendous mountains and beaches that could not survive without insulation.

"You have plenty of deer and rattlesnakes up in there," said Daryush. "And more rattlesnakes than deer." He straightened his aviator sunglasses.

We were on our way to a conference of translators in Malibu. I translated Arabic. Daryush lived in Van Nuys; he was an Iranian Jew who had come to Los Angeles via Israel, and did Persian and Hebrew court interpreting. We were carpooling, because Daryush, who, like much of the Iranian community, had been in LA since the 1970s, pointed out to me that if every commuter in LA drive-shared just once a week, air pollution could be cut by 20 percent. So I had picked him up in the Valley, and now we were weaving south through the Santa Monica Mountains to attend "Mosaics: Cross-Cultural Aspects of Translating in Los Angeles." It was being held at a private house on Pacific Coast Highway, only a few miles south of Zuma Beach. Always the practical LA native, and a passionate surfer, Daryush insisted that we bring bathing trunks and towels in case it turned out to be boring. After all, we were going to be just two miles from Zuma, and should head there afterward anyway. He had packed a snack of fresh Persian bread, pickled turnips, raw onions and radishes, a watermelon, and a bag of lemons. "The lemons are for meeting girls," he explained. "You'll see."

I had forsaken a journalistic career in the Arab world a few months before and was now living tentatively in LA; not sure I would stay, I had begun translating for a living, and had become friendly with other translators, mostly from the Middle East. The Malibu get-together was a regional meeting of a national translators' association I had joined, and I was curious to see what a roomful of LA translators would look like—a conclave of surfers? I had begun doing adult literacy tutoring, too. I had made the usual vow of new Angelenos to learn Spanish—even on noncable television there were three Spanish channels—but so far had failed. Daryush already spoke good Spanish.

"Look at the street names," he said as the car climbed from the Valley up into the enfolding green hills. "Even up here they have Spanish names. Look. De La Guerra. De La Luz."

Topanga Canyon Boulevard was lined with seventy-foot eucalyptus trees, poplars, willows, and cypresses. As the car wound through the hills, following the switchbacks, we could peek through the trees at the hairpin turns to see the valley floor, already far below. Daryush pointed out the shining black glass bank towers, shopping malls, and expanses of tract housing; his brother worked in an upscale hair salon to the south, in Woodland Hills. To the north lay Hidden Hills, which, appropriately enough, was not visible.

There was nothing in sight but more towering, scrubby green slopes undulating around the road, which curved so lavishly that sometimes a new wall of green loomed beyond the closer hills and I wondered whether we were going the right way—whether that was another mountain range, or we were heading back the way we had come. There were few landmarks—scattered clapboard businesses, countrified with sloping roofs and wooden porches. Some sold health food, crystals, gardening equipment, or videocassettes.

"Deep Canyon Video Rental," read Daryush. "Canyon Car Care. So many old trucks. The trash cans are old. They are not good consumers in the canyons."

That seemed true. There were old pickups with rolled hoods and chrome grilles loaded with sacks of feed or bicycles for rent. We shot past a rusted old railway car poised over a narrow gully off the road, apparently being used as a covered footbridge between the canyon road and a one-story house obscured by jacaranda trees. And this just a mile or two from LA's shopping malls.

I had already noticed that LA had no center of gravity, where you stood and knew that you were at the heart of the city. Downtown LA, visible from almost anywhere, was both overbuilt and empty, designed to be unfriendly—the bus benches were shaped like logs so that homeless people could not recline on them. There was no equivalent of the Mall in Washington or Central Park in New York. This meant that every spot in LA was almost equal—the center was wherever you were.

The shape and size of the place bewilders first-timers. Only a few weeks previous, I had done an interpreting assignment, escorting a group of visiting Egyptians and Palestinians. They were staying at a Holiday Inn near Los Angeles International Airport, and no matter which of LA's dozens of Holiday Inns we passed, most of them called out, "Our hotel!" Was it possible that, with the dizzying array of beaches, freeways, and tall buildings, they thought LA's time and space could be pulled inside out like a sock, putting us back where we had started? Or perhaps they thought that by some miracle the city's five hundred square miles were mostly contained in a few kaleidoscopic, eye-fooling blocks. I explained that Holiday Inn was in reality a very popular chain of hotels, but not before getting a glimpse of the sort of otherworldly expectations that even the most sophisticated visitors have of LA. There were actually more pedestrians in this isolated canyon than there had been on the residential boulevard below. Most were long-haired men, and women in peasant dresses. An ocean breeze had already begun to work its way through the mountain passes as we swerved by Topanga Creek.

"This strikes me as a very pleasant city for exile," I remarked. I did not want to add to this obvious understatement the equally obvious implication that it was especially so compared to his homeland, which at the time was at war. LA's exiles tended to be young and comfortable. Their image, as I had perceived it among those left behind in the Middle East, was of lounging by poolside and cursing their luck. The reality was that they generally became productive Angelenos who slowly became incapable of living anywhere else, least of all in their homelands.

Most of Daryush's family lived right over the hill from him, in Beverly Hills. And he had no intention of going back to Iran or to Israel, which he had enjoyed only for as long as was necessary for him to acquire citizenship. He talked Israeli politics, supported the Labor Party, and regularly read the local newspaper *Israel Shelanu* ("Our Israel"), but dismissed the Jewish state as "Little Liberia—a Liberia that works. So far." Besides, the surfing was better here. It seemed incongruous to me, since I thought of all surfers as blond, but Daryush said all you needed was upper-body strength and a love for the ocean and solitude.

Now we were rolling downhill into a vast pillow of cool

ocean air as the canyon unwound behind us. I almost hated to get to the end. This was the kind of countrified drive that was the perfect mixture of machine and nature—the unfolding view of mountainsides carpeted with chaparral and heather, and the sheer joy of handling the road's tight curves. I had the thought that Los Angeles is probably the world's most beautiful city for driving.

Eventually, with a few final twists and turns, the canyon road ends, like a roller coaster having its last fun with you before you roll to a stop, and we swooped down to the end of the road and an aqua horizon. The white wooden arrow at Pacific Coast Highway pointed north and said *Malibu 7*.

Sometimes it is easy to think that LA is surrounded by water, because the city seems so physically oriented toward its open horizons, to the west and south. The whole city, draped over the curved Santa Monica mountain range and the long flat basin up to the ocean's edge, has been compared to an amphitheater, and faces 270 degrees of water; the drama must be playing halfway around the world. Even the Europeans discovered it from its western shores and not from the east across the continent.

Daryush was enjoying the ocean view and the almost startling explosion of the surf on the wide beaches, but I was enthralled by the traffic. We were still in Los Angeles; even Malibu was just a city neighborhood, though a few years later it would secede to become a city in its own right. Los Angeles was always criticized for its inadequate public transportation, but the very thought seemed ludicrous on this little two-lane highway. Not only because of the staggering breadth and width and variety of LA, but because despite the flat endless valley floor and the basin over the hills, this was no city like any other, with streets, stoplights, and some sense of relative compactness.

Even the cars gave me pause. A sort of eternal present is suggested by the cars Angelenos drive—they seem forgotten by time. Not only do people garage and maintain their cars, the climate is extremely forgiving. Cars live longer, without rust or salt stains. My small car was briskly passed by 1953 Chevies, 1961 Thunderbirds, and early Mustangs that all looked right out of the box, and they were not being driven by haughty collectors, but by little old women wearing barrettes and teenage boys wearing baseball hats backward.

In a city people love to interpret through clichés, the biggest one of all is that you can get around only by car. In part it was true, because of the odd shape and topography, and lack of comprehensive and frequent public transportation. Only rarely do LA's observers seem to consider the corollary: that you need to learn to drive, to maintain a car, and to read. Of all the cities I have lived in, Los Angeles demands the most skills. My first literacy students all needed to improve their reading or their English for automotive reasons. LA is short on taxis, buslines, and landmarks—or, with its chain hotels, has dozens of duplicates, and so has high expectations of its guests. As a result, its natives are not mellow airheads, but strivers.

The downside to all the driving is the mode of interruption that cars add to life in LA—I already knew that. It made the city lack impulsiveness. Distances were long, you had to make sure you had gas, there were the unpredictable traffic factors, and then you had to find a parking space and probably pay for it. It was like being a nicotine addict, making sure that you always had cigarettes and matches and were not far from an ashtray. This was, I guessed, the difference at the root of all the differences between LA and other cities. Perhaps the seriousness with which Angelenos took their cars was what made the driving so good. I seemed to notice a Zen of driving:

smooth merging, safe passing, full and complete stops at red lights. LA people groaned about the terrible driving, especially on the freeways, but I saw more courtesy displayed in a single day in California than I had seen in months anywhere else.

We passed a half-dozen blond teenage girls in very short print dresses and cowboy boots walking by the side of the road.

"I hope the conference is dull. Look at those blondes," said Daryush. We had reached the open stretch of Pacific Coast Highway where bathers parked for free along the ocean side of the road and walked down to the beach. Most other beaches had signs for paid parking.

"I thought you were dating someone. A blonde from Glendale."

"The Armenians get all the girls," said Daryush, and added, "There's Betty Sue's place," pointing to one of a row of garages set along Pacific Coast Highway.

"The first segment of our symposium will be a discussion of how tax law applies to translation agencies and self-employed translators and interpreters," announced Betty Sue Najafabadi, our hostess. "Then we'll have a short break. Feel free to have coffee and doughnuts then, before we move on to our very exciting intercultural insight orientation from our wonderful guest speaker, Fred Upledger, because we know that many of you are new to the Los Angeles area."

That was putting it mildly—many were not citizens, and almost none of us were within a generation even of being Americans. She herself was one of the few Angelenos. In the brief registration session inside the door of this near-beach-front mansion, I had noticed that people were speaking all the languages one might have expected from a room full of translators: Spanish, Persian, French, Japanese, Chinese. There were many native speakers. On top of that, there were the marriages that had given so many of the group exotic names, like Betty Sue's—there was also Marie-France Scoggins, Ermenigilda Fong, and Guadalupe Nykvist.

The house stood on a slight elevation over the famous beach. We could clearly see the sun on the ocean from the rows of folding chairs facing Betty Sue's hostess table with its tape deck. All that stood between the sands and this huge living room, with its massive slate fireplace and Southwest look—bunches of dried red peppers, wooden rattlesnake art, beige and terra-cotta surfaces, potted cactuses, and oversize white furniture—was a row of large but undistinguished beach houses built directly on the sand. I was standing on the flagstone terrace near the Jacuzzi, puzzling over the strange zoning that allowed these poor beachdwellers to build there, when I noticed Betty Sue pointing some of the beach houses out to another guest.

"That's Bill Cosby's place. That's Linda Ronstadt's. Martin Sheen. Way up there is Malibu Colony—that's where Cher and John McEnroe live. Not together, I mean. Peter! You'll love Fred. He's another Bodhi Tree person."

Betty Sue had steered me to the Bodhi Tree—"Books to Illuminate the Heart and Mind"—to find a Koranic concordance in Arabic I needed, and now it somewhat whetted my interest in hearing Fred. I had thought of LA as a beach city, but this bookstore in West Hollywood was a whiff of the Himalayas. You could hear its steel and copper wind chimes half a block away, and once inside it exhaled an olfactory cocktail of barky incense smells: frankincense, jasmine, sandalwood, cedar, cinnamon, patchouli. I was sure I had the wrong place—this was the head shop of the stars. There was a display of divining rods. The wall above the cash register was adorned with a row of photos of swamis and yogis, including a plump and smiling sepia yogi with flowing black hair who looked especially familiar. He was labeled Paramahansa Yogananda, and he looked familiar to me, I realized, because his enormous book *Autobiography of a Yogi*, whose cover was adorned with his photograph, had been a paperback cult favorite when I was in college in the late 1970s.

Knowing that the Bodhi Tree was Shirley MacLaine's favorite bookstore should have prepared me for the elaborate wooden labyrinth of rooms equipped with benches where adults might scan the works of Sri Aurobindo, Baba Hari Dass, and Madame Blavatsky, or children might skim *The Lovables in the Kingdom of Self-Esteem* or selections from the one of the largest collections of fairy tales, traditional and Third World (*Jahangir and the Kukri*), I had ever seen. The adults' myths-and-legends section, though, was even bigger, and centered very heavily on the English tradition: there were dozens of books on legendary Britain, King Arthur, Merlin (*See also* Merlyn), Guinevere, Gawain, the Grail, and the land of Avalon, with related sections on the Rosicrucians and Freemasonry. I only had to turn halfway around from the mists of Camelot to reach for books on Hassids, the Gnostics, Quaker/Amish subjects, Feminist Witchcraft, Voodoo, and Self-Enfoldment (a system of "inner perceptions," not yoga positions).

Customers sat on the benches raptly reading *The Diamond Sutra* and *That Which You Are Seeking Is Causing You to Seek*, herbals, and magazines like the New Age *Shaman's Drum*, *Longevity*, and *Alternative Medicine*. The newsrack was largely dedicated to living longer through exotic herbs, cures, and exercises, and the theme was carried on in the adjacent room, where the Hemlock Society section (*Dying with Dignity, A Graceful Passage, Final Exit*) was opposite the one on reincarnation.

"Would you mind scooting over just a bit? Or maybe just hand me that *Astrology of Wealth*? Oh, I thank you!" a short woman wearing noisy nail jewelry said to me pleasantly. All the browsers were smiling and elaborately polite. Several seemed to be strangers recommending books to one another. More LA politeness—was it the sun? I was used to climates where the heat made people slow and rude; here, it made people mellow—a word that just around that time was falling into disfavor as too brainless.

Waylaid by crystals and astrological software, Ayervedic mud baths, I Ching coin pouches, tarot cards, UFO books, zafus (pillows) and zabutons (meditation mats), I finally found the Koranic concordance I needed, in an Islamic section unsurprisingly dominated by Sufi texts. There were a fair number of good books, though, both history and literature, in many of the sections—one young man leaving as I left had a sheaf of fliers on Reichian Therapy, Feet Awareness, and Private Sessions with Wanda, tucked into his just-purchased copy of *Anna Karenina*.

I did wonder what Fred's presentation would be like. I asked him where he was from.

"Brooklyn!" he said as if I should have known all along, and immediately added that he avoided fellow New Yorkers in LA. All they did was complain about La-La Land and the mindless entertainment industry. "And they spend their time writing television scripts that would do very little to improve anything. These campy things, you know? They write a sitcom script and brag about how bad it is, and just laugh. They want it to get sold, and if it doesn't they just hate LA more, but it's themselves they hate. I know that, as an informationologist. And kvetching about not being able to get thin-crust pizza! Now, you sound like a New Yorker, too."

"You've been out of Brooklyn too long," I said, but he cut me off before I could say any more.

"Do you know what the least-sought-after airline routes in America are, among cabin attendants?" Fred asked. I shook my head. "The routes between LA and New York! My steward friend told me that people who travel between New York and LA are 'the scum of the earth'! I strongly believe that going back to New York, even for visits, is what prevents New Yorkers here from finding their energy."

"Time to sit down!" said Betty Sue.

The tax man, from Beverly Hills, looked princely in a charcoal-gray silk suit and open white shirt, but the most ironic thing was the glamour of his address, on Doheny Drive, combined with this Malibu meeting place. None of us earned very much—there was a saying that in order to survive, translators had to work at a second job or be independently wealthy. Betty Sue's husband was a rich real estate developer, so she was giving us a welcome glimpse into a better-upholstered world.

"The group is mostly women," I commented to Veronique Lamy during the break following the tax adviser's explanation of what constituted an independent contractor.

"The answer is money, my dear," she cackled in her husky cigarette voice. She did translating and subtitling for French movies, and had told me that she was one of "the clique of California's biggest fans—European women." She shrugged. "Men have always been able to make better money. The old way was the translators were clerical, not professionals. Something for ladies to do—secretaries and housewives. Welcome to the club, my dear."

"Let's go, people," said Fred, and clapped his hands. He turned around to slip a cassette into the tape deck on the table and turned back as we started to gather and sit down. I recognized the opening bars of Bob Marley's "I Shot the Sheriff."

"Up-up-up-up! Don't sit down. I want to start by getting you moving. I want to get you touching. Let it out. Come on. I want everybody up." He clapped his hands in time to the music and began to shimmy his shoulders and dance from side to side, with perfect unself-consciousness. Slowly, some of the translators, many of whom were very old and frail, most of whom were at least clapping, but all of whom were deeply mortified, began to sway, and almost as quickly sat down again. I sat near the front; Daryush was back by the coffee.

"I've got to wake you up after that tax man," he said, and I saw Betty Sue frown, because the tax man had been friendly and interesting, and had not made us dance. "And work off those doughnuts!"

"I'm awake!" said Veronique in a tone of voice that implied "enough already."

"First, some introductions. I'm a refugee from New York," said Fred earnestly. "I'm a real new kid on the block here, but I love it. There's lots of energy. I live in Venice—I love the energy down there. I love the crystals for sale, the madness, the let-it-all-hang-out mind-set. Every skateboarder is important to LA; I truly believe that. There is something very Third World about this place, very connected, very attuned to its surroundings—very LA. I just might be here to stay. But I'm not here to talk about myself, but about you, and your clients. How to interact, how to work interculturally, as befits good Angelenos. And I believe in never underestimating Angelenos!"

He locked his hands behind his back and squinted down the room.

"Who are we? Are we the work that we do? Which way does LA face? I'm a corporate adviser on diversity—I assist intercultural insight and oversight. Am I more than that? You are translators. You deal with intercultural communications every day. Am I on thin ice? You guys speak in tongues, and hey—I hardly get along in English! But do you know what it feels like to be blind to another culture? Do you? To be dominated or exploited by another culture? Are you the messenger or are you the message? The medium or the message? You are not a telephone—you are cultural mediators. You are part of the message. I mentioned cultural domination. That's a problem. Are you part of that, too? We're going to play a game."

He strode among the folding chairs and stood still, his eyes closed.

"I want you to write down a number. A percentage. The percentage of drug addicts in the United States who are white. Just write it down fast. Guess. Make me a guess."

Everyone dutifully wrote down a number. Fred strode back toward the table with the tape player and turned to face us again.

"Let me hear some of your guesses."

"Are Persians counted as white?" called Daryush.

"Uh, no. No—yes. No," Fred answered.

"Seventy-five percent," guessed Daryush.

"Eighty percent," insisted Tillie Albright.

Others called out guesses of between 50 and 85 percent. Fred nodded slowly and crossed his arms.

"Well, you're an exceptional group, because most people guess lower than that. I've heard ten and fifteen percent, and that's from some of LA's top corporate personalities. Eighty percent happens to be the right answer. And yet why does most of America persist in perceiving most drug addicts as black?"

"Parlor use of drugs does not make the news, but the street-level violence of drug dealing does," suggested Wendy Krantz, a court interpreter for Spanish. "The black gangs, as well as Hispanic gangs, are visible because of violent drug crime, especially in Los Angeles."

"Also, because there are few public cultural expressions of drug use among the white people?" Guadalupe Nykvist guessed. "Middle-class drug use is clandestine, but gangster-rap music, which is a Hispanic but mostly black genre, glorifies both drugs and the associated gang violence. That is actually promoted and marketed."

"Marketed by whom?" Fred crooked an eyebrow. He may have meant his previous question to be rhetorical. "These are some of the things we need to think about. I mean, I don't think too many record companies are owned by blacks."

"I thought we were talking about drugs," said Wendy. "Though I don't remember why."

"We are talking about perceptions—about appearance versus reality," Fred pointed out. "For example, about how you treat people. Let's look at this. How are we supposed to treat others? How did our mothers tell us to treat others?"

"The way you want to be treated. I mean, the way one wants to be treated himself. One is supposed to treat others in the manner in which oneself wishes to be treated," offered Gaon Shabazi.

"*Three* wrong answers," marveled Fred, as if impressed. "I

mean, that is what our mothers said, but Mother wasn't on the money, was she?"

"What others?" I asked. "Our customers? Our coworkers? The next-door neighbors?"

"Your employees and coworkers. We are being a teensy bit corporate at the moment. Pretend you have a large and diverse workforce. Pretend that you are Northrop or the Bank of America. And remember that the slow poison of prejudice at work in every American body," he intoned, "begins with thinking everyone is like *me*. Everyone should be treated like *me*. Others wants to be done unto the way *I* want to be done unto. This is our egoistic culture. I am going to ask you again, and this time I want you to think before answering. Tap into those beautiful LA minds of yours. How must we treat others?"

The beautiful LA minds were locked inside puzzled faces of various ages and hues, until the performer in Fred came alive again. He scratched his head bewilderedly and appeared to be getting the glimmer of a brainstorm.

"Could it be—do you think—could it *just possibly be* that we should treat others the way they *want* to be treated? How about that, people?"

The longish silence was broken by the gay laughter of Tillie Albright, a Dutch-to-English translator with a small agency who blithely violated Association rules by pitting translator against translator when a non-Dutch job came her way ("Peter, I can get this done for twelve cents a word, with no rush surcharge, by a mutual friend. Now, do you want bread on your table or not?").

"You are very young, my dear!" She actually shook her finger at him gently. "Do you know how people want to be treated? Like kings and queens, if you please! Believe me, translators would love to be treated as if the words 'hard work' and 'discipline' were not in their dictionaries. Treat me as I wish to be treated? Lots of coffee breaks, and martinis at lunch! A little discreet harassment from the right person will not be a problem! Even some dancing!"

"We will come back to this point when we get to our role playing," Fred announced, to cut off the laughter she had set off by winking at him.

Two or three hands were raised, but he motioned a change of subject.

"Let's look beyond our borders—in LA that's easy! We have all the nationalities of the world here. I have visited Iran," he suddenly boasted. "You probably don't think a sane person would go there! But I am a very culturally curious person. The Islamic Republic! That evil ayatollah! I want you all to take a piece of paper and write down the first word that comes to mind. The *first* word. This is a little free-association game. Just write it down as soon as I say my word. My word is 'Iran.' Okay—go."

He put his hands on his hips and gazed out at the jade-green horizon for a moment before turning back to us. He quickly wrote *Media Messages* in red marker on the white board. He snapped his fingers and pointed at Guadalupe, then opened his hand interrogatively.

" 'Patriarchal,' " she read.

"Uh, uh-huh." He pointed to Carol Zazula, a Pasadena native who did Polish, and to the others at her table.

"Rigid."

"Xenophobic."

"Omar Khayyam" was Peggy Boyd's answer.

"Theocracy" was Pam Alger's.

"What were you doing in Iran?" Daryush asked.

"A corporate assignment. Anyone else?"

"Persian language, a poetic language," someone said.

45

Fred nodded, smiling and yet looking slightly let-down. Possibly he was wondering whether we had disappointed him innocently or were playing with him. Clearly he had been looking for "terrorism."

"In Indonesia," Fred resumed, having apparently jettisoned the rest of the Iran lesson, "there is something called unity in diversity. There's a very good lesson in that for our city here. We are a very mellow place. But I know of something better—strength in diversity. What I would like to hear now is a definition of affirmative action."

"I had to deal with it the other day," said Carol Zazula, who was prone to get conversational without notice. "In Polish it sounds Orwellian—it sort of means 'positive action' or 'the good deed.' For a source text, it conveys no meaning, and the receptor language needs a gloss. It's sort of like 'pro-life'—I mean, who isn't, if you put it that way? Or 'pro-choice'—I mean, what's that all about—smoking or not smoking in restaurants? It's a cultural thing. All cultures have euphemisms. So in the end, I had to—"

"That's very interesting, and I want to hear the rest of that. I just want to move on just a little bit. We're going to do a little role-playing, but first—" He pulled the cassette out of the tape deck and was about to insert another when Betty Sue, seated closest to him at the front, held out a folded slip of paper that had apparently been passed up from the rear.

"My goodness, I hope this isn't serious," he said as he read the note. "Which one of you is Peter Theroux? Could you please take Mr. Daryush to Zuma Hospital?"

"That's why I surf," Daryush explained as we sped farther north. "Imagine if we had spent the whole morning listening to that."

Actually, some of what Fred had been doing was like literacy tutor training, some of which often involved writing with the wrong hand and a small amount of role-playing, but the role-playing was generally limited to the process of tutoring adults. No one seemed to get what Fred was trying to train us to do.

After passing Point Dume, a small prominence of land sheltering a Marine station, we could hear the insistent thud of waves hitting the beach, like an irregular heartbeat, even though we could not see the beach yet.

"Whoa! Park here and we won't have to pay," said Daryush.

We put on our suits in the large changing room. It looked impossible to swim at this beach, and I had to wait and build up my nerve before even trying. The waves, which lurked and moved like sea monsters far out before rising high and racing in, formed a huge, glassy-green pipeline that crashed in a six-foot-high explosion of foam, which, Daryush pointed out, could break your neck.

The western end of the Santa Monica mountain range encloses the long south-facing beach from the west and north, but today the peaks were veiled in mist.

"Ocean fog and mist, not smog. The air here is perfect. You stand out—look how white you are," said Daryush. "There aren't that many white people on the beach."

None of the white people were white, of course—everyone on the beach was brown, some from birth, others not.

"Spanish and black people love the beach the most, and surfers," said Daryush, surveying the heaving mountains of water crashing onto the sand. "White people are afraid of skin cancer. Los Angeles and Long Beach are mostly families at the beach, mostly families not speaking English, with food and chairs. Now I wish I had brought my guns."

"Your *what?*"

"My surfboards." He smiled.

Daryush surfed in Malibu and beaches to the north, outside of LA, claiming that the best surfing was found in central California. On one of his rare trips south, however, he had surfed and approved of Huntington Beach in Orange County, and he shot a whole roll of film in the town's International Museum of Surfing. I sat in his condo in Van Nuys one afternoon inspecting snapshots of the longboards, the killer-wave murals, and the statue of the founding surfer, the venerable Hawaiian "Duke" Kahanamoku. California congressman Dana Rohrabacher's own surfboard was on display, too; he had grown up surfing.

"Surfers are friendly—the museum people are terrific," he reminisced. "It's a religion. You have Hawaiians, Fijians, Australians, and Americans. We talk about surfing in California, New York, Florida, and everyplace. It's a family. Some surfing areas up north you have localism. That means they don't want outsiders coming into their areas, and surfers consider that the most despicable thing. Surfers are the most ecological people in the world. They have hundreds of beach closings every year in this state, and surfers suffer the most. But you still don't find surfing news on the sports page."

I thought that over; it was true.

"Why don't you write a surfing column for a Hebrew or Persian paper here?" I meant this as a joke, but he shook his head resolutely.

"I've wanted to, or to translate some pieces from the surfing press. The terminology would be a great challenge. But those people only care about themselves."

It was no wonder Daryush embraced the surfing community so warmly. He harbored a huge grievance against his own Iranian compatriots in LA. Although there were between 200,000 and 400,000 Iranians here, he often complained that there was little sense of community. Their religious communities—Muslims, Jews, and ethnically Armenian Iranians—had little interest in one another. Much of the community had lived outside Iran since the 1970s and had been opposed to the late shah, and many others—the richest ones—had left Iran only with the fall of the shah; the two groups still had little common ground. What most LA Iranians did have in common was a wish to be invisible, which may have stemmed from the anti-Iranian feeling during the U.S. hostage episode in the late 1970s, or from a disillusionment with politics in general. Most further distanced themselves from their modern homeland by calling themselves Persians.

There was some surfing going on far down the beach. I could only make out the black forms of surfers paddling out. The curving waterfall of the bigger waves tended to hide them as they rode in.

"It's not such a great day for surfing." Daryush had followed my gaze. "There have been no hurricanes, and no Santa Ana winds. Just chancy."

"Why do they wear those black body suits?" I asked. "I thought surfers wore baggy bathing suits."

"Amateurs do, and people who want to show their behinds, and surfers just fooling around. For serious surfing you have a wet suit, because it lets a layer of water in that warms your whole body."

"They don't look comfortable."

"They are, but you shouldn't surf anyway. You could bodysurf—you can learn that in two weeks. Or boogie-board, in the shallow water. Or even sand-surf, right on the sandy part of the beach. Kids learn that way. Not at this beach, though."

"They don't do it here?"

"No, I mean you shouldn't do it here. You should practice where people can't see."

I went into the water. It was like stepping into the small tentacle tips of a monstrous octopus—even in four inches of water you could feel the urgent pull of the water racing out or the force of it boiling back in. Once you're in, the depth fluctuates violently with the movement of the waves. Every third wave rolled in like an arched emerald wall, rearing up with a thin white crest—the oceanic equivalent of a cobra spreading its hood, and nearly as unnerving. Every crashing wave spun me wrong side up if I was swimming, or sent me somersaulting underwater if I was treading water. I swam out to be clear of the breaking waves, only to find out that they looked more frightening from the other side.

There were two young blond women visiting Daryush when I staggered in—he had his lemons out and was giving them advice.

"Just rinse or shampoo your hair at the shower there, and squeeze these on and run them through in slices."

"Like, can I have a bunch?"

"Take them!" He laughed. "I can help you if you need."

"Except we're going to be in the changing room," one said, and the two women exchanged a slightly wary look. "We'll catch you later."

"They're from the Valley!" Daryush exulted. "One of them works in the Nordstrom at Topanga Plaza—I can look her up there."

"Were you giving them lemons for their hair? Is that a Persian habit?"

"No! Thanks to my brother. If blondes swim with dry hair, their hair soaks up the sun and water and it can turn green! Hair is a sponge. Shahram told me that you can use eggs, mayonnaise, or mashed bananas, but lemon juice is the best."

"Are you kidding?"

"This isn't Iran, Peter," Daryush pointed out. "Women don't use bathing caps. The sun makes their hair dry, and the ocean discolors it. The other best thing to do is to mash a banana and mix it with mayonnaise."

"And eat it?"

"And coat their hair! And lie out in the sun. And then shower it out."

"What if a dog got to it first?" Or flies? Or even a toddler, if the banana-and-mayo beachgoer was asleep? It sounded revolting.

"California beaches all have showers, and no dogs," he pointed out.

"What do you do to lure women to you, just set out your lemons and wait for them to get green hair?"

"No," he said very seriously. "I juggle the lemons, and then they get interested, or they need them. All California girls know these things. And I have a watermelon all sliced for a snack. It's a fruit trap, you can say."

He offered me some watermelon.

"It's your color," he warned, pointing to my shoulders.

It was time to go, thanks to the melanin-impaired member of the group. Daryush left the last two lemons on the sand and stuck his business card between them, and we trudged away from the boiling waves back to the changing room.

"Surfing is all about being alone," Daryush explained as we piled back into the car. I had asked him why he would take up such a dangerous sport—it was not unknown to encounter sharks along the coast. "No one can see you. I don't surf at noontime—that's why I didn't bring my longboard. I paddle out in the late afternoon, when the beach is getting empty. No one in the city can see me. It's just me and the ocean. Surfing is for remote places."

"Like Los Angeles?"

"It's a Hawaiian sport."

It is true that you don't see surfers at most LA beaches. They seek out wild weather patterns and beaches without swimmers. It came to California late, and its Los Angeles image was magnified by the entertainment industry. The Beach Boys were Angelenos, from nearby Hawthorne. Surfing movies were Hollywood products, whether the beach-blanket variety or *The Endless Summer*. Singers Jan and Dean had donated some of their gold records to the Surfing Museum.

"But most of all, surfing is international. It connects you with the ocean—it's not about the beach. It's humane—you see fish, you discover pollution, you rescue people." He came back to the point. "Really serious surfers leave California, because the real weather and waves are in Hawaii, but I'm not that serious."

Who could get that serious? I shifted into fourth gear where the highway passed through Pacific Palisades. This day seemed to me the proof that LA lost nothing in translation. City, suburb, mountain, forest, ocean, freeway, and a rainbow of languages. And this was a workday.

It had been a perfect day. We yawned from the heat we had absorbed, the bracing coat of salt from swimming, and the clean breeze from the west as we traveled down the coast and into Santa Monica. The air was cooling off, and a light fog was blowing across the road. The car swooped into the tunnel that marks the beginning of Interstate 10, which is locally known as the Santa Monica Freeway but runs east all the way to Jacksonville, Florida. We reemerged into the light and toward the road's identifying billboard. When the highway shows you its big green business card with its full name, the Christopher Columbus Intercontinental Highway, you feel that the world is just a few exits away.

3

Literacy in Long Beach

The San Diego Freeway has ten exits in Long Beach; it is the next-biggest city in LA after Los Angeles itself. Like LA, it was settled successively by Shoshones with roots in northeast Asia, Spanish conquerors, and Americans from the Midwest. Its flat miles of grazing land were so thickly settled by Iowans during the Depression that annual Iowa picnics would be a city fixture. For decades, these fairs divided the acreage of public parks into sections of picnic tables divided by which Iowa county the families had come from. Obituaries in the local Long Beach paper, the *Press-Telegram,* frequently mention towns like Audubon, Cherokee, and Oskaloosa, Iowa, as the birthplaces of its longer-lived citizens.

That reputation died hard—all southern California's images seem to die hard, leaving a shimmering mirage. People flocked to Orange County, for example, because the aura of its open spaces and orange groves lingered long after it became one smoggy, overbuilt suburban sprawl, with gang crime and a freeway problem (the "Orange crush") rivaling LA's. In the same way, Long Beach's image as a staid suburb of craggy old Midwesterners, enlivened only by the devilment of its thirty thousand sailors, remained after the naval base was closed and the proportion of white students in its premier high school, Polytechnic, dropped to 24 percent. Because of its port and its low rents, Long Beach became a major point of entry for immigrants, especially Cambodians and Mexicans. The result is a city that is diverse and tolerant without being flashy, with a few rich ghettoes: a country-club neighborhood and a marina with gondoliers, which the city fathers called Naples, probably since LA already had a Venice.

Long Beach is part of the vast so-called "cemetery with lights"—the LA County cities south of the Artesia Freeway and east of the Palos Verdes peninsula. The metaphor, sometimes quoted in Hollywood-oriented guidebooks, means, of course, to suggest suburban somnolence, not pitiless mayhem. On the map it is bounded by the Los Angeles and San Gabriel rivers, Compton and Watts on the north, and Orange County on the east. In reality, there are no borders or landmarks—in dry seasons the rivers do not exist and are marked only by the huge concrete gutters that locals call "the flood control" instead of "the rivers." To the south is Terminal Island (formerly Rattlesnake Island) and its prison. The island was once the site of a Japanese fishing village, which constituted LA's largest concentration of Japanese until the community moved inland to Compton. Beyond that and the oil-drilling islands lie Santa Catalina Island and the undersea mountain range called the Channel Islands, whose humps rise like a sea serpent's from San Pedro Bay.

Like the rest of LA, Long Beach was carved out of Mexican ranchos—its Alamitos Avenue, which bisects the city, was once the boundary of the Los Alamitos and Los Cerritos ranchos. It was bordered by Rancho San Pedro to the west, which became the town of San Pedro and was annexed by Los Angeles city to serve as a port. To the north lay Rancho La Tajauta, which later became Watts and was annexed by LA as well. Long Beach was founded on Los Cerritos ranch land purchased as the "American Colony" of an English visionary, William Willmore, and later renamed Willmore City and then Long Beach, in 1888, when it incorporated as a city to avoid being swallowed by the upstart and very expansionist Queen of the Angels. Some of Long Beach's streets—Stearns, Temple, Bixby—commemorate the early-nineteenth-century New Englanders who arrived, married into Spanish ranch-holding families, and made their fortunes with the beef-cattle herds that ended up in the barbecue pits of Gold Rush miners up north. (A dozen years later, these ranchos enjoyed a sheep-ranching boom, with the wool all sent east—"dyed both blue and gray," one historian wrote.)

I had fallen into the rhythm of living here, attracted by the clean air and excellent library. The city had very little image to live up to, except its old values of hard work and clean fun. These were extolled even on the old hotel advertisements posted in the lobby of the Willmore, the building where I eventually bought a tiny condominium. It had been a grand hotel in the 1920s, then an apartment complex, and was now a historic landmark condominium building. The old virtues had survived into a decade where Long Beach was known for its well-established lesbian community and uncounted breakfast restaurants, the best in the county, and its large population of "seniors." The city hosts meetings of Better Breathers, advising its cardiorespiratorially impacted citizens on "Traveling with Oxygen." On some streets you can get

nearly run over by busy wheelchair-bound travelers connected by tube to their portable oxygen supply as they go
bombing past the coffeehouses of east Long Beach.

Long Beachers have the endearing habit, common
throughout the county, even in its most chokeheld inner suburbs, of referring to LA as though they were not in the middle
of it. "Up in LA" and "Well, over in *Los Angeles*" are phrases
you hear not only in Long Beach and Santa Monica but in
San Pedro, Wilmington, Venice, and other parts of Los Angeles that prefer to go by their neighborhood names. And yet
in Orange County, some people refer to themselves as living
in LA. Both attitudes are informed by a certain defensiveness
which it is hard not to adopt. I had not lived long in LA when
I felt the first twinge of it. I was doing a favor, showing a car
that a friend of mine was selling to a young couple who had
come down from Sherman Oaks to look at it.

"Dick Snapper," said the man warmly, and I realized that
he was introducing himself.

"Our church has a branch in Long Beach," said the
woman, Lydia, as the car crept out of Temple Avenue onto
Ocean Boulevard and its view of the blue-and-white towers
(camouflaged oil derricks) on the Thums Islands. "But we
haven't been here in a long time. We don't have any friends
here. What's that noise? That clicking."

I did not hear any clicking.

"Good night! Could it be the timing chain? Don't tell me
that's the Pacific Coast Club."

This was a funny castle on the beach, built in 1926, beside
the Villa Riviera, two 1920s resort properties gracing what
was once California's most spectacular eight-mile beach,
along with LA's best pre-Disneyland amusement park, the
Pike. Until the beach was halved and given a breakwater to

ease port expansion, meaning the destruction of the Pike, Long Beach had been a resort that prided itself not only on the crashing surf and raucous amusement parks, but on the sober Iowan morals that prevailed. ("No Saloons" was a boast prominent on almost all the Wilson-era travel posters.) I had met a Texan oil heir who spoke wistfully of the biggest pre-bust amenity of Dallas oil wealth: a compartment on the Santa Fe Chief across the Southwest, a suite at the Pacific Coast Club, the Villa Riviera, or the Willmore, and two weeks being blissfully knocked to pieces by the breakers of San Pedro Bay. Clean fun had been a Long Beach selling point since the 1800s, and in the year of its incorporation—in part to maintain its prized "dry" status—a guidebook assured visitors:

Long Beach contains elegant hotels, a large Methodist Episcopal church, a Congregational church, stores and livery stables, but no saloons. In Long Beach, no saloons are tolerated and all objectionable elements of society are kept out.

"Yes, it's the Pacific Coast Club," I said. This was three years before it was demolished to make room for an empty luxury block of condominiums to preside over what some bitter locals called, after the harbor expansion, Short Beach.

"I think our church is out that way," said Snapper, motioning west, and Lydia smiled meaningfully at me. I had already reasoned that since mainstream churches were found everywhere, the fact that they remarked on a branch of their church here meant it was one of the small New Age denominations with "science" in its name that were really tax-free gospel-of-success scams.

"Or it might be in Huntington Beach. I'm a little ditzy," said Lydia with a crooked smile.

"Power steering," said Snapper approvingly.

We turned left onto the reclaimed land where the "Coney Island of the West" had stood until 1979. All that remains of the Pike on the beach is a lone tattoo parlor and the domed building housing the Lite-A-Line pavilion. The Lite-A-Line frenzy—the game is a cross between bingo and pinball—peaked in the 1940s, when the Pike was the largest amusement park west of the Mississippi, but has outlived the merry-go-round, Cyclone Racer ride, Majestic Dance Hall, and all the other attractions. As late as the 1970s, though, the Oklahoma Mummy Man, an actual mummified corpse, was on display, in the tradition of Western carnival sideshows, which almost always had a bandit's remains in stock.

"I don't see that many sailors. Good night! This used to be all tattoo parlors and sailor bars," commented the husband. We had turned from Shoreline Drive, the western terminus of the "Hands Across America" nationwide chain in 1986, up to Long Beach Boulevard, formerly American Avenue. "Here we go," he said, with evident satisfaction, as he noticed a short row of run-down bars ornamented with the painted silhouettes of hourglass-shaped women with very big hair—some had SAILORS WELCOME signs. One, the U.S.S. Somewhere, flew an American flag.

"Just like you said, hon," said Lydia.

Snapper shrugged. "We are *not* in Sherman Oaks."

This was common. Everyone wanted Long Beach to be trashy and down at the heels—it was the navy reputation, tattoo parlors, and the very existence of the huge port. While the town was clearly far from LA's other big population centers to the north, it was the quintessential LA city: a combination city and suburb with suburbs of its own, a small, Midwest-type settlement beside a port that had brought Lindbergh and Emperor Haile Selassie through town, a favored location of Mack Sennett movies, and an influx of immigrants. Long Beach was known as Little Phnom Penh for hosting the world's largest expatriate Cambodian community. Most of all, here were miles of the classic LA suburban "look"—the overgrown small town. Nearly all of Long Beach, the Valley, West Los Angeles, and the basin had been expanses of one-family houses with yards, driveways, and children on tricycles. Now the explosion of LA had overlaid a big city on these suburbias. The most noticeable results were the car-crowded streets. You could never find a parking space. Belmont Shore, which had been one of Long Beach's small seaside neighborhoods of California bungalows and quiet streets, now churned with the busy traffic of visitors drawn here by the shops, beaches, and restaurants. Residents sitting in their front yards to enjoy the night-blooming jasmine could watch the chess game of motorists cruising for parking spaces and even inching onto the sidewalk when none could be found.

Throughout LA, people had forgotten what the place had become. One example was the way Long Beachers craved homes in Belmont Shore, long after it had ceased to become a refuge. It was one of the most congested parts of the city. It reminded me of the way concertgoers at the Hollywood Bowl loved to picnic outside; the famous amphitheater does have grassy areas and does a lively business selling food and drinks, but the picnickers could evoke nothing but pity. In their minds, this was Glyndebourne or Wolf Trap. They half-reclined on spread-out blankets with cushions, eating tiny sandwiches and sipping wine, anticipating an evening of Mozart or Ella Fitzgerald, oblivious to the fact that they were, actually, awkwardly sprawled on a cramped median strip with a line of cars puffing exhaust into their faces, with no view beyond the wheels and bumpers inching past.

I drove past the slope of Hinshaw Park, dense with trees, and pointed out that the San Diego Freeway was just four blocks away.

"I thought it would be a lot farther than this," said Lydia, who then marveled, "This is nice!" She repeated it again, this time sounding, somehow, disillusioned: "This is *nice!*"

One of the city's attractions was its southerly location, just inside LA County but with two major freeways cutting through it. It was axiomatic that few of my Westside LA or Valley friends came down here much. To my best friends I would reveal the secret that it took under half an hour to get here; to everyone else, I had been known to say things like "I'd love to see more of you, but I live down in Long Beach." I was able to flee boring parties easily by pleading the necessity of having to drive, drawing out the words as heavily as I could, all the way back down there to Long Beach. Off the hook, I would zip down the San Diego Freeway where Long Beach's little downtown sprang into view after Los Angeles International Airport and the satanic oil refineries of Wilmington in the "shoestring," the skinny, twenty-mile long strip of the city of Los Angeles annexed in 1909 in order to connect its downtown to the seaport site.

We turned east to Signal Hill and up to the top, where the Snappers crowed at the gleaming view of the downtown Los Angeles skyscrapers, the San Gabriel Mountains, and the barely visible Hollywood sign on Mount Lee. To the east lay flat Orange County and the purple Santa Ana Mountains.

"And look at the ocean!" said Snapper. "Look up that way, Lydia! Good night! I didn't think you could see all the way to Century City from down this way. Is it always this clear?"

"Most days," I responded. It took me a few seconds to understand why I lied: I was stung at their belief that the town was nothing but tattoo parlors, and their satisfaction at having spotted one. "Los Angeles is not really that far. Or rather, it's far, but the air here is clean enough that the view makes it seem near." I knew Sherman Oaks was in the Valley and, despite the grand houses and trees, had, thanks to smog, the stuffy air of a high school lab or old attic. I was developing an LA attitude, but did I want to belong or not?

Snapper took the wheel, and we cruised down the hill. They got engrossed in talk about the brakes, and Lydia asked me whether the water pump and distributor cap were original with the car, which was several years old.

"See, sometimes the insulation on the distributor wires gets real old, and when it rains it locks up and won't start. It doesn't rain much out here, so you don't think about it. You think it's the battery, but it's not. Or it gets moisture in the distributor cap, and you need to dry it out."

I thought it remarkable that a churchy housewife, even a New Age one, who had already described herself as "ditzy," would have this detailed knowledge of mechanics, but this was LA.

To the south, the sea-monster backbone of Catalina Island lay on the blue Pacific horizon, a misty backdrop for the trim silhouette of the *Queen Mary*. The old Scottish liner had, since 1967, given Long Beach a stab at an identity besides Iowa-by-the-Sea. The city began to call itself Queen City, lending seagoing glamour to local concerns that quickly renamed themselves Queen Beach Printers, Queen City Bank, Queen City Meats, and so on.

Long Beachers knew that the huge imported bauble invited all kinds of derision—the *Press-Telegram* had a radio commercial selling its very local coverage with mock eavesdropping on the *Los Angeles Times* newsroom, where reporters confused Long Beach with every other coast town in the county, finally remembering, "Yeah! Long Beach is where they put London Bridge." The ship was, of course, a glorious relic of the 1930s, with its ballrooms (unless a beer or perfume commercial is being filmed there, it is a favorite location of Elizabeth Taylor), bars, windy decks, staterooms, and troop-carrying facilities. Even the engine room is a huge attraction, with a haunted passageway. The largest and fastest ocean liner of its time even survived the temporary ownership of Disney Inc. Until 1990, visitors boarded the ship for free, with the option of taking a guided tour, strolling around, or eating in one of the restaurants or bars. Disney almost choked off the *Queen Mary*'s tourists by charging $17.50 for each ticket, plus parking; Disney threw in admission to Howard Hughes's *Spruce Goose* (then parked under a giant dome nearby) and to London Towne, a tiny walled-in assemblage of Tudoresque half-timbered T-shirt and postcard shops. Disney further made itself odious to Long Beachers by introducing strict employee dress codes on the *Queen Mary* and enforcing Disneyland's iron rule against facial hair for male employees. When Disney pulled out, the city took over running the ship.

Dick said they were not ready to buy the car right away; they would pray on it and see.

"What islands are those with the colorful structures?" asked Lydia as we parted back on Ocean.

"Oil islands."

The Thums (the name is an acronym: Texaco, Humble, Union, Mobil, Shell) Islands were reminders of the oil fields that had once covered Long Beach and this enclave city, Signal Hill (formerly Cerritos Hill), which in the 1920s had been the world's most productive oil field. There still were oil pumps clacking along at various intersections in Signal Hill, only one of the little touches that made this, my refuge from the Middle East, seem like an Arab world theme park—there was the hot sun, the nearly eight miles of sand along the beach, and the long guns of the U.S.S. *New Jersey*, which had shelled Beirut in the early 1980s, visible as it rode at anchor in its home berth at the Long Beach Naval Base. There was the mosque, the Masjid al-Shareef, on Orange Avenue, and the lights and flaring gas of Wilmington's oil refineries just north of the port, the very image of the Saudi industrial city of al-Jubayl on the Persian Gulf.

Not that I needed any reminders of the Arab countries. I had spent my first many months in LA translating the Arab novel *Cities of Salt,* ordering in food, discovering cable TV, and otherwise feeling out a crude prototype of "cocooning," aided by fax and phone. Galled by the incongruity of monastic monomania amid the sun and adventure of LA, I got more involved in the local scene by becoming a tutor in an adult literacy program. After all, I was a writer and translator. Didn't I have a vested interest in people learning how to read? And it was a chance to meet more of my fellow citizens. And there were more and more of them. People were pouring into southern California.

This was 1986, and all over Los Angeles cars sported WEL-COME TO CALIFORNIA, NOW GO HOME bumper stickers, far outnumbering RESPECT ORGANIC REALITY and I ♥ TEHUANTE-PEC. Perhaps there was too much competition for jobs—you could gather that from the desperate appearance of many of these drivers *and* their cars, and the frequently accompanying license-frame motto *Hit Me—I Need the $.* But you even saw the "welcome" bumper sticker on expensive cars in LA's richest and most liberal suburbs, in Santa Monica and Silver Lake. What was their problem? It was annoying to see the grumpy NOW GO HOME admonition on bumpers in Long Beach, where most out-of-staters were whiffle-headed seamen who had driven out here, complete with their Michigan and Idaho and Texas license plates, to serve the Stars and Stripes at the Long Beach Naval Base, the Long Beach Naval Shipyard, or the U.S. Naval Weapons Station a few miles down the beach, where Los Angeles gave way to Orange County.

The military were recognizable not only by their short hair, occasional tattoos, and out-of-state plates, but by the way they watched movies. They tended to go to theaters in threes, with two sitting four or five seats apart in one row and the third sitting between them, but two or three rows back. The corners of this triangle, nearly connected by spread-out arms and elevated legs resting on seat backs, exclaimed "Damn!" and "Yes!" throughout the movie, prompting some other moviegoers to mutter, "Squid." And without the sailors, I would probably never have noticed the city's many lesbian bars. These were spotted by the combination of women in line to get in and mystified sailors watching warily from across the street. The servicemen were seeking places with lots of women and few men, but an inner voice was telling them that this actually was too good to be true.

There were dozens of literacy programs in LA, mostly offered through the public library systems. I chose Long Beach Project Read, the best-run and best-funded program, run by the city library system. It served much of southern LA County beyond Long Beach's borders, with a paid staff of two, plus about two hundred volunteer tutors. After being trained and certified, I was given a confidential assignment: to tutor a policeman who lived in Long Beach but served on the force of a neighboring city. He had made it through the police academy, and could read, but could barely spell or write. He was under pressure to write police reports of incidents he had handled, a responsibility he always left to his patrol partner. His name (his "name," for confidentiality) was Cedric Laubach, and all the librarians were in love with him—he was tall, muscular, and chatty, always giving them tips about personal and car safety. To me he confided his pet peeve, gangs, and his satisfaction that California's ban on the death penalty had decreased not executions, but trials.

"That just moved the death penalty to the street. I'm not going to put my ass to extra risk for someone who can kill without being killed. I don't give any gangbanger the benefit of the doubt."

"You mean you're more inclined to shoot first and ask questions later?"

He just smiled.

"You should go on a ride-along," he said. "We're getting understaffed, so we can't afford too much of our time for that kind of thing, but do it in Inglewood or Compton."

This was before the rap album *Straight Outta Compton* had made that city globally famous for its gang warfare and thriving drug trade, but already its murderous streets were legend in LA. By the time I eventually decided to call one of Laubach's Compton colleagues to look into doing a ride-along with night patrolmen, the city had canceled them—local journalists in addition to camera crews from as far away as Japan and Australia had overburdened the small department's resources.

"I have a basic formula for helping to write reports," he

told me, and passed a sheet of yellow lined paper along with the Police Academy vocabulary sheet and some sample police reports across the round wooden table—for anonymity, we were meeting in the deserted magazine room of the Burnett Branch Library in central Long Beach. He had chosen Burnett as a meeting place not only because the literacy program was based there, but because it mostly served children and was quiet during school hours. His basic report formula, he assured me, worked for most of the incidents he handled, but when he began to realize that he would eventually need six or seven basic formulas, he decided it would just be simpler to improve his writing.

While proceeding northbound on _____ Ave./Blvd, suspect/s were spotted engaging in _____ in the _____ block of the street. Upon observing this suspicious behavior, we made a U-turn at _____ and proceeded to the scene, where at that time suspect/s then attempted to flee on foot/in a vehicle. At that point in time the suspect dropped a small beige rocklike object to the ground. At that time I subdued and handcuffed the suspect, all the time never losing sight of the small beige rocklike object on the sidewalk. . . .

"Crack?" I asked him, and he nodded. "How do you never lose sight of it?"

"You have to say that," Cedric said. "If you don't, then in court their attorney will ask you, 'Well, how did you know that rock wasn't already on the sidewalk?' You have to be sure that it was their own crack."

Fortunately, most of the police reporting process was a matter of checking boxes ("Partially/Fully Disrobed" "Obscene Epithets/Gestures"), and Officer Laubach's spelling did not need as much work as he thought. It all came to him much more easily when he learned to pare "at that time" and "I then proceeded to" from his prose. The multiplicity of cities in LA allowed even more anonymity than was available in most big U.S. cities. Adults who wanted to learn to read and write could usually get free tutoring either nearby or miles from home. Although the program for which I tutored was, strictly speaking, for native speakers of English who qualified as functionally illiterate, sometimes south LA's multifarious population of immigrants from abroad, who spoke English but didn't always write it well, were given tutors. I tutored an elderly Vietnamese woman, Mrs. Nguyen, who was one of the wave of older Asian women who approached Project Read in the late 1980s. Even the small door-to-door outreach effort of which the program was capable had turned up a surprising number of Japanese, Korean, and Vietnamese women who had never learned to read. All their bills, taxes, and other reading and writing tasks had been handled by their American military husbands, who generally were, by this point, late husbands. Their situation must have been common throughout southern California, with all of its air and naval bases and military retirees.

This group of East Asian widows was distinct from the large number of Vietnamese and Cambodians, both here and in Orange County. These quiet communities produced a young generation of gangs, who, like most mafias, tended to prey on their own people through extortion, scams, protection rackets, and drug dealing. When it came to fighting over turf, the Cambodians fought most lethally with Latinos. Their graffiti, newspaper accounts of their occasional gunfights, and the translator meetings I attended taught me that

LA was not about color. America's three centuries of white, red, and black had ended. From now on, I thought, it was about language.

Mrs. Nguyen proved to be a fast learner when matched with a retired woman tutor; older women working together generally did well. They were warm and frank and empathetic, and often baked cookies for each other. Once I met Mrs. Nguyen being helped into the lobby of my building by her son, and we all became friends. She had high blood pressure, but her son was a doctor. "He worries too much," she confided, but she did not know what I did: that his male roommate had undergone his first hospitalization for AIDS-related complications.

Although well over 90 percent of the literacy students were American-born and English-speaking, I was assigned many nonnative speakers, and my next student was Israeli. Dimpled, dark-eyed, dangle-earringed, fortyish Shula was a fountain of optimism. "I *love* it" was her most often used expression. I once asked her about her tour of military service in the Tsahal, just to see if she would say "I love it," and she did. She was another exception to the rules at the literacy project, since she spoke, read, and wrote English passably well. She had turned up one day seeking help with her cosmetology homework—she wanted to be a beautician. In the meantime, she gave Hebrew lessons to members of the city's small Jewish community. Shula (short for Shulamit) was a poor speller, but could give a flawlessly clear explanation of electrolysis, her favorite procedure ("I love it—it's great," she gushed), and I offered to take her on. She was a former Tel Avivian from a family of Jewish refugees from Basra, Iraq, whose spoken Arabic was especially charming—an Iraqi poet, Saadi Yusuf, had written of "the tang of apples in its accent," and this was detectable even in the little Arabic that Shula retained. Despite several years of living in Long Beach, she had retained the native Israeli's deep, guttural *r*.

"Do you know what a 'scroll' is, Shula?" I asked her when the word came up, ready to help her along with *megillah*.

"Oh, yes, I love it," she said enthusiastically. "The *scrrroll* is the little gray one with the big bushy tail, no?"

Eventually Shula did pass her cosmetology exam and moved to the Fairfax district, a mostly Jewish neighborhood near the sprawling CBS Studios. When Clinton was elected president years later, I imagined Shula giving out her address and saying, "I love it," because her condominium was on Clinton Street. It was "mostly Russians and bad traffic," but she loved it.

"Some days I could believe I am in Tel Aviv. I can have falafel and every Jewish thing, you know?"

"Why do you want to live here if it's so similar?" I asked her.

"There's no war or threat here, the economy is better, I can make money and a good reputation as a beautician here. Maybe I will go back to Israel as 'the famous Shula.' "

"What kind of problems do you find here?"

"I wish I know why American men wear boxer shorts. To me it's funny! And all my family wants to come here, too. I get plenty of visits. People from Israel, and my friends who have got jobs in New York. They like it better here for visits. I love it, but when will I study?"

We were both learning that people who live in enjoyable places never lack for reminders of the outside world.

4

Much Moor

The colossal, clogged freeways hold LA together but are great murderers of spontaneity. My first out-of-town visitor was a Saudi houseguest who jumped eagerly into my car for an excursion to the Watts Towers Festival. After nearly an hour of crawling traffic and no scenery but brick barriers and retaining walls decorated with INSANE GANGSTER CRIP, EAST SIDE LONGOS, and PREEN HO HO HO, Talal glared incredulously at the hideousness around him, then scowled at his watch and muttered, *"Al-medina hadi maqbarat lil-waqt"*— This city is a graveyard of time. "And look at the fog!" he said. That was grim, too—the basin's morning haze does not burn off until about eleven o'clock. "Will there be gangs there? Look at these cars!"

A car idling on a freeway symbolizes almost everything wrong with LA. The wasted time is one of the city's huge headaches, considering that every minute of unmoving traffic keeps workers out of their workplaces, pours airborne pollution into the air, and slowly builds up the vast miasma of temper and rage that expresses itself in freeway shootings and angry, reckless driving. The famous freeway shootings of 1987 (followed by bumper stickers that read KEEP HONKING, I'M RELOADING) were not the most lethal result. The aggressive driving of motorists who are frustrated or just running late results in accidents that cause not only fatalities but more traffic jams, more murderous frustration, and so on, until a fresh tide of metal, glass, and fossil fuels has risen and ebbed to erase the detritus.

Talal was deeply annoyed by the slow traffic and the ugliness of a city he expected to be a veritable Paris on the Pacific—as an Arab he would not even notice the sunshine when it burned through the haze—but he agreed with me that these were the politest motorists he had ever seen.

"No one is honking his horn—that's spooky,"

I pointed out that southern Californians disliked confrontation—they liked to think that everything was fine. I was making this up as I went along, never actually having asked myself why the sound of auto horns was so rare on the city's 510 miles of freeway, but then started to believe it. It was part of living in an eternal present that ignored yesterday's earthquake and tomorrow's drought. This was epitomized in the common sight I would show Talal the next day: the big houses built on shelves and stilts hanging off the steep hillsides of Malibu, Hollywood, and Pacific Palisades. The very sight of them was like an editorial cartoon of the mind of LA, but they were real. Honking a horn would remind everyone within earshot that something was wrong somewhere. The noise would bruise the air. And these were the happy-face Reagan years.

"Stop philosophizing about zombies," Talal interrupted

before I could go on about the image of eternal youth that hung over the city in its eternal present. "Get off this bridge and let's take a normal street."

"Jackknifed big-rig in the number two lane at Slauson. Sigalert," I said, quoting from the radio, turning it up so that he could hear the nation's most elaborate traffic report. Just when you thought they had updated you on the condition of every freeway in LA, they moved on to places you had scarcely heard of: "Injury accident on the San Bernardino at City Terrace, you'll find red taillights backed up to the Downtown Slot. East LA Interchange cleared up after that load of spilled mattresses on the northbound 101, but that southbound audience still has things backed up to Beverly Boulevard. Try to stay clear of the 60 eastbound in Chino, where a stall in the number three lane has things going slow. Riverside Drive is your alternative; looky-loos westbound have things tied up almost to the 15. Looking at Orange County, there's a definite situation developing with that hazardous material spill at the El-Toro Y. . . ."

"That hardly sounds like English. Is he watching all those areas from one helicopter?"

I pointed out that the helicopter was staged—the omniscient freeway czar was sitting in a Pasadena studio with a sound-effects panel and a box of doughnuts—but resisted the clichéd remark that nothing in LA was what it seemed. Feature articles about LA always harped on nothing being what it seemed, claimed that this was a Potemkin city in a million cute ways, but surely that was true of every place on earth. I switched the radio to 97.9 FM so that we could hear the traffic report as a torrent of Spanish studded with bursts of *"también* Coldwater Canyon" and *"problemas en el Y de El-Toro."*

"Amazing," said Talal. He was probably still thinking of

the daily pollution report printed beside the daily weather forecast in the morning newspaper. I had shown it to him because it had been a relatively good day, at least near the coasts:

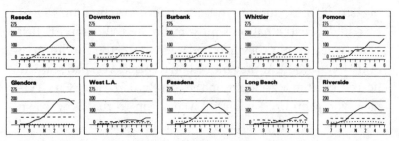

The daily air quality report gave a futuristic feel to the morning paper, enhanced by the occasional excommunicatory advisory that the air was "unhealthful" or "unacceptable." I had sampled that sort of air just once, on an outing to an auto-parts salvage yard in the town of Duarte, built on the basin side of the San Gabriel Mountains. This was the last stop for the smog, a cauldron of all LA's exhaust fumes and chemical emissions. The air was as heavy and brown as suede, an ethereal sewage that stung my eyes and tongue; it only took about ten minutes for me to start breathing like a chainsmoker. I never bothered to read a weather forecast in Los Angeles, but after that day never missed the air quality forecast.

We started to work our way over to the right, through the hundreds of cars holding a driver and no passengers—this was a refinement of the terrible spectacle of a stalled freeway: three tons of metal and steady pollution occupying a couple of hundred square feet, and all that just to move one body, or keep it stalled. We headed east on Compton Boulevard.

There is now only a small segment of the street known by that name. As gang murders continued to poison Compton's reputation, neighboring cities crossed by the street changed its name to Redondo Beach Boulevard or Somerset Boulevard, anything but Compton Boulevard.

We headed up Central Avenue, the main street of this historically black section of Los Angeles.

Now beyond the retaining walls, Talal marveled at the attractiveness of Los Angeles. "No apartments—all villas!" The little houses were small, neat, and painted a palette of colors. The lawns were grassy and fenced, and the palm trees were just as majestic as those in Saudi cities, and there were more of them here. Even the shabbiest parts of LA look pretty and lively when you swoop off the hypnotic freeway, where a car trip is really a state of suspension, with little sense of progress or changing landscape. We had snapped out of it and were now heading north on a surface street—LAspeak for street, as opposed to freeway; half of all newcomers mishear the term as "service street," imagining some kind of narrow access road, before realizing that even Pacific Coast Highway and Sunset Boulevard are mere surface streets.

The visual divorce between freeways and neighborhoods means that the city is almost always seen from a distance, and as the freeways only get more heavily traveled, and the city more heavily populated and noise-sensitive, rooftops may someday become entirely invisible, with the construction of more and higher sound barrier walls. In the literacy program, I had interviewed a woman who had been driven to seek reading help by sound walls. She lived in Santa Ana and worked in Torrance, and since she could not read the freeway signs, she depended on landmarks—a department store, a fire station, a bank—to find her way. Otherwise, the freeway was all the same, and time was a poor gauge, because the traffic was so unpredictable.

"The day I saw them closing off the lane to brick up a wall between the 405 and those neighborhoods," she confided, "I knew I would have to learn how to read those signs. That's why I'm here now."

"You could use gas stations as landmarks, because they make their signs high enough to be seen, or go by the mileage on the odometer," I suggested, then added, because these tricks were subversive to literacy, "or learn how to read." I hastily praised her courage for coming in to the program.

"This was never a problem in Yucaipa," she said—her desert hometown.

No, probably not. Her story struck me as a wonderful example of the sort of skills that LA forced its citizens to learn.

"Cages," said Talal, pointing to a doughnut shop, a beauty shop, and a fried-chicken joint whose outer walls were clad with bars from the ground to the eaves. The bars, at barely three-inch intervals, did made the small structures look like traveling cages for circus animals—the House of Curls looked like a mobile elephant house.

"To keep the animals out," I said. Since crack dealers and addicts had unleashed themselves on LA, anything worth two dollars in exchange for a small beige rocklike object was a motive for murder. This simple fact, and the struggle for a share of the drug market among gangs, accounted for LA's horrific rate of gang-related murders, which was then nearly two per day.

Little was left of the former glory of Central Avenue, once a lively strip of businesses, jazz clubs, and the legendary Dunbar Hotel, which from its opening in 1928 until its conversion to a retirement hotel in the 1960s put up every visiting member of America's black aristocracy—Duke Ellington, W.E.B. Du Bois, Bill "Bojangles" Robinson, Joe Louis, Nat King Cole, Cab Calloway, Langston Hughes. It had been the official black ghetto of LA: this street with three blocks on either side, as far south as Slauson Avenue. Until 1948, blacks in Los Angeles were denied union membership, barred from county nursing schools, and—LA being a subtler place than the South—while not barred from department stores, harshly overcharged for every purchase in order to discourage their business. There was a neighborly feel here, but the show-biz glamour was gone, and half the signs were in Spanish. The citizenry was well over half Spanish-speaking, and by 1993 the *Sentinel*, LA's venerable African-American community newspaper, would have abandoned Central for West LA. The end of segregation had deprived Watts of many of its blacks. Even before the 1992 riots, in the decade preceding them, nearly 75,000 blacks had fled from the crime, drug industry, and police brutality, despite the "Don't Move, Improve" movement sponsored by local churches. There was about a 20 percent drop in the black population, which was not one of the most desperate in the country. Despite the fact that its roots were in the Depression's massive poverty-stricken exodus from the South, even in the 1930s, Watts boasted the highest proportion of black homeowners of any city in America.

The loss of Central Avenue as LA's Harlem is generally portrayed as a terrible tragedy. But in fact, as with much of LA's young, fast-forward culture, its zenith—its whole span, in fact—had been short-lived. Most of the population in the first half of the twentieth century had been born in the South, and it was only one generation later that the exodus started. Watts had started life as a rancho, La Tajauta, and, like much of LA, was settled by Yankees. In 1874 it was inhabited by farmers from Maine, who wanted to incorporate as a town called the State of Maine. In the 1880s, Charles H. Watts, an Ohioan who had settled in Pasadena, bought it up, and when the Pacific Electric Railway planned its Red Car route through the land, it became Watts Junction. A golden age of real estate speculation followed, and the tract was touted as a splendid new bedroom satellite city accessible to Los Angeles by bus and the "Big Red Cars." Seven-to-ten-year mortgages were offered: lots cost anywhere from $350 to $500, and the Golden State Realty Company started a tempting "$1 Down, $1 a Week" plan.

When Watts finally won incorporation in 1907, it was a diverse town of Germans, Scots, Mexicans, Italians, Greeks, Japanese, and blacks, but the city's board of trustees was all white, and in May 1907 they voted to put the calla lily on the city's official seal. Only in 1910 did black migrants, mostly from Texas and Louisiana, begin to settle along Central Avenue and in the area south of Watts called Mudtown. Most of southern Watts was a farm area cultivated by Japanese with close ties to Japan—a Japanese flier shot down at Pearl Harbor was found to be wearing a Compton High School ring, and the woman who would broadcast from Japan as Tokyo Rose, named Iva Tagori, lived in Watts and also attended Compton High. ("It sure was a blow when that happened with Iva," one of her schoolmates from early in the century recalled in MaryEllen Ray's *City of Watts 1907–1926*.)

"Watts—Hub of the Universe" was the city's slogan, because its streetcars linked Los Angeles, Long Beach, Huntington Beach, and Newport Beach. Like Long Beach, it was a Prohibition battleground and a stronghold of the Women's Christian Temperance Union. In 1918 the WCTU succeeded in briefly shutting down its "social clubs," which had excluded Asians and blacks anyway. Within a few years, they were back doing such lavish business that there was a whole series of movements to change Watts's name—the "liquor element" had damaged the reputation of a city already notorious for its bad repair and racially hostile policing. In 1925, a Ku Klux Klan speaker came to organize Watts, and the city's first cross-burning took place in Grape Street the following year. The Klan did not take over, but moved to Compton, where they occasionally lined up on horseback along the town line to remind blacks and Mexicans to stay in Watts.

Los Angeles annexed Watts in 1926, largely for racist motives—there were fears of a black city with its own black government rising to the south. It rapidly became something of a transit area. As often happens with new additions to LA, nonresident developers built it up to the maximum, and the overbuilding and small lots quickly made it unattractive to people with money. Cheap rents did attract newcomers, though, and it grew quickly. Pacific Electric and defense manufacturing industries employed most of the 650,000-strong black community of 1965, up from little more than a tenth of that, 75,000, in 1940. Despite being the neighborhood of UN diplomat and Nobel Peace Prize laureate Ralph Bunche, Watts received little general attention until the summer of 1965, when the arrest of a young man named Marquette Frye set off the Watts riots, or Watts Rebellion. Racist policing was the detonator—"We never laid out no rugs for no nigger prisoners," one LA cop had been quoted as saying. The conventional view of white LA at the time scarcely considered the years of hostile policing that had nurtured the problem:

"The arrest of a drunken Negro youth at seven o'clock on August 11, 1965—an extremely humid Wednesday night—

triggered the violent action of the Negro mobs," wrote W. W. Robinson in *Los Angeles: A Profile* (in the Centers of Civilizations Series) shortly afterward, in a tone typical of the times. "Ten thousand Negroes, in menacing, marauding bands, took to the streets. . . . Throughout all of Los Angeles, white citizens were buying guns."

There was little sign of the arson that had destroyed much of Watts then, but one look told you that little had changed in the district: it was very neglected and loaded with liquor stores. Before 1965, Watts's merchants and cinema owners had mostly been white, and when they fled, black businessmen could not get the bank loans they needed to buy up the businesses. This sort of economic discrimination would do as much as drug dealing to perpetuate local poverty.

As in many parts of the city's southern flatlands, in summer the air was like breathing fire. Despite the wide flat neighborhoods and freestanding wood-frame houses, many in the classic California bungalow design, it had a very un-LA feel: too many pedestrians. You could see the lack of local supermarkets in the number of old ladies in hats and carrying net bags, walking down the street or sitting at bus stops to do the day's marketing. The signs read PANADERIA, TAQUERIA, and CARNICERIA Y PRODUCTOS LATINOS, and these were abutted by the bodegas and *botánicas* selling the goods and services of Santeria. This voodoo variety of Catholicism was, appropriately enough, rooted in Africa, with an elaborate system of Yoruba gods aligned with Catholic saints. All were fastidiously barred, though. Almost nothing was open at eleven o'clock on this weekday morning.

To see more of Central Avenue, we continued north past Watts into central Los Angeles.

"Oh, no," said Talal, pointing off to the right.

I flinched at the sight of a billboard adorned with an immense portrait of Saudi King Fahd—the same flattering icon that adorned every office and airport in Saudi Arabia. It advertised the future construction of the Masjid Bilal Islamic Center near the intersection of Central and King. Bilal, historically a friend of the prophet Muhammad and one of the first converts to Islam, had been an African slave, and mosques in African-American neighborhoods were often named for him, just as Catholic churches in the same neighborhoods were generally named for the great martyr of color St. Martin of Porres, or, in the South, Our Lady of Sorrows. As a political dissident, Talal was depressed to see a glamorous billboard of the Saudi king, but I was actively annoyed. Inside fanatical Saudi Arabia, the king maintained a ban on the construction of churches, illegally extending the ban even to foreign diplomatic premises, but was clearly delighted (it was a very jolly portrait) to be hypocritically exploiting the religious freedom of tolerant infidels.

"They are cutting a stick for their own back," said Talal firmly. "Look at all the mosques they built in Lebanon to promote movements sympathetic to them. They spread the fire of rivalry and subversion *in spite of their noses.*" The Saudi royals, he said, who were anything but Islamic in their own deeds, were looking for trouble by spreading Islamic fervor— if the converts to Islam were sincere, they would turn against the monarchy. The events that followed the Iraq war years later proved him right. Not only that, Los Angeles would become a city with a significant Muslim population; I thought of it as a hilarious revenge, in vast time and space, of the Muslims on the Spaniards—defeated and expelled from Spain, only to pop up in a former colony. I explained this to Talal, adding that the next turn of the screw was that South

Central LA and its missionary mosques were turning Spanish again. These *reconquistas* among Moorish descendants, reduplicating centuries of Old World nationalism and religiosity, were happening on the turf of a single city. "That's good news," he said. "The Arabs, the Spanish, and the Africans have done things of great genius together."

Though Talal was tantalized by the Oz-like cluster of downtown skyscrapers, so tall that they loomed magnificently while still several miles away, we both took Fahd's portrait as a totemic sign to turn around and get to the Watts Towers Festival.

Porky billows of barbecue smoke rolled over the old train tracks on Willowbrook Avenue and through the tree branches. Talal inhaled and worked his eyebrows in anticipation as we drew nearer the barbecue grills set across barrels sawn in half lengthwise. Long sides of pork ribs painted with crimson sauce crackled on the spits. There was also chicken, beef, chitterlings, and tubs of collard and mustard greens. Talal's facial expression partially registered confusion; he did not recognize any of these smells.

"Don't bother to ask," I told him. "You'll go to hell if you eat any of it."

"Especially with Fatso looking down on me," he agreed, jerking his thumb in the direction of the king's portrait fifty blocks north.

Bookstalls sold African and African-American histories, Egyptian religious books, Caribbean calendars, and bales of self-published local history. Artists displayed oils and charcoals of Martin Luther King, Jr., Malcolm X, Marcus Garvey, Elijah Muhammad, Bob Marley, and Emperor Haile Selassie. There were "Queens of Africa" posters sponsored by a beer company, jewelry, Watts Towers T-shirts, African cosmetics, caps, robes, and rows of food booths selling hot meals, corn-bread, and sweet potato pies. One stand sold videocassettes of old *Amos 'n' Andy* episodes—"Kingfish in Trouble," "Sapphire's Phony Romance," and a dozen more.

"Welcome," said a smiling man wearing a knitted skullcap and loose African shirt called a dashiki in the 1970s. "I am pleased to welcome you brothers to the Watts Festival." He gave us discount coupons for a hot links stand and advised us to buy our sweet potato pies from Miss Emma's front yard on Hickory Street, then asked where we were from. When Talal said Mecca, he and the man—who introduced himself as Karim—got into a long talk. Karim was a Muslim who yearned to go on the pilgrimage.

"I wish I knew Arabic. I just know the basic prayers," he said.

Karim was not the only nonlinguist in the crowd. While the two of them chatted, I strolled by the tent of empty folding chairs where a jazz quartet was gearing up and encountered two portly women in white gowns and hats handing out lime-green leaflets. They were almost entirely in Hebrew except for the word "Yahweh" printed twice in English with graphics, and a brief anti-Semitic blurb ("white racist Cossack/Khazar Zionists") in English. Neither woman offered me one.

"May I have one, please?" I asked the first woman. She looked away and gave me one. I scanned it but could make little sense of the poorly printed miscellany of phrases. *"At mdeberet 'Ivrit?"* I asked pleasantly.

They must have been members of the Black Hebrews, a nutty wannabe sect that taught—though I doubt even they believed it—that Africans were the only true Jews. I was disappointed that there were no Black Hebrew men around, because they sometimes wore turbans, sashes, and even scimitars on television, but the sisters—I am sure they called themselves sisters, even though they weren't talking—refused to answer my questions. I kept the leaflet, but wasn't it funny that a group with Judaic and African pretensions would be known only for celebrating this sort of perpetual Klannish Halloween? To say nothing of the oddity—given the dark persecutions of Jewish history—that such well-padded Baptists would want to play at being Jews.

Talal did not want to look at the Hebrew flier and refused to go near the Nation of Islam booth, dismissing it with the word "slaves"—fortunately in Arabic. "Let's see the towers," he suggested.

Like surreal rockets, the transparent Watts Towers—hollow filigree steeples of steel-and-concrete hoops encrusted with glass and ceramics—soar nearly a hundred feet over 107th Street, just where it reaches a narrow dead end. Admiring them in the mid-1970s, Jan Morris found the eccentric splendor of the towers in the poor neighborhood to provide the most magical spot in LA—"you might easily suppose yourself in some African railway town, in the Egyptian delta perhaps"—and the towers have an almost Egyptian-scale mythology. They were built over more than thirty years by Simon Rodia, an Italian immigrant, and are composed of steel rods and pipes, without scaffolding, connected by iron mesh and wire and coated with mortar. He never allowed himself to be photographed, left Los Angeles upon completing the work in 1954, and never returned. There were rumors of hidden treasure behind the plates in the walls and in the fanciful "boat of Marco Polo," which encouraged vandalism on a pharaonic grave-robbing scale. And in much the same way that ancient Egyptian temples gave life to modern Egypt through multibillion-dollar tourism, the towers have given a symbol and tourist destination to one of LA's flattest and most dangerous neighborhoods.

"Notice the decoration, which includes seventy thousand seashells," a guide was telling a group of children. "Look up. What else do you see?" They were too busy chewing on ribs to answer. "Pieces of dishes and glass, 7-Up bottles—see that green glass?—and that blue is from Phillips' Milk of Magnesia. There are tiles and mirrors, and pieces of flower pots. The children of the neighborhood helped Mr. Rodia find these ingredients of his artwork."

Riots apart, Watts is known mostly for these towers, which are a great but inappropriate metaphor for the city. Their lofty grace has survived only because both neighborhood vandalism and the city's attempts to pull down the towers—using ten thousand pounds of bulldozer pressure—failed to destroy them. Rodia did not come from LA and did not stay here, and never applied for a grant to create the city's greatest work of folk art. The irony was inescapable in a city that had a pathological quest for quaintness, always trying to create street festivals and ethnic events. Poor little Olvera Street, one of the oldest streets in the original pueblo of Los Angeles, had been turned into a market lane on steroids; it was jammed with plaques and souvenir shops where you could buy plastic bananas with the inscription "I went bananas in LA." By comparison, even Rodia's majestically weird towers, untouched by boutiques and official culture, seemed austere.

"I don't see any gangs," said Talal.

This was true, though he sounded disappointed. The crowds around the Watts Towers Arts Center, both black and Latino, were overwhelmingly local, but no one looked gangy. The voice of black LA in the entertainment media was rap music. People unfamiliar with the actual communities often got the idea that they were crawling with drug gangsters.

"They go about at night, and I just stay in," said Miss Emma, handing us single-serving sweet potato pies for one dollar apiece. She was tiny, wearing a hairnet and apron, and walking from table to cashbox in her front yard in a half-crouch, but beaming through her wrinkles. She stopped beaming for a moment. "This is a Crip neighborhood. They sell crack they buy down in Tijuana."

"How much better for them it would be, if only they were consuming your fine pies, instead of drugs," said Talal gallantly. He was proud of his grasp of verb tenses. "You should be charging more than one dollar each."

"Honey, my philosophy is live and let live, and I do just fine," said Miss Emma.

"Is it expensive to live here?"

"You ask this gentleman what the black tax is," said Miss Emma.

"What did she say?" asked Talal. She was already serving pie to the man in question, obviously a neighbor, since he hugged Miss Emma and she tried to refuse his two dollars. He smiled at Talal.

"High interest on home loans, high car insurance, high store prices."

"And high blood pressure. And the police, and these schools, and the gangbangers," added his wife.

This was before the gang truce that followed the 1992 riots. Even when that came along, of course, it only reduced crime among gangs; it would give a fabulous boost to the gangbangers' crimes against society at large. This part of Watts was indeed a Crip neighborhood: there was not a trace of red clothing anywhere, but lots of blue, especially in the navy paisley handkerchiefs knotted around young men's heads. Talal was vastly amused both by this and by the sagging—the gang look achieved by wearing pants nearly a foot lower than normal. The saggers' fat round rumps exposed underwear, almost always clean and often jazzy. Along 103rd Street, the patterns ranged from musical notes to silly red polka dots, and their belts were girded tightly around the middle hips, exactly where the bottom part of a belly dancer's costume begins.

"It is a diversionary tactic. They do it so the police will not look at their faces," concluded Talal, sounding very pleased with his analysis. "Did you know that? If you see two men with their trousers half down, and big bottoms in funny underpants, you will look at their bottoms. It buys them time to shoot. For the gang boy to shoot at the police."

I disagreed. What about escaping? How could they run? One teenage boy chatting up a girl at the corner of Central ("How can she accept to talk to him with his pants down?" marveled Talal. "She must be a very cheap girl") had his waistband so low that it was actually underneath the curve of his ass; he had to waddle with his knees together to keep his pants from falling down.

"He'd have to make sure he shot all the cops after him," I said. "How fast do you think he could get away?"

"Drugs," said Talal. "He does not ask himself such a question."

Our gangster, or wannabe gangster, was wearing a blue paisley handkerchief tied around his forehead, a baseball cap, dark sunglasses, and gold chains to complement the swath of white combed cotton that hugged the fat loaves of his buttocks. It was all out there—even if his jeans descended completely, there would be nothing more to see. His slightly staggering waddle was a reminder that the word "Crip" may have come from "cripple," describing the spastic strut that had been the trademark of the OGs, or Original Gangsters of LA, twenty years before. Anyway, all dangerous gangsters drove around in packs, with sawed-off shotguns and booming music; even walking beside a beautiful girl could not save this pedestrian from looking as if he had just been the victim of a swarm of demented attackers who had robbed him, disheveled his clothing, and humiliated him by cramming loud rags on his head and loading him with chains big enough to suggest bondage or captivity rather than glamour.

"Nice villas," commented Talal as we headed up Compton Avenue. The word sounded foreign in this run-down neighborhood, but of course the neat if peeling houses, grassy yards, sunflower patches and tall palms, and particularly the rows of freestanding "villas"—instead of the tenements that composed all Middle Eastern ghettoes—gave Watts a glamorous cast in Talal's eyes. And of course these houses were wooden; in the Arab lands, only marble was more expensive for construction. Few writers—John Rechy was one, in his novel *Bodies and Souls*—noticed the physical appeal of Watts, a "deceptive prettiness . . . which continues, lingers, never completely disappears."

"It's not like home," was Talal's comment as we sped into the sunset on the Santa Monica Freeway, enjoyed the uncommon speed and space of this cross-city flight.

We were on our way to see friends of his in Beverly Hills. Not only did all your old friends always visit you when you lived in Los Angeles, they always had other friends here, no matter where they came from. And though almost all of my old friends originated in obscure places, they always had a cousin in Culver City or an old neighbor from Aleppo to visit in Glendale. The tricky thing—for a host doubling as chauffeur—is that all such people in southern California abbreviated their whereabouts as "LA," and anyone who lived in the two hundred miles between Long Beach and Mexico seemed to give out his address as "LA—near Disneyland."

"Or maybe it is. It's a little like Manfouhah," Talal added. That was a poor market neighborhood on the outskirts of the Saudi capital, Riyadh, where newly settled bedouin got their first taste of urban life. It had Watts's diversity, if only in the sense of tribes mingling. "Of course, it's much nicer. Why does it seem so scary to people?"

Comfortable though it may feel, something in Watts—the hot sun, the small wooden houses, the aroma of tar roofs, the honeysuckle and sunflowers, the glimpses of cornstalks in some back gardens—gives it an Old South feel that offends the notion that this city is the world's capital of material glamour. Nor did it feel like a coastal city, since the whole wide horizon and Zen of the beach are absent. In a Third World setting, Watts would be upper-middle-class, partly because its drug dealers would have been long since executed. Transported to the Midwest, Watts might be considered a lively and diverse, if crime-ridden, success. Fifteen minutes from Hollywood, the incongruity of its peeling paint and barred windows leaves an unspoken indictment hanging in the air.

5

Hollywoods

Hollywood is the destination, but it is not one of the easier places to reach, thanks to its freeway-resistant steep hills and tony neighborhoods. The Hollywood Freeway itself runs through downtown Los Angeles and cuts a corner of east Hollywood, almost as if physical throughways could not quite close in on the place that Robert Redford has called "a state of mind . . . definitely a state of mind." Whether for work or play it is Hollywood's movie-capital status that makes LA a destination.

So, arriving in Hollywood is the biggest cliché of all. It is the big giveaway in half the books written about the place—giving away the fact that the authors are starting at best from zero, at worst from unreal preconceptions, when they take their first look. The look is very simple: new, lots of skin—this always makes a big impression, because so many visitors come from colder and more conservative climates—and rife with commercialism, too. Everyplace is commercial, but visitors

love to pretend to be shocked and amused that Sunset Boulevard is all about billboards or the freeways all about bumper
stickers. The laissez-faire sluttishness of Hollywood is what
usually detonates the smirking note-taker first, with a torrent
of arch first impressions.

"Southern California rolled past the windows" of the car
carrying Jeremy Pordage, the Aldous Huxley stand-in of
After Many a Summer Dies the Swan (1939), who, in the first
chapter, has just arrived in LA:

> The first thing to present itself was a slum of Africans and
> Filipinos, Japanese and Mexicans. And what permutations and
> combinations of black, yellow and brown! . . . At every corner
> there was a drug-store . . . a vast, untidy, suburban world of
> filling stations and billboards, of low houses in gardens, of va-
> cant lots and waste paper. . . .
> EATS. COCKTAILS. OPEN NITES.
> JUMBO MALTS.
> DO THINGS, GO PLACES WITH CONSOL SUPER-GAS! . . .
> The car sped onwards, and here in the middle of the vacant
> lot was a restaurant in the form of a seated bulldog, the en-
> trance between the front paws, the eyes illuminated.
> "Zoomorph," Jeremy Pordage murmured to himself. . . .
> ASTROLOGY, NUMEROLOGY, PSYCHIC READINGS.
> DRIVE IN FOR NUTBURGERS. . . .
> CLASSY EATS. MILE HIGH CONES.
> JESUS SAVES.
> HAMBURGERS.

The same glib documentary of first impressions would be a
permanent favorite of literary newcomers. Fifty years later,
when Huxley's countryman Richard Rayner landed in LA,
about to write the novel *Los Angeles Without a Map* (1988),

little had changed but the mode of arrival—Pordage had come by train, and Rayner's Chapter 1 is set in the jet age.

> Hours later the plane began to descend. I looked out of the window and there was Los Angeles, huge and sprawling, stretched out in the sun, an endless possibility. . . . The cab was blue and white, a Chevrolet. A sign hung from the mirror, saying "Welcome to California. Adjust your Attitude."

Like many other literary visitors, Rayner suffers the delusion (or pretends to) that he is in a movie. "What an interesting movie I'm making," he muses on the plane from London to California, and when he has, in fact, finally found happiness in a Los Angeles hotel room with a real Angeleno ("My tongue explored a route down her body, past breasts, across belly and thigh . . ."), he marvels to himself that "a fantasy had sprung to life. I was, actually, *in a movie.*"

In his excellent *Naked Hollywood,* the companion volume to a television documentary of the movie industry, Nicholas Kent records the impressions of a newcomer to whom LA's setting—the light, the sky, the ocean, the palms—are already familiar from having seen so many movies, and that is without even leaving the airport. It is the opening of his book. Then, he writes, you leave LAX and head for Sunset Boulevard.

> . . . you head north on the 405 to Sunset. By now the sense of cinematic *déjà vu* is so potent that you are feeling like the lead player in your own biopic. Take a left on Sunset, past the manicured lawns on Bel Air and Beverly Hills. A perfect backdrop. Roll credits.

Never mind that he is obviously lost (the 405 and a left on Sunset would take him *away* from Bel Air and Beverly

Hills)—he is a lead player in his own biopic. After a guilty U-turn not recorded in the book, he does discover Hollywood:

> The reality is a disappointment. Hollywood today is a dormitory suburb, and the boulevard that bisects it is made up of images from a handful of tatty postcards—a star-studded sidewalk, an ancient steakhouse, an elaborate Chinese movie palace, a gaudy shopping strip for trippers.

It is the very fact that LA's stranger visitors (the kind who believe they are starring in a movie) head for Hollywood Boulevard first that has turned the street into a T-shirt-and-photo-op ghetto. Locals have no such insane delusions. An Angeleno can drive by acres of perfect lawns without it crossing his mind that he is in a movie. Visitors to southern California, on the other hand, *want* the place to be glamorous, silly, prurient, superficial, rich, and pretentious, with a dramatic layer of *noir*. It is a place that no one wants to see through native eyes. And opening these novels with arrivals was surely the result of movie influences, as so many movies—westerns in particular—begin with the stranger riding into town. It was subliminally cinematic.

Some of LA's gaudier crimes have been committed by showbiz-fixated out-of-staters, most notoriously Charles Manson, who came to LA, lived on a movie-set ranch, and wanted a record contract. The Sharon Tate murders happened only because Manson, in his quest for stardom, wanted to terrify the former occupant of the house, record producer (and son of Doris Day) Terry Melcher, and his girlfriend, Candice Bergen. And, of course, Hollywood stardom was also Adolf Hitler's dream for Eva Braun, once the Third

Reich had extended its dominion over the Hollywood Hills. Some LA books start not with arrival but with the first dissatisfied day. The heroine of Alison Lurie's *Nowhere City* notes:

> All the houses on the street were made of stucco in ice-cream colours: vanilla, lemon, raspberry, and orange sherbet. Moulded in a variety of shapes and set down one next to one another along the block, behind plots of flowers much larger and brighter than life, they looked like a stage set for some lavish comic opera. The southern California sun shone down on them with the impartial brilliance of stage lighting.

There is always the snappish reminder that something out here is phony—the very sunshine is scolded for not being quite real.

LA-set books by people who have lived in the place never begin with arrival and in fact tend to be short on description, good or bad. This is the case with Gore Vidal's *Messiah,* in which the city merits only the comment "Egypt one knows without visiting it, and China the same; but Los Angeles is unique in its bright horror."

Hollywood Boulevard is the emblematic LA street, famous for being famous. It is celebrated for its vulgarity, but really has not capitalized even on vulgarity—it has no pretense at all. It is supposed to be fun to look at, and full of places to spend money. Unlike the great promenades of Europe, it has no looming cultural or religious presence: no cathedrals or museums, nothing to suggest spirituality or authority—because this is not a capital city, either. The bright commercial brainlessness of the street can magnify a wonderful mood or turn a bad mood dismally black. The humorist S. J. Perelman found nothing to smile at on his first arrival here.

Hollywood Boulevard . . . creates an instant and malign impression in the breast of the beholder. Viewed in full sunlight, its tawdriness is unspeakable; in the torrential downpour of the rainy season, as we first saw it, it inspired an anguish similar to that produced by the engravings of Piranesi. Our melancholy deepened when the mem and I took an exploratory walk around the hotel. As we sat in a Moorish confectionery patterned after the Alcazar, toying with viscid malted milks and listening to a funereal organ rendition of "Moonlight in Kalua," the same thought occurred to each of us, but she phrased it first.

"Listen," she said. "Do we really need the money this much?"

That's the giveaway: even the great Perelman was here for money—in his case, to write Marx Brothers movies. LA is a land of promise, of fortunes to be made. It is not incidental that Huxley's Jeremy Pordage, a scholar, is coming to Los Angeles at the behest of a colossally vulgar millionaire to be royally paid to perform a relatively frivolous research job. The protagonists of *The Nowhere City* had come to LA for the money, too. Writing about and visiting LA always seem linked either to a bitchy school of anthropology or a profit motive. The writers do not so much name-drop as detail-drop (MILE HIGH CONES) to show that it is not they but Hollywood that is nuts. They live in a place they are imagining, and there is no bad weather—except for Perelman, who needed contrariness to flourish—to remind them that the place is real.

The money incentive is an important one because it put the money seekers on the defensive. People who came here for any more altruistic reason would never have become as venomous as William Faulkner, who called LA "the plastic asshole of the world," Bertolt Brecht, who called it a "coal-mine" and "sewer" (after having originally seen it as "Tahiti in metropolitan form"), and Aldous Huxley, who in his drug-clouded LA years—when his conversation could scarcely have been at its most sparkling—swore that "no man could find a better spot on earth, if only he had some intelligent person to talk to." Thomas Mann, Anthony Powell, and Evelyn Waugh all loved Los Angeles and gave it the same sort of ritual hazing to show that they had not sold out, though more often than not it was the proof that they had done just that.

It was the sun that brought the movies to southern California, even if the first local filming, some scenes from the 1907 feature *The Count of Monte Cristo,* was done in downtown Los Angeles on South Olive Street ("Over there," say LA Conservancy tour guides, pointing to a spot about three blocks away, not worth the walk; 751 South Olive is now a parking lot.) Hollywood's first movie was Cecil B. De Mille's *The Squaw Man,* made in 1913. Not only the sun drew moviemakers, but the proximity of the Mexican border, a refuge from patent agents from the East, who came to LA seeking out violations of the patent on Thomas Edison's filmmaking equipment. The glamour of filmdom and LA's lush natural setting—the county was still half orange groves—made Hollywood grow through the teens and the twenties, and attraction built on attraction. At least a dozen Angelenos I know have wondered aloud about why LA people are so good-looking; then decide that it is because of all the inbreeding of pretty movie hopefuls. And people expect the city to be pretty, too.

If you are not a movie buff, on the other hand, you do not expect Hollywood to look fabulous. In fact, you find its "bright horror" quite attractive. You know this mostly not from Hollywood Boulevard, which is the shortest of Hollywood's major boulevards, but from Santa Monica Boulevard. I first knew the east Hollywood segment of the street from the prosaic standpoint of a translator of Arabic. The particular Hollywood I needed stretched from the Armenian neighborhood near Vermont Avenue to the Lebanese consulate in a high-rise building near La Brea (it was not listed in the lobby directory, which added a hint of secretiveness to the loud, bright boulevard). I went there weekly for the new Beirut and Cairo newspapers, recordings, and the occasional supply of stewed fava beans for which the Armenians and I had retained a fondness.

There was a touch of Beirut in the driving; this was the only part of town where motorists ran red lights and swooped on and off the freeway like stuntmen. The width of Santa Monica Boulevard seemed to invite speeding, and my first LA speeding ticket was at Santa Monica and Alexandria Avenue, within sight of the double-spired Armenian church. I moaned about the ticket to all of my friends.

"Better to get a ticket for going too fast on Santa Monica Boulevard than for going too slow," said one of them meaningfully.

This was not only because east Hollywood was where you found current issues of *al-Watan al-Arabi* and *al-Ahram*. Its main street was a meat rack for prostitutes, mostly beefy males. I was slow to realize that. I had thought these hairy young men waiting for buses, half reclined on the bus bench, shirtless, legs in ripped jeans and spread apart, one hand lazily resting on the crotch, cocking an eyebrow at the traffic, were displaying some extremely laid-back LA mannerism. Subsequently I did notice that they eventually got rides in private cars rather than the RTD buses.

There was a slow evolution away from Arabic culture in east Hollywood, however, once the Soviet Union started to crumble. The Levantine neighborhood, which spoke Arabic and Armenian, became more strongly Armenian-speaking with the arrival of Soviet Armenians. The names—Garo, Arta, Arax, Arka—between Vermont Avenue and the Hollywood Freeway did not change, but the script did: from Arabic and English, to Armenian, to Russian. The little ethnic microclimates were visible in the video stores too, and the newsstands, where the bilingual English-and-Arabic *Beirut Times* gave way to trilingual English/Russian/Armenian papers. Fava beans and falafel were still for sale, but the script changed. The process was still going on, as one could see from the Aeroflot Air Express Transport trucks always parked near the corner of Santa Monica Boulevard and the freeway.

Old World Hollywood was also heavily Jewish. My literacy tutoring led me into immigrant tutoring; I taught conversational English to Russian immigrants. There were more Iranian Jewish immigrants, but like the Armenians, they had established communities to glom on to, in which they invested and intermarried, showing only the most casual interest in learning English. The Russians had to turn to social programs, and, in the case of my student, eventually to Occidental College. Her English had improved quickly, though her accent remained stubbornly Russian—even after a full year at what she could only call Accidential College.

The Jewish Resettlement Center was just south of Hollywood, in a building also housing the Israeli consulate and the local headquarters of several Israeli banks. Among the businessmen and diplomats who came and went were the center's kerchiefed old *babushki* and little Russian girls in old-fashioned frocks with foot-long bows on their pigtails. The graffiti in the men's room were the politest I had ever seen, in a city where graffiti were often six feet tall, slashed across the sides of buildings. Russian-Jewish LA graffiti were written in minuscule ballpoint letters in the narrow grout between the tiles: *Death to the Intifada, Death to Radical Feminism, Death to Pamyat.*

Immigrant Hollywood fades as you move west and the rents get higher; it ends altogether on the block of Santa Monica Boulevard where El Al Israeli Airlines once had a majestic billboard displaying the Hollywood sign and the Dome of the Rock, with the legend FROM ONE PROMISED LAND TO THE OTHER, 3 TIMES A WEEK. This promised land, Filmdom, is one of the few LA places that signally fail to become theme parks, and not only because Hollywood Boulevard is slummy, but because LA willfully destroys its past and its holy places. Would that the other promised land were so sane. Fanaticism over sacred real estate—the Jerusalem Syndrome—can never take hold in Hollywood, where the Brown Derby, Disney's first studio, the Garden of Allah, the Hollywood Canteen, Pickfair, Schwab's Drug Store, the Trocadero, the Mocambo, and the MGM back lots have all been razed to make room for parking lots or condominiums. There is nothing but the present in Hollywood, an eternal, if sometimes shabby, present. Only one movie studio, Paramount, is left. Many studios, however, return to the old place to launch a new movie.

Not even a genuine Hollywood premiere makes you feel you are actually in a movie, but it can make you feel like a star off the set. I had been given a pass to a premiere by a journalist friend, expecting to be in the audience, unaware that the evening starts having an audience of one's own. Any premiere at Mann's, formerly Grauman's, Chinese Theater fills a half block of Hollywood Boulevard with *Day of the Locust* mobs throbbing behind barriers and rubbernecking cops. But the walk by the throngs passes too fast. Life on this side of the velvet ropes should last more than twenty seconds. I had been on the other side, as an idle newcomer to LA looking for celebrities outside the Academy Awards venue, the Music Center in downtown Los Angeles, and seen Federico Fellini, Jane Fonda, and Glenn Close stroll in. In real life, in the impartial light of First and Grand, they could have been mistaken for a monsignor, a beautician, and a Westside real estate agent. Also, on that occasion there had been demonstrators adorned with sandwich boards reading BURN HOLLYWOOD BURN, DOWN WITH DIRTY MOVIES, and DIE HOLLYWOOD SCUM, but this social set passes on premieres. Now, clutching my ticket and strolling down the carpet that stretched from McCadden Place to the boulevard, where the Chinese Theater stood, I tried to look like the somebody who looked like a nobody, wearing sunglasses and giving the yelling crowd as little of my profile as possible—one full-frontal look at my face would confirm the worst, that I was a diversion from something bigger. I was almost immediately rewarded with screams of "Tom Hanks!" Unfortunately it was the real Tom Hanks they had sighted, easing out of a limousine with his wife ("Rita! Over here!" shrieked the crowd) into the brilliant glare of the forecourt of the theater. It was dusk, but the forecourt was a well of white light.

The red carpet was everywhere, and the electrical cables for the lights covered the hand- and footprints of movie stars. The quarter acre of footprints are far more famous even than the theater's weird Hollywood-Chinese roofline; the idea for the slabs came from Mary Pickford, after her little dog, Zorro, ran across her freshly set cement driveway. Realizing that she now had permanent keepsakes of her beloved pet, she telephoned Sid Grauman, who was then building the Chinese, and suggested that the theater display movie stars' footprints in the forecourt.

At this moment, it was filled with packs of journalists armed with lights, microphones, and cameras; like schools of fish, they would drift toward a target, and then instantly scoot away in concert upon discovering that it was a nobody. But the red carpet wound, like a funhouse track, past the cameras and booms, into the cavernous space of the theater, which was packed. The gold-and-red-tasseled ceiling and high Chinese screens—built in 1927, Early Bronze Age by Hollywood standards—reverberated with gleeful schmoozing.

I knew that Westside Los Angeles audiences often applauded the credits of movies. In smaller houses like the Nuart, Laemmle's Royal, even the Bay as far south as Seal Beach, a few hearty claps at a name as it glimmers onto the screen is a sleek assertion of rank, like recognizing a fine wine, if the name is obscure, or an announcement that this person is a close friend, if it is a Name. In any case it is a statement of belonging to the filmmaking community. So I should not have been surprised at the cannonades of applause that greeted the flicker of names on the gigantic screen.

The Columbia Pictures logo (the lady with the dazzling torch and background of sapphire clouds, briefly transformed into Columbia's corporate logo, then back again) came and went, but A FOGWOOD/INDIEPROD PRODUCTION brought down the house, with new cascades of clapping and even, I swear to God, a few bravos, for A DAVID SELTZER FILM, SALLY FIELD, TOM HANKS, and the name of the movie, PUNCHLINE. Unfortunately for the featured players, most of whom were sitting around me in this audience, applause for the rest of the cast was very up and down—pianissimo for JOHN GOODMAN, whose television career had not yet been launched, a medium burst for KIM GREIST, an explosion for PAUL MAZURSKY, and a slight trailing off for MAC ROBBINS, MAX ALEXANDER, TAYLOR NEGRON, BARRY NEIKRUG, PAM MATTESON, down through ANGEL SALAZAR and DAMON WAYANS. This heavily industry audience rested their hands, except for localized bursts, during the casting, editing, production design, and director of photography credits, though there were tremendous reprises of handclapping for PRODUCED BY DANIEL MELNICK AND MICHAEL RACHMIL, and WRITTEN AND DIRECTED BY DAVID SELTZER.

There would not be as much enthusiasm shown again until the party, which was frantic, and even more rubbernecky than the screening, because not only was it a premiere party, loaded with celebrities, agents, and press—it was being televised. It would be broadcast on HBO as "The Punchline Party," with a huge lineup of standup comics on the stage above the Hollywood Inn parking lot, and an audience full of famous faces.

There was Martin Mull, and Chevy Chase, and Jerome Hellman, who made *Midnight Cowboy,* and actresses Ally Sheedy and Valerie Bertinelli, producer Sherry Lansing, actors Christopher Lambert, Jason Patric, Kirk Cameron, director Paul Mazursky, and Phyllis Newman, the famed Broadway actress whose autobiography, *Just in Time,* had recently been published. I had noticed it in Book Soup on Sunset Boulevard because of the staggering roster of star blurbs praising her book from its jacket: Leonard Bernstein, Lauren Bacall, Neil Simon, Liz Smith, and even Betty Friedan.

"Phyllis, meet Peter Theroux—he translates Arabic novels," said my journalist friend.

("From this he makes a living?" someone behind me murmured in real bewilderment.)

"I know your very admirable work," bluffed the still-beautiful star of *One Life to Live*—she had played the shady Renée Divine. This was even better than the premiere. Here you felt famous because people pretended to know you—or, God knows, actually believed you were someone important.

"There is Dawn Steele," said someone; the diminutive lady was head of Columbia Pictures and was basking in praise of the picture we had all seen. Behind her back it was a different story.

"She is such a cow."

"This is actually a very bad vehicle for Tom Hanks."

"She started out thinking up designs for toilet paper—she made a fortune in New York selling toilet paper with the Gucci coat of arms all over it."

It had turned into a real industry party—almost none of the executives were watching the string of comedians perform on the other side of the tables that were piled high with chicken, pasta, and exotic breads filled with walnuts or sun-dried tomatoes.

I got talking to a Creative Affairs executive from RKO Pictures about how influential American movies were abroad, but the megasmashes tended to be trash. I was thinking of the runaway success of the Rambo and Rocky films in places like Lebanon. Terrorists seemed to thrive on Hollywood's most violent fare. It stoked both their fascination with and resentment of America. He nodded.

"High concept. Teen shit—foreigners love it. The better-written stuff is too hard to follow in the Third World. It's an important market, now, especially for videocassette sales. Too bad it makes them think less of us. But heck, it's their taste we're catering to."

I had not thought of it as a vicious circle, but here it was from the horse's mouth, smack in the heart of Hollywood Babylon itself. I got some food. There was Sydney Pollack, a gray eminence in this very young crowd, which was mostly talking about the packaging of the upcoming Jetsons movie. It reminded me of a growling letter from S. J. Perelman I had read, where he sneered at the young generation of Hollywood moguls as "agents and ten-per-centers" who had been "whipped and worn smooth by the hot blast of television." I found a table.

"You cannot have a small dinner party in this town," said George Christy, the *Hollywood Reporter* social columnist. He was busily forking in Caesar salad and taking notes with the other hand as he looked around at the milling guests holding plates. I looked at his pad and read *Tom Poston Larry Kasdan & Meg, John Lithgow*. "You invite ten people. They all RSVP. Your secretary phones around the day of the dinner to double-check. Everyone's on board. Dinnertime rolls around and half of them don't show up!"

We had been comparing LA and New York; despite the moderate LA-bashing of this renowned symbol of Hollywood, sloppy social manners were the biggest outrage he could come up with.

John Goodman settled down at our table, holding a beer, and nodded hello.

"Great movie. You were terrific," I said.

"Thank you," he said, glancing around. Tom Hanks and Sally Fields had disappeared after a brief appearance on the stage before the start of the comedy acts, which George Christy would describe in the following week's *Hollywood Re-*

porter as "Very Low-Grade Las Vegas . . . tiresomely raunchy and depressingly scatological." Goodman, though, was not only staying but chatting with ordinary folk. Perhaps he still felt in-character—he had played an insurance salesman in the movie—or perhaps his heavy build and kindly ordinary-joe looks expressed his real nature.

"I'm very privileged to meet you," a star-struck young woman at our table said, and asked for his autograph. She had been asking him what it had been like to work with Tom Hanks and Sally Field, and he had answered, "Great." Her smile, like mine, expressed her pleasure at having lucked into a celebrity that neither gushed at nor snubbed fans. His short answers, though, might have expressed a certain wariness of the stealthy actors and scriptwriters who might at any moment try to spring a script on him or send a tape. "I mean, you could have gone over and sat with Teri Garr!" she explained.

This was true. There were a couple of empty seats at the neighboring table, where the blond comedienne was holding court with a collection of famous faces from Second City Television, and Marsha Mason had stopped by to say hello to her.

"Teri Garr?" said Christy, looking around. "Thank you." He set down his fork firmly and went over to her.

"Well, I'm sorry, George—oh, for fuck's sake," Teri sputtered.

We could not hear what Christy was saying, but he filled us in when he reappeared and resumed his fork and pen.

"What was I saying ten minutes ago about dinner parties? I invited *her* to dinner and she RSVP'd and then didn't show. That is so typical of this town! I said, 'Look, I can pick up the phone and get Nancy Reagan' "—who was still living in the

White House—" 'and I don't need this kind of nonsense.' I told her off."

"She's dating Woody Harrelson from *Cheers*," said the star-struck girl.

The comedians were winding down and the exits were already getting congested. Not only is LA a notoriously early town, its people are freeway-conditioned to avoid rushes and traffic jams. Even though there would not be serious traffic anywhere at this hour, almost midnight, the beat-the-traffic gene ordered the partygoers home. Letter writers kept the *LA Times* informed of new and outrageous examples of the "seventh-inning escape"—from Hollywood Bowl concerts and plays as well as Dodger games.

The night was perfect, dark and starry. It was a Friday night, and people were discussing weekend plans as they filed out: Malibu, Santa Barbara, Laguna. "I still have the shack in Palm Springs," Christy was saying to someone, "but it's still too hot." It was September. Troubles, I suddenly thought, make you yearn for the past or for the future, but the serenity of LA makes you think only of today.

As Santa Monica Boulevard continues west, it passes through one of LA's more famous villages, as the city of Los Angeles gives way, at La Brea Avenue, to the city of West Hollywood. Despite being a busy town, it has a vacationland feel and an inarticulate feeling that tomorrow doesn't exist, and this may well stem from the lack of small children. West Hollywood is famous for being a gay city—the world capital of the gay adult film industry, as San Diego is capital of straight adult videos. "The Creative City" is what the signs officially welcome you to—the creativity is expressed in film, interior design, restaurateuring, and fashion. Its birthrate must be only slightly above Vatican City's.

Not that any of this is new. When West Hollywood was incorporated as a city in 1984, becoming LA's eighty-fourth city, it had only 575 children—about 1 percent of the population. The demographics of the place were distinct: only 16 percent of the residents had been born there, and more than a third had been born outside the United States. In the battle leading up to incorporation, an anticity group, the Keep West Hollywood United movement, was accused by the local press of creating fears of a "Jewish takeover" or a "gay takeover." These minority communities, diluted at the county level, might have loomed large in a tiny city and made war over the Book of Leviticus. Actually it was those two groups that did the most to promote the city's tolerant atmosphere.

There was no Jewish takeover, except on weekends when hundreds of elderly Russian Jewish immigrants took over Plummer Park in their baggy pants, print dresses, and stout old black umbrellas to protect them from the sun. Sometimes they brought their grandchildren—the girls were always wearing hair bows two feet in diameter. Every bench and chair was taken up by the old immigrants, who read Russian newspapers and played dominoes and fended off ("No green card yet!") the Democratic and Republican party workers who were always circulating with clipboards, trying to sign them up.

The gay takeover was somewhat more successful. With a quarter to a third of its inhabitants being gay, West Hollywood elected America's first openly gay mayor, Valerie Terrigno, as soon as it became a city, and its stretch of Santa Monica Boulevard was much more a gay ghetto than Watts was a black one. The inward-looking curse of the ghetto lay still even on this most liberated community, where pink fliers on telephone poles urge their readers not to serve in the military ("Let the hets die for this country. You have more creative things to do!''). Such nasty paranoia is rare, though—if anything, West Hollywood is the epitome of southern California's good humor and informality, especially in dress, which in summer is so scanty that you would swear there was a beach half a block away in this landlocked city.

Like most other LA cities, West Hollywood started out as grazing land for livestock, with the name Rancho La Brea. At the turn of the century, Moses H. Sherman, a railroad man from West Rupert, Vermont, built a station for his Los Angeles Pacific Railway on the former rancho land, to connect LA with Santa Monica and allow the rancho to sell its peas, beans, and fruits to LA. In no time the twelve-acre settlement was renamed Sherman, and marketed to pioneers seeking a new life on the fringes of the nascent silent movie industry. Sherman, its promoters boasted, was conveniently located "between Hollywood and Beverly," both "peopled by a high class of citizens."

Time was already running out for the high class of citizens in between. As Hollywood proper was part of Los Angeles, movie stars and other fun seekers, gangsters among them, during Prohibition, looked toward the unincorporated land to the west, which was off-limits to the Los Angeles police. Like that of Watts, Sherman's character was shaped by the freedom its unincorporated status offered. Unlike Watts, though, Sherman had rich neighbors. Its boosters were not absentees, and its lots were drawn larger, especially north of Sunset Boulevard, a segment of which now became the Strip. The result was a resolutely upscale city. As early as the 1920s, most of LA's hot spots—Ciro's, the Mocambo, the Trocadero, the Garden of Allah—were here. Gangsters, of whom Bugsy Siegel was just one, thrived. Like Industry Hollywood, founded by fugitive patent scofflaws, West Holly-

wood prospered on the initiative of new residents who
wanted to be beyond the reach of the law. Its gay reputation
dates from the same period: harassed in the jurisdiction of Los
Angeles police, Westside gay men and women moved their
night life beyond its reach, to West Hollywood, and then
started to work and live there. The West Hollywood Historical Society states bluntly that, in addition, "gays [were] attracted in part by the interior design establishment" and the
profusion of houses and apartments, cheaper than in Beverly
Hills, that made it "a quiet little Greenwich Village of sorts."
A town with all this gaudy sin for sale was not going to remain
"Sherman" for long.

Sherman did not know what to call itself. In the mid-1920s
it toyed with strictly descriptive names like Cahuenga Valley
and climatological choices like Magnetic Springs, even
though it had, in practice, already succumbed to the dream-
factory town next door, calling itself West Hollywood, and it
stuck with that name when it incorporated. It is the epitome
of Hollywood, too: unlike the Hollywood district of Los Angeles to the east, it is clean, prosperous, and lavishly residential. None of its bookstores, like Book Soup and the Bodhi
Tree, or star-crowded restaurants, like Chasen's and Spago,
are more than a block from immaculate middle-America suburban streets. There are high rises old and new, especially
along Sunset and in the hills, but south of the Strip the typical
dwelling is a little Sherman clapboard behind high hedges
with only a glossy BMW or new Bentley in the little driveway
to demonstrate the solid gentrification of the place. West
Hollywood never wanted to be part of LA, and in fact is unlike it, in its compactness and many pedestrians, even its lack
of male prostitution—who needs it amid all these crowded
gay cafés with their dozens of AND NOW FOR MY NEXT TRICK

T-shirts? Its residents never wanted to be annexed by the city of Los Angeles, though before incorporation some wanted to merge with their neighbor to the west—this inclination could be seen in other possible names for West Hollywood, such as Beverly Park and East Beverly. But such a jaded suitor could not interest Beverly Hills.

6

BH

You have not left movieland behind at the West Hollywood city line, where bars and florist shops give way to broad lawns and "Maps to the Stars' Homes" stands: the "Welcome to Beverly Hills" sign informs you that this is the sister city of Cannes, France. In fact, Beverly Hills has a serious case of Francophilia, evident in street names like Charleville, Nimes, St. Pierre, and St. Cloud. (At least Beverly Hills doesn't have the diacritic addiction you see elsewhere in LA, where you find business names like Eleganté, Belmonté, and Trendé.) The dominant architecture is a variation on a chateau, a confection of stucco with oriels and wildly oversized mansards. There is a French-owned hotel in the neighborhood, too, a flesh-toned chateau on steroids called the Ma Maison Sofitel, where California girls answer the telephone with an airy "Ma Maison Sofitel, *bonjour,*" but are stumped if you take French any farther than that; *bonjour* is official policy, but none of them actually can speak French. With its tiny surface area and relentless glamourocracy, however, it is not France but Monaco that Beverly Hills is emulating.

Beverly Hills is even more a city of the imagination than Hollywood, but whereas Hollywood is everywhere, an industry, a state of mind, an attitude, Beverly Hills is a relentlessly limited and excruciatingly well-defined place with fanatical borders. It has always wanted to be small. It resisted annexing land east and west, and nearly panicked when West Hollywood put out merger feelers in its direction in the early 1980s. "Keep it limited and keep it precious," as one city leader put it.

The city's history is the stuff of a sweeping miniseries, and it is incredible that *The Beverly Hills Story* has not been made into a staggeringly star-studded television extravaganza, in which all the celebrities would play themselves in the final half hour. The introductory irony would be that Beverly Hills was founded by hillbillies.

It was the Valdez family from Sonoma, Mexico, who would be the ancestors of Beverly Hills: young newlywed Eugenio Valdez, his wife, and their parents emigrated to California in 1781. The Ferrer Villa family emigrated from Sonora the same year, bringing their six-year-old son, Vicente. About twenty years later, the Valdezes' California-born daughter María Rita married Vicente and they settled in the Mexican land grant known as San Antonio. She was still living there in 1831, a widow with eight children, when she had to fight off a claim from an abusive cousin, Luciano Valdez, who had built a house on the land; for a settlement of $17.50 she got rid of him and became sole owner of the Rancho Rodeo de las Aguas (Ranch of the Gathering of the Waters). The spread lay at the base of Benedict Canyon and Coldwater Canyon, which included not only all of present-day Beverly Hills but bordering areas of the future Bel Air Estates and Westwood on the west, and Rancho La Brea (the La Brea Tar Pits) and Rancho La Cienega to the east. After fires and Indian attacks, María Rita sold the whole ranch for four thousand dollars in 1852, for use as agricultural land. But after one successful crop and one failure (one of the buyers, William Workman, shot himself), it was sold to Pioneer Oil Company in 1862. The land yielded no oil either, and was put to use as pasturage for sheep. Subsequently the territory was divided up into lots for sale at ten dollars each, but there were no buyers.

It may have seemed that the rich but petulant soil of the future Beverly Hills refused to do anything as plebeian as sprout wheat or spew oil, but things looked up when it was found that lima beans grew beautifully throughout the rancho. In 1887 the railroad came through, rechristening the land Morocco, after the name of the local train depot. In 1906 a little city was mapped out by the Rodeo Land and Water Company. The section on the flats between Wilshire and Santa Monica boulevards was given the tony name of Beverly—the inspiration was President Taft's vacation house in Beverly Farms, Massachusetts. The other, mountainous half of Morocco, from Santa Monica Boulevard north to the hills, was named Beverly Hills, and in 1914 both areas were incorporated as the city of Beverly Hills (pop. 550).

Advertising—"boosterism"—was, as always, the engine of southern Californian growth. While Long Beach trafficked in morality and amusement park rides, Beverly Hills sold salubrious weather, aided by the pseudoscience of "climatology," devised by one of LA's legendary boosters, Lorin Blodget. The movement was aided by terrible cold spells in the northeastern United States in the late nineteenth century:

"Cold with moisture leads to pulmonary diseases; heat with moisture leads to malarial fevers; and pulmonary and malarial afflictions are two of the main causes of mortal disease. In California the air is dry and pure."

Just as big a draw as the healing climate was Pickfair, the old hunting lodge high in the hills at 1143 Summit Drive that Hollywood's two most glamorous stars, Douglas Fairbanks, Jr., and Mary Pickford, converted into a palatial home. It had the first swimming pool in Beverly Hills—one hundred feet long—man-made canals and a beach, and even the romance of wilderness; Fairbanks, who loved hunting, was living in the midst of a natural deer and coyote habitat. The two movie idols were married at Pickfair, and entertained all the royalty in Hollywood as well as the foreign-born variety, of whom Prince George of England, Lord and Lady Mountbatten, and King Alfonso XIII of Spain were only a few. Dry and pure air, plus the glamour of movies and the West's most vertiginous social ladder to climb, sealed Beverly Hills' luxurious fate.

Not only the air, of course, but the land was dry, and in 1923, a citizens' movement began promoting annexation to Los Angeles, mostly to gain access to Los Angeles' large water supply. It was up to the rich and famous, who wanted to retain Beverly Hills' exclusive character, to campaign vigorously against annexation, and the city of 844 registered voters defeated annexation by 507 to 337. Eight great stars among the city's movie community are immortalized for the anti-annexation activities by a black monument of a spiraling strip of celluloid surmounting an octagonal base with bas-reliefs of the heroes (Douglas Fairbanks, Harold Lloyd, Tom Mix, Conrad Nagle, Fred Niblo—director of *Ben Hur*—Mary Pickford, Will Rogers, and Rudolph Valentino), which still stands at the corner of Beverly Drive and Olympic Boulevard.

Despite being the headquarters of Hilton Hotels, Litton Industries, and Earl Scheib Auto Paint & Body Shops, Beverly Hills is all about retail shopping. The boosterism that built the cities of Los Angeles lives on here, but the vocabulary effort that used to be put into climatology has been converted into the smooth pitch of this little El Dorado's purring consumer salesmanship. You cannot look into any Visitor Center brochure or walk down Rodeo Drive for ten minutes without seeing the words "elegant" and "finest" thirty times each. Wherever you look you will, you are assured, enjoy a Continental atmosphere, European ambience, luxurious amenities, impeccable Old World charm, personal attention, world-renowned cuisine (sophisticated lunching, intimate dining, gourmet creations, and truly celebrated confections), gracious warmth, legendary personal service, unsurpassed comfort, prestigious salons, exclusive showrooms, and luxuriously appointed facilities; you will acquire distinguished apparel, deluxe jewels, distinctive furnishings, classic menswear, extraordinary fragrances, unique glassware, superbly handcrafted luggage, exquisite silks, elegant accessories for discriminating purchasers, tasteful linens, customized leather goods, signature mechandise, upscale fabrics, one-of-a-kind gemstones, internationally acclaimed silver, meticulously designed fragrances, painstakingly created ceramics, unforgettable furs, superlative crystal and exceptional china, unparalleled financial services, and, when you must regretfully leave, full destination planning and chauffeured ground transportation. It is a bit of a theme park—Rich Land.

The city officially encourages a "Golden Triangle" walking tour, which mostly encompasses the Rich Land theme park below Santa Monica Boulevard. The mansions above are covered by the Homes of the Stars tours, which the city does *not* encourage—the maps and tours generally come out of Hollywood, not Beverly Hills—and the really spectacular ones are hidden by walls and hedges.

Stop #1 on the Golden Triangle tour sounds an ominous note: at the corner of Beverly Drive and Charleville, you are faced with the same crosswalks, restaurants, and drugstores that would greet you at the main crossroads of any little town in the world. The only signs that you are in LA are the men with luxuriant black manes and women with wild blond ones, all tightly swathed in the same black spandex and Ray-Bans. "You are surrounded by the Four Corners, which are four separate buildings on four separate blocks built and owned for many years by the screen actress Corinne Griffith," reads the printed guide. Even the most enthusiastic trekker suffers a twinge of sarcasm crossing Charleville: let's see now, four *separate* buildings on four *separate* blocks? Oh, my! And this was *the* Corinne Griffith?

The tour moves north on Beverly Drive to the busy intersection with Wilshire, and the brochure calls your attention to the beautiful white Moorish-style building with the onion-shaped dome; formerly the Beverly Theater, it was built by an architect who gloried in the name L.A. Smith in 1925. Now it is the Israel Discount Bank. The Mediterranean theme is continued at Stop #3, Two Rodeo Drive, "one of the most expensive retail centers ever built," a tiny shopping mall accessible from Wilshire by the Spanish Steps. These are, well, steps, leading up to Via Rodeo, a theme-park Spanish street with the José Eber Salon, assorted chocolate purveyors, and a café. The mixed Italian-Spanish street name is a sign of the city's rather lame Latinate touch, which Evelyn Waugh and S. J. Perelman lampooned with street names like Via Dolorosa and Alta Yenta Drive.

You go north on Rodeo Drive, a neat two-block-long

B H

street equally famous for its expensive shopping and very plain looks. Everyone knows that Hollywood Boulevard is a letdown, but at least its gaudy squalor makes an impression—it *looks* like the famous Boulevard of Broken Dreams. The guidebooks should call Rodeo Drive "inimitably understated" instead of "fabulous," which would dull the letdown of seeing one of the most boring streets in the city. Number 32, though, was designed by Frank Lloyd Wright—Anderton Court, a short white office building with a jutting front and an open ramp zigzagging from floor to floor, up to a high spire. The building is not one of Wright's greatest, as it is a minor thing with obvious problems—the ramp seems to be too small for handicap access, for example, and even the official walking tour guide calls it "one of Wright's lesser and zaniest creations." It is, however, almost the climax of the walking tour, notwithstanding being Stop #4 out of a total of twenty-one.

There are very few pedestrians, meanwhile, but they are the same ones you would see at any theme park in the world: Japanese and European tourists, all with maps and cameras but almost none with shopping bags, American families with videocameras, and the equivalent of park staff: doormen and security guards outside Van Cleef & Arpels and Fred Joaillier, the occasional Ambassadear (the city's red-uniformed guides), and the police (this being the best-policed six square miles in LA). Instead of sighting Mickey Mouse or Snow White, you may spot Ted Turner, Julia Roberts, Cher, or some other Rich Land character getting in or out of one of the long cars that frequently cause limo-lock all the way down the block.

The next landmark is the Rodeo Collection, a marble shopping mall, selling mostly apparel, fragrances, and truly distin-

117

guished beauty supplies, built by an Iranian entrepreneur, Daryoush Mahboubi-Fardi. Across the street is the boutique owned by Mahboubi-Fardi's compatriot Bijan. He is known for running one of the city's few clothing shops for which appointments are necessary ("However," notes the Historical Society's illustrated coffee-table book *Beverly Hills,* "if you are covered in diamonds and chinchilla they just might let you in").

In LA at large, Bijan is best known for his billboards on the San Diego Freeway near Los Angeles International Airport, which show his doughnut-shaped glass bottles of Bijan perfume and the creator himself, all in white, his tanned face distorted in what must be a frantic scream of delight—as you round the South Bay Curve, you almost drive into his mouth. The current one shows him and his wife, in black, doing the scream.

I chiefly remember Bijan, however, for his dictator clocks. He once designed a tribute to his international clientele by filling his store window on Rodeo Drive with a clock for each major client, adorned with the customer's name and that country's flag, and of course the clock was set to the homeland's local time. The joke, certainly lost on Bijan, was that he had created a unique, tasteful, elegantly crafted, superbly realized rogues' gallery. Prince Ahmad bin Abdelaziz, Saudi Arabia, 10:00. Jean-Claude Duvalier, Haiti, 2:00. Omar Torrijos, Panama, 2:00. It was hard to believe that it was not intended to be subversive, that it had not been done with the assistance of a massive California Arts grant, and that it was an advertisement in a Rodeo Drive shop window instead of an installation on the wall of one of LA's ludicrous galleries of horrible state-funded art. There on the right would have been a scrapped car, entitled *LA: Unsafe at Any Speed.* On the left you would have three scorched cereal boxes—*LA: Snap, Crackle, Pop*—that would be a commentary on the riots. In the middle, the wall of dictator clocks, with a placard reading "Time Is Running Out." Even the clocks could have been given an LA theme with the motto from the sundial of the local San Gabriel Mission: *Ora Omnia Vulnerat, Ultima Occidit* (every hour wounds, the last one kills).

Moving on, you notice that Beverly Hills is strong on galleries, selling what is immediately recognizable as Big House Art: rather mediocre, hugely oversized, and, oddly enough, not hugely expensive, possibly because with art fashions changing so quickly, all of these brushed-nickel nymphs with Mardi Gras masks, rough spheres of green distressed copper, and bright Disney reproductions are considered disposable rather than durable goods. It was all made for big boardrooms, big bedrooms, big living rooms, and big vestibules. Some of the stuff you never see outside Beverly Hills: actual expensive representative art like life-size peacocks, ballerina statues with real silk tutus, painted harlequins with gold-trimmed shoes, and classical reproductions like the ones in the gift shops in Caesars Palace in Las Vegas: an imposing soapstone Pericles head, a row of faux-marble caryatids, and a bevy of snow-white vestals.

Beverly Hills has a pale Waspy reputation, but in fact it is a surprisingly brown city. As elsewhere in LA, the nannies pushing strollers are Latinos, as are the sweepers, car-parkers, and the one or two very furtive panhandlers, who generally are found only on Rodeo. Iranian boys with gold ID bracelets lounge with tennis rackets over their shoulders or tool around in Porsche convertibles or BMWs with LA's uniquely Persian signature: white bodies, white door handles, and white hubcaps. There is a distinct Middle Eastern air to the place, which goes far beyond the hot sun and towering palm trees. "In the 1950s there was a large influx of Jews, who built synagogues and schools," states the city's official history, produced by its Historical Society. "The Arabs began arriving in the 1970s, and their children account for 40 percent of the school population."

Actually, the Arabs' flirtation with Beverly Hills was brief and mostly investment-oriented. Their principal footnote in Beverly Hills' history was the episode of eccentric young Sheikh Muhammad al-Fassi, who was related by marriage to the Saudi Arabian royal family. He owned a mansion of an ugly green shade on Sunset Boulevard and painted skin tones and pubic hair on the Greek statues that adorned his front lawn. It was destroyed in an arson fire in 1980 and finally razed in 1985. Plus, these Arabs were all from the nouveau riche Gulf states, with hardy bedouin roots, and must have been insanely intimidated by Beverly Hills' cosmopolitan and well-established Jewish and Iranian communities. As I turned right on Rodeo onto Little Santa Monica Boulevard—a shopping lane parallel to the boulevard itself—it was my luck, as a translator, to happen upon a Lebanese lady and a child who appeared to need my services; I knew they were Lebanese from the three-year-old's East Beirut accent, not the woman's. I then saw, however, that she was a mother, not a nanny, and that she was probably just trying to make her child worthy of Beverly Hills. She was bouncing him on her arm as she looked through her pink figure-eight sunglasses at some Big House Art—a naiad made of antiqued green copper—in a gallery window near the corner of Beverly Drive.

"*Aseer, Mama, biddi aseer! Biddi aseer halla!*" He was squalling that he wanted juice, Mama, juice, *now*, and refusing to look into the showroom window.

"Silence, chéri, tu peux prendre du jus un peu plus tard, mon petit chou, assez, donc," cooed his mother, pushing his hair out of his eyes. *"Regardes cette belle déesse."*

"La, biddi ishrab aseer!" He didn't want to look at the pretty goddess, and probably had no idea what his mother was saying.

The tour directs you to continue down Little Santa Monica Boulevard to see the city's airborne-looking "Jetsonesque" gas station (the roof is a colossal populuxe wedge that looks like a forty-ton red corn chip). Beyond Little Santa Monica, on Santa Monica Boulevard's thundering six lanes, I was suddenly struck by a lurking fear. People who live in Los Angeles are asked by others, Don't you worry about landslides? Aren't you afraid of earthquakes out there? What about riots? To which, it now struck me, there was only one answer: No, I am afraid of not having a car. The small scale of Beverly Hills had just given way to this tremendous highway, which was, as usual, a two-way chariot race of chaotic traffic. A big bus was sneezing to a halt at the bus stop before Crescent, but the bus benches were jammed with shoppers, busboys, waiters, and salespeople on their way home to Hollywood, and the bus was already full. There was not one taxi in the traffic.

"This city sure loves its cars," marveled a tourist to his wife, who were standing beside me behind the crosswalk.

His wife responded by actually taking a picture of the traffic. I was sure she was focusing on a cream-and-chocolate Rolls-Royce stopped at the light.

Does LA love its cars? This was an apt point at which to puzzle at the status of the car in California. Here we are famous for "car culture," and yet I had read in the *Los Angeles Times* that in 1993, Californians "owned fewer vehicles than the national average: .73 per person versus .75 nationally. We use less fuel in a year: 520 gallons per person versus 560 nationally. And we drive less: 8,400 miles versus 8,500 miles." LA is not known for its public transportation, but Europe—of which one is forcefully reminded, a block from the Beverly Hills' Italian Renaissance post office, with the river of Mercedeses and BMWs flowing gently down the street, in a town where even the Arabs speak French—has excellent public transportation, and yet its use of cars has increased three times faster than in America. Here, the weather was too good not to use cars—wasn't the convertible LA's iconographic car? The extra freedom was essential for creative changes in plans, and then there was the sheer size of metropolitan LA, about a thousand square miles. There was certainly no special love affair with the car, as Charles Lave, the *LA Times* writer, had pointed out; I knew what he meant. Having grown up in Boston, I knew that you could resent cars because you sometimes had to dig them out of the snow, and their wheels made whining and screaming noises as they spun, trapped in icy ruts. Cars here were looked upon more fondly, that was all. You could feel panicky without one, and the next moment delighted to be strolling around town, free of your two-ton steel anchor.

A banner was strung across Crescent Drive: "South Central Los Angeles and Beverly Hills in Harmony: GOSPEL CONCERT at Beverly Hills High School."

Stops #8, #9, and #10 take the now footweary explorer to the Beverly Hills Fire Station, Civic Center, and Post Office. The Renaissance post office may have "vaulted ceilings covered in mosaics and murals"—the murals are set dizzyingly high, depicting scenes of workers and toilers in egg tones—but it is the library that is interesting.

The Beverly Hills Public Library is a very different world

from the posh mixture of predictable glitz and unexpected boredom of the city's downtown shopping area. I walked through its cream, green, and purple lobby, where a lady wearing a cherry-red silk pajama outfit shuffled with her walker and a stack of books toward the circulation desk. There an Asian-American boy with waist-length black hair and round black Harold Lloyd glasses took the patron's selections: Barbara Taylor Bradford's *Angels,* Wendy Hornsby's *Telling Lies,* and a trashed paperback of *The Zodiac Killer.* Six boys in identical white shirts, charcoal-gray trousers, and black leather yarmulkes swept into the corner area to tap away at the computerized Info-Trac system for locating books. They were speaking rapid Persian, interspersed with words like *"Not!"* and *"I'm so sure!"* and when they had started tracking the books they wanted on the black-and-apricot monitor screen, I could see that it, too, was in Persian. Beverly Hills High is noted for its diversity—perhaps these were some of the gospel singers who might be performing in the LA and Beverly Hills in Harmony extravaganza. In the library vestibule, there were fliers posted for a poetry reading in a Crenshaw district park (PEACE LA: THE POETICS OF GANG TRUCE) and a City of Beverly Hills New Youth Team Program HIP-HOP Workshop for sixth-to-eighth-graders (WE'RE IN THE HOUSE IN FULL EFFECT . . . *One of the hottest dancers on the L.A. scene, Chonique Sneed, brings a unique flair to this workshop*)—this really was gracious, this seeking out of cultural ties with the southern side of the city.

In the periodicals room off to the right, blond and Asian teenagers were retrieving copies of the *Economist, Senior World,* and *YSB* from the tables and slapping them onto reshelving carts. There were grandmothers, two Latino girls reading a skateboarding magazine, and a glamorous young woman in spike heels and a pale lavender bouffant flipping through *Worth,* but by far the most attentive readers were the balding men devouring the new issues of the *Hollywood Reporter, Variety,* and *Billboard.* The tables were also full of local newspapers; this is a reading town, and as the *Beverly Hills Courier* immediately reminds you, a small one. Some of the news items could have come from a little town anywhere:

A Beverly Hills landmark, Pauline's Girdle and Lingerie Shop, closed its doors earlier this week. "This store has been here 49 years," said Pauline, who ran the location for the last 20 years under her own name. "It's kind of like the end of an era." Pauline's was well known for its incredible collection of women's intimate wear, which attracted shoppers from all over.

Of course, no small town has personals like the ones in Beverly Hills. Every single ad bristles with subtle codes establishing who might be offering money and who might be after it (the former are "financially secure," "generous," "successful," or just outright "wealthy"; the latter tend to specify someone "classy," or to make a pointed reference to appreciating "the finer things in life.") And you would scan the *LA Times* in vain for a:

MUSLIM AMERICAN Princess, private European schools, well traveled, resides in BH. Russian/Kashmiri born in Pakistan, seeks cultured Valentino/Sir Walter Raleigh, Caucasian/Mediterranean, discreet.

There were long lines at the circulation desk. Beverly Hills library cards are gold.

Ironically, the official walking tour goes downhill just as you leave the flats for the edges of the famous, much more fashionable hills, going west on Santa Monica Boulevard and then north up into selected sloping streets. You pass Beverly Gardens, where the Morocco Junction train station used to stand, and are directed to the O'Neill House, an example of Gaudíesque Art Nouveau. The Gaudí is a rest from the gaudy, but a slightly strained note is struck by a rich city's tour guide sending you three blocks out of your way to an interesting house, merely to see its "art glass windows and skylights." On this block, Hollywood had upstaged Beverly Hills. Across from the house, on Park Drive, were two parked back-country jalopies with spoke wheels, held together with rope and festooned with kegs of moonshine ("XXX"). The *Beverly Hillbillies* movie was being filmed here this spring.

The streets and homes, though, are the little city's real monuments. The splendid houses and beautifully laid-out streets are really the envy of the world. I remembered watching *Beverly Hills Cop* in a Jerusalem cinema in 1985 with an audience which enjoyed the plot twists politely but gasped with longing at the real estate. Every exterior or interior shot of a fabulous Beverly Hills house provoked an admiring "Tsssssssss!" from every moviegoer in the house. The wide streets, the luscious furniture, and the fabulous hotel lobby scenes were viewed with unhidden vicarious bliss, and the sight of the mansion where the final shootout took place nearly got a standing ovation.

It is to avoid shootouts like these that the rows of mansions are bristling with tastefully semi-concealed cameras and discreet signs proclaiming Westec, Armed Response, Bel Air Patrol, American Home Security, and Protection One. Everyone who writes about LA—everyone who visits LA—comments on the profusion of these small but menacing signs. The private security business is huge; the amount of what needs protection in an underpoliced city like Los Angeles is ever mounting. Beverly Hills may look overpoliced, even though its police are friendly and nearly all handsome (Zsa Zsa Gabor described the cop she slapped in 1988 as "gorgeous"), but given the worth of the city's property, every house wants its own little force.

At Santa Monica and Camden and stretching a full city block to Bedford Drive is the Cactus Garden. There is nowhere to sit, but then there is not much to look at. This rectangular ranch of prickly exhibits is one of the largest cactus collections in the world, the Golden Triangle guide boasts, but not even the most beautiful cactus merits more than a glance. Besides, you are nearing the frontier: you are almost back in Los Angeles. A small dirt park with unfriendly plants and nowhere to sit, with nothing to look at but the huge concrete boulevard, and its intersection, just three short blocks ahead, with thundering Wilshire. You go on to Walden Drive on the right for a glimpse of the Witch's House, built in 1921, with its rickety fence, tiny moat, and steep, crooked peaked roof. On the inside, says the guide, it is like any suburban home, but on the outside it looks like a storybook witch's house. At the corner of Santa Monica and Wilshire is a fountain, donated by Harold Lloyd's mother. Turning down Wilshire heading east, the guide urges you to take in Home Federal Bank with its "window boxes trailing real vines." And being invited to admire *real vines* is the thing that finally propels you out of Beverly Hills.

1

Confronting Santa Monica

Luis was functionally illiterate in two languages; he could read at about a third-grade level in English, whereas he could hardly read his native Spanish at all. His religious ideas, however, were fully formed: he was a born-again evangelical Bible Christian. We had our first meeting, ironically, in front of the statue of Saint Monica at the coastal point where Wilshire Boulevard meets Ocean Avenue in Santa Monica; he was carrying an adult literacy workbook and a dogeared Bible with floppy black covers. He lived in Wilmington, the Los Angeles harbor district just across the Los Angeles River from Long Beach, but worked on construction jobs all over the county. He had been tutored for a few months at a time through library programs wherever his work took him—Long Beach, Torrance, Lynwood, and Palos Verdes. Now he was working on a huge house being built in the northern, old-money section of Santa Monica, staying temporarily with a friend of a friend in a rent-controlled apartment on Arizona Avenue. He did not know where the library was, so I told him to meet me at the statue at the end of Wilshire for our first meeting. Walking six blocks to the library would give us a chance to get acquainted, but it was hard to leave this greatest of LA's ocean vistas.

Santa Monica is set high on miles of mountainous palisades, and Palisades Park, the long strip of magnificent palm trees and benches which runs along Ocean Avenue above the beach, commands a glittering sapphire panorama of Santa Monica Bay. Looking out at the hundreds of miles of whitecaps into the stiff Pacific breeze is like standing at the prow of an ocean liner, sailing between the extended forearms of the Palos Verdes peninsula ten miles to the south and the Santa Monica Mountains ten miles to the north.

"That's a piece of shit. That's a sign Los Angeles is the devil's city," Luis said when he saw the cream concrete statue. Built during the Depression by the Federal Art Project, the statue commemorated the mother of the North African Saint Augustine; during the saint's notoriously delinquent youth, Monica prayed and wept, with the conviction—her most famous quote—that "the son of these tears can never perish." In 1789, when a Spanish force camped at the coast with Christian missionary Father Juan Crespi, the gentle waves reminded the priest of Saint Monica's tears, and they named the bay and local springs after her. The theme was carried on by a local Protestant diocese, which in 1988 built St. Augustine-by-the-Sea Episcopal Church. Luis shook his head disgustedly at the glass jam jar of violets that someone had placed at the base of the statue.

There were not many "adult nonreaders" in Santa Monica. The city library had a literacy program, which dealt largely with members of the city's legendary homeless population, or people from nearby Venice, the lively beach district just to the south, famous for its resident movie stars like Dennis Hopper, its lively beach life, and its violent drug-dealing gangs. Many wealthy communities had too many eager volunteer tutors and no adult students, while more run-down areas, like Compton and south LA in general, had hundreds of willing students and few tutors. There was little crossover of resources, because undereducated adults tended to have complicated lives (children, odd working hours, spotty mobility) while tutors, the majority of whom were older women, generally hesitated to travel long distances to poorer cities. Long Beach had it about even, with about two hundred tutors and two hundred learners at any given time, but since its library system vigorously supported the literacy effort and the training of new tutor classes every two months, there was almost always a small overflow of Long Beach tutors. That is how I happened to tutor Luis Frenes.

On our way to the library, he nearly got run over crossing Ocean Avenue because he was trying to find an apposite passage in his Bible. Not that I was trying to argue with him; I was thinking that we could use his religious beliefs to lay the groundwork for a "language experience" writing exercise or piece of writing where he would set out his ideas logically. Like nearly every born-again nonreader I had ever met in LA, Luis wanted to be a preacher. Something in the literacy ordeal added fire to their religious ambitions.

We crossed Ocean at Lawrence Welk Plaza, an office development built by the late North Dakotan bandleader—the name of the adjacent apartment block, Champagne Towers, was a reminder of his bubbly music and of this city's more conservative past. When we reached the library at Sixth and Santa Monica Boulevard, Luis was impressed by the building but immediately peeved by a tribute to the lost Indian tribes. We worked our way through the snoring drunks in the reading room and found a quiet spot for tutoring in the reference section. "They're the devil's children," said Luis with a sad shake of the head. "They're not going to get saved here." I began to wonder whether this was a sort of built-in punishment for fanatics, the fact that *everything* got under their skin. More interestingly, here in America's largest Catholic archdiocese—thanks to Latinos like Luis—he was a throwback to Los Angeles' middle past.

LA was founded by priests and Catholic settlers, but in the late 1800s, in the period when its population multiplied a hundredfold, it became a Protestant city. Early Yankee settlers like John Temple in Long Beach and Eugene Plummer in Hollywood had been eager to convert to Catholicism to marry the daughters of Mexican ranch lords; *they* changed their names, becoming Don Juan Temple and Don Eugenio Plummer. But the big waves of Midwest immigration became too big to assimilate; they overwhelmed the population, and from the turn of the century until 1960, Los Angeles recorded the highest percentage of native-born white Protestants of any large city in the United States. Additionally, black settlers in LA during the Depression and World War II were nearly all Protestant. In the 1960s, though, Mexican immigration started to tilt the scales back in favor of the Vatican in a remarkable spiritual Reconquista.

In the end, it was the schismatic nature of Protestantism in LA, spawning endless breakaway sects and cults, both fringe and fundamentalist, that started to form a sea of strong American waves crashing against the Roman Church. Despite the vastly dominant scale of Catholicism in Spanish-speaking LA, about 20 percent of the county's Latino Catholics have converted to non-Catholic churches.

The Santa Monica Public Library is a monument to the town's literate values and its intensely liberal conscience. You are greeted at the entrance to the library by a long, narrow aerial photograph of the city's shoreline set above a panoramic shot of the old, uninhabited hilly coast. There is an elegantly carved text set beside it, from Dee Brown's *Bury My Heart at Wounded Knee,* which Luis had asked me to read along with him (a confidence-building technique called duet reading):

California Indians were as gentle as the climate in which they lived. The Spaniards gave them names, established missions for them, converted and debauched them . . . after the discovery of gold in 1848, white men from all over the world poured into California by the thousands. . . . No one remembers the Chilulas, Chimarkios, Urebures, Nipentais, Alonas, or a hundred other bands whose bones have been sealed under a million miles of freeways, parking lots, and slabs of tract housing.

"But those Indians were the worst kind of pagans and idolators," sputtered Luis crossly.

"What was it about the statue you didn't like?" I asked him in the middle of our lesson.

"Worshiping statues drags people to hell. Drag my mother and my father. He died of cancer. My sister wasn't a Christian—she kept pictures of the saints, and the devil gave her a miscarriage. She died and she wasn't saved."

"That's a very enlightened view, Luis, but Catholics don't worship statues, at least they're not supposed to. They're just reminders, like a photo of your kids."

"The Book says no graven images. Idol makers are gonna taste hellfire. There's no substitute for being right with the Lord."

"You've been tutored in Long Beach. You know the statue of Abraham Lincoln in front of the library? Is that wrong? Statues of saints are the same thing. They keep a memory alive, you might reverence them, but no one worships them."

I was beginning to feel uncomfortably like Father Crespi himself, but Luis was maddening. We turned to literacy: he was in the second workbook of our prescribed reading series, so we read a selection on how beer was made. "I don't even drink nonalcoholic beer," Luis pointed out severely, but soldiered through the piece slowly until he came to the word "fermentation."

"Jesus," he said.

"What's wrong?"

"I'm just calling on my holy spirit." He scrunched up his face and looked away, making a fist with his elbow resting on the table. "Frustration."

"Don't be frustrated."

"It's not 'frustration.' It's . . . 'frantation.' "

"Look at the word, Luis."

"I'm gonna call on my holy spirit."

While Luis consulted the oracle, his eyes clenched tightly shut, I gazed around the library at the displays on women's issues, AIDS/SIDA information, brochures on housing issues, and some of the homeless patrons sitting nearby. The unshaven derelicts with their whiskery, hot-pink faces had been a *cause célèbre* in this LA town half the size of Long Beach, which prided itself on its tolerance but relied very heavily on the spending of tourists whose eyes you could see widening in horror at the transients pissing into the daffodil bed in Palisades Park. Ocean Avenue and this park were famous for their aggressive panhandlers, who also haunted the pier and the open-air restaurants and built makeshift trash camps across from the city's best restaurants, high on the Ocean Avenue bluff overlooking the beach. There was a widely publicized public debate over whether sleeping patrons who reeked of urine and bourbon were legitimate library users, and this tolerant city decided that they were. The city had a large homeless population, drawn by the warm climate and hospitable municipal government—there was an official feeding of the homeless at the city hall every week. The mass feeding was temporarily suspended when the city's tolerance started to wear thin—Ocean Avenue had become a mecca for vagrants, many of whom were mentally ill or had drug problems, and all of whom, even the teenagers among them, claimed, well into the 1990s, to be Vietnam War veterans. This was why Santa Monica businesses now handed out colorful cards to shoppers:

Make your Change Help, Not Hurt
SAY NO TO PANHANDLING

The cards go on to urge you not to provide money for drugs and alcohol; to contribute to charity; to call the police if you feel harassed or threatened; and to "walk with confidence—the streets of Santa Monica belong to all of us." In the meantime, on Ocean Avenue, I Cugini, Ivy at the Shore, Kenny's Steakhouse, and other restaurants over the ocean have put up Plexiglas barriers around their roadside dining areas, shutting out the sea breeze along with the growling and deeply tormented panhandlers.

Jerry gave up on his recalcitrant or illiterate holy spirit and learned the word "fermentation." After going through the rest of the piece, he had had almost enough for one day; all he wanted to do was to have a look at a newspaper to check out available apartments. He was getting tired of sleeping on his friend's couch, and missed his family back in Wilmington—he saw them only when he could get a ride down to the harbor area, or on weekends, because he had to change buses several times, making the trip too time-consuming for a commute. We decided to meet weekly at this library for as long as his local construction job lasted. He would bring his *Challenger* book, some blueprints, which he wanted to learn how to read, and some of his AA reading materials. In the meantime, we would have a look at a local paper's apartment listings.

"I wish I could stay up here—it's a lot nicer than Wilmington," he said. "There's no construction going on up here, though. There's lots of demolition going on, but those crews are pretty tight. They got a lock on all that work."

"Demolishing what?"

"Apartment buildings, mostly. I made a lot of money on that work like ten years ago, but being down in Wilmington, I lost out to all the guys up here. Listen, I need to use the bathroom and wash up. Then we can check the newspaper. Where's the can?"

It was upstairs, necessitating another trip through the dormitory-like reading room.

There was an interesting reason Luis had made so much money destroying Santa Monica property; it was ultimately traceable to the town's affluence. Since 1860, the town had been a summer resort; at the turn of the century, Pacific Electric introduced the Balloon Route, a circular railway passage from Los Angeles to the spectacular beach at Santa Monica, but that was only for day trips. With the construction of the Santa Monica Freeway in the 1950s, which linked the city to downtown LA, real estate prices rose. The city attracted residential light industry, the Rand Corporation, and thousands of LA commuters in addition to its longtime retirement community. The inflation made housing hard to afford, and by the 1970s, 80 percent of Santa Monica's residents were renters. Interest in rent control stirred. In 1978, California's famous Proposition 13 was drawn up to lower steeply rising property taxes; tenants, the bill's proponents rashly promised, would get a trickle-down benefit when property owners passed on their tax savings in the form of lower rents. So tenants helped to pass Proposition 13 and soundly defeated a rent-control initiative, Proposition P, on the same ballot.

But property values went up with the lower taxes, and hundreds of Santa Monica landlords sold their properties to cash in; the new buyers had to pay higher mortgages, and so actually raised rents. Largely with the help of the Campaign for Economic Democracy, formed by local celebrities Tom Hayden and Jane Fonda, Santa Monica put a new rent-control bill, Proposition A, on the ballot for a 1979 vote. It provided for the rolling back of rents to April 1978 levels, the creation of an elected rent control board, allowing the city to forbid the demolition of property, and the near-prohibition of the then-booming business of converting apartment properties into condominiums. Luckily for Luis, the campaign for Proposition A brought on a bonanza in tenant eviction and home demolition as Santa Monica's frightened landlords put their hopes in rent loopholes for new construction put up after the passage of the bill. The demolition was especially prevalent along the yuppified Wilshire corridor of the city. Prop A was sure to pass in a city whose interventionist views, according to university researcher Robert Nozick, permitted "every kind of behavior except capitalistic acts between consenting adults."

It was an issue hard to stay away from in Santa Monica. While Luis used the men's room, I browsed through the upstairs videocassette rental section: right beside *How to Marry a Millionaire,* starring Marilyn Monroe, Lauren Bacall, and Betty Grable, was the locally made instructional video *How to Prepare for a Rent Control Hearing.* It was clearly for tenant, not landlord, use.

When Luis emerged, we went back downstairs to the periodicals department and sat down with a couple of Westside papers. We chose the *Los Angeles Times* first—after computers, newspapers are the greatest intimidators of new readers, and so overcoming this taboo was frequently a shortcut to a major breakthrough. The *Times'* "fast format"—a brief synopsis of each article between the headline and the text—makes the job easier for the functionally illiterate. Its frequent errors of English usage and occasionally unedited silliness allow for those lighthearted moments when new readers have their self-esteem boosted by the errors of the fully literate. *Times* writers used *"ex cathedra"* to mean "outside of the cathedral," "unprepossessing" to mean "unpretentious," and "grizzly" to describe murders that had nothing to do with bears. A front-page review of a novel in its *Sunday Book Review* contained the reviewer's admission that "I don't read much fiction." All this made it a valuable literacy tool, nearly as nonthreatening as the New Reader's Press special newspaper, *News for You.* Today, however, we were out of luck—the *Times'* gigantic classified section ("Southern California's Marketplace") had no listings for Santa Monica.

"That's incredible," I muttered.

"No problem, nothing to copy down," said Luis wryly.

"Let's try the Santa Monica paper," I suggested, and handed him the copy of the *Outlook.* He found the classified section and flicked through it to the real estate pages, which we then studied carefully. There were thousands of apartments for rent, but nearly all were in Brentwood, Venice, and the nearby Palms neighborhood in Los Angeles. The initials SM in the tiny listings nearly always led to a house or condominium for sale. Luis made a note of some telephone numbers but grumbled, "It's probably like the last time I used the papers that were stapled to the telephone poles—they are just subletting for a couple of months, and the place is already taken."

Rent control is not an easy subject to examine in the Santa Monica library, because all of the books and manuals relating to the law and how to get around it are always checked out. Elsewhere in Los Angeles I was able to learn that Santa Monica had the country's lowest vacancy rate—1.8 percent. I checked a free rental guide from a curbside dispensing machine, *Apartment Magazine*. It officially covered all of Los Angeles and the Valley, but did not have a single listing for Santa Monica, even though every surrounding area—Brentwood, Westwood, Beverly Hills, and Venice—had hundreds of properties for rent. There were even full-page ads for Beverly Hills apartment buildings that offered "1 Month Free with 1 Year Lease" ("Call for details on receiving an additional $500 off!"). Beverly Hills is a much smaller city than Santa Monica, but there is no question which LA community is more exclusive in terms of competition over scarce property. The enforced low rents discouraged further building: Santa Monica granted 697 building permits in 1978; in 1979, the year rent control went into effect, the figure had gone to 555; by 1983 it had sunk to forty-three, and by 1984 to nineteen. This was to say nothing of units taken off the market, kept vacant, or rented only among family members.

New building was almost all condominiums.

Long Beach voted down rent control, though it had nearly as high a proportion of tenants as Santa Monica (66 percent versus 80 percent), because of its largely working-class population. The result was that Long Beach developers overbuilt in the optimistic 1980s, which meant very depressed rents in the 1990s, and endless pages of cheap rentals in the Long Beach paper, the *Press-Telegram;* the market had accomplished in Long Beach what rent control had failed to do in Santa Monica: create affordable housing for the masses. A dogmatic opponent of rent control would probably draw a parallel between Santa Monica's lack of affordable housing and the lavish growth of its homeless population.

At least rent control had a life-giving effect on Santa Monica's businesses: with the money they saved on rent, affluent Santa Monicans spent twice the state average on shoes and restaurants, and three times the state average on televisions and music equipment.

Luis did not want a lift back in the direction of Wilmington, because he had to be on the job site first thing in the morning, and had some shopping to do.

"Everything here is expensive, man. I'm going to be living on oranges."

"Because they're cheap?"

He laughed.

"They're free, man. Some of my friends sell them on the street. You know where you always see a guy or a lady selling oranges at an intersection, or the freeway on-ramp or off-ramp? I used to do that. I sold flowers, too, but mostly oranges."

What he was describing was one of the commonest sights in Los Angeles. Some vendors sold bags of peanuts, too.

"Did you ever make any money at it?"

"Not bad. It was enough when my wife was working, but she isn't working now, so I had to find something better. Besides, you get bothered by the panhandlers. Every time a Latino gets a ramp site for selling oranges, a black or white guy comes along with a 'Will Work for Food' sign. You never see a Latino carrying one, not even at Pico and La Brea."

This was the intersection where illegal immigrants lingered by the dozen, waiting to be picked up for day work. You often saw the drivers of pickup trucks slow down and show them two or three fingers, then go down the block and slow down for them to board.

"Those panhandler guys bother you, man."

"Do they try to get free oranges?"

"They don't want *oranges*, they want money. When you tell them no, they say 'God bless you,' and that bothers me even more, because none of them are righteous, and they scare off customers. But I didn't like it anyway. I used to have to stay out in the sun all day long, and, man, did I get beaned out." He smiled at my curious look. "That means brown."

The desire not to be too brown was something Luis shared with most Santa Monicans. As in many seaside cities, it was the out-of-towners who slowly baked themselves on the sand, while the citizenry resorted to sun block, sunhats, and in the case of Santa Monica's little old women, parasols. This was something I had seen only in West Hollywood, where elderly Russian women protected their fair complexions from the California sun with big black rain umbrellas.

Luis and I parted, and I made my way through the town's famously varied cityscape, past the sign-up table for the Rainforest Action Network and the four South Americans in black trousers and fedoras performing a dance to the accompaniment of Andean panpipe music from their portable tape player. The Monica 4-Plex cinema was advertising *Mudar*, an Iranian film directed by Ali Hatemi, with the tail of the Persian word for "mother" twisted into a valentine. This would be for the city's omnivorous film community, not local Iranians, of whom Santa Monica had relatively few.

As is the case in most of LA's cities, Santa Monica's residential streets outside its downtown are lined with small-town clapboard houses and modern apartment blocks, though the houses get larger as you move north, toward Pacific Palisades. The city's rich neighborhoods are as full of television and movie stars as Beverly Hills, though they tend to be younger: Ted Danson, Amy Irving, Oliver Stone, Michelle Pfeiffer, Wesley Snipes, and Jason Bateman are just a few. Beverly Hills' ironclad *nouveau riche* reputation for quiet and elegance may be a bit of a posture, but Santa Monica's young, hip, rich, and mildly activist image is real. Tom Hayden, who was a member of the Chicago Seven, might possibly have married Jane Fonda and lived in Beverly Hills, but he would never have been elected assemblyman there. The richer and smaller city to the east is diamonds and charity balls; the beach town to the west was food kitchens. And here was Step Up on Second, one of the help centers listed on the anti-panhandling card. It was a thrift shop with a private area in the back—was that where the feeding of the homeless went on? A sign in the window advertised the services: helping the mentally ill homeless to "manage anxiety" using writing, drama, art, and music.

The main settlement of Santa Monica's homeless community is a shabby camp at the loveliest corner in the city, Ocean and Colorado, where the road leads down to the pier and the beach. Scabby, sunburned, and very introspective—policemen on horseback were patrolling the intersection, probably because of a near-riot at Venice Beach the day before—the homeless were surrounded by tables and chairs, bedrolls, bicycles, bags of trash, piles of clothing, old luggage. Beyond, the surf lands on the smooth beach with a regular thud. I felt an instinctive throb of sympathy for both the homeless and for the Step Up on Second people who taught them how to manage their anxiety—teaching people to read was surely a snap by comparison.

"Buy some books?"

A bedraggled but sane street woman in a stocking cap was lugging a small carton filled with papers on her hip. Most were back issues of *Vanity Fair* and *Redbook*, but there were some paperbacks and a heavy pile of what looked like gigantic term papers in cheap binders. I bought two magazines from her and asked about the fat term papers.

"Those are screenplays, honey. You a writer? These fuckers don't sell. This is the second time they aren't selling. Maybe the tenth time. You passing on them too?" She cackled, ripping an eight-cylinder rumble from her lungs, along with a gust of cigarette breath.

"These are screenplays? Where do you get them?"

She must have had two dozen of them. This was Easy Metaphor Heaven—even beggars were sneering at unsalable screenplays, and knew some of the lingo. I imagined a bag lady selling a shocked screenwriter a copy of one of his works to allow him to sit on a Palisades Park bench without getting bird shit on his trousers, which was probably a likelier scenario than an actual executive buying a screenplay for the same purpose, then deciding to produce it.

"I find 'em in the trash. I get some from the bookstores, too, because they put them on the outside bookshelves with the cheap books. The ones they don't care if they get stolen, see. I figure I'm doing them a favor. Some of 'em aren't too bad. Have a look."

She handed me *Dead Street* and *Altogether Elsewhere Vast.* Each was about three hundred pages long, and they were by the same writer. I flipped open *Dead Street,* expecting to read "FADE IN. Exterior, Day. Tall grass comes into focus. Sharpen focus, PAN TO graffiti-covered wall" or something of that sort. Instead the first page read

> I dedicate this screenplay to my first screenwriting professor, Alvin Nichols, who instilled in me my love of this craft; to my parents, my wife Shira, and all the wonderful . . .

I felt a stab of true LA *noir*—a screenplay with a dedication, even though these things are not meant for publication. You might as well dedicate a lawsuit brief or your library card application.

"Make that eleven times someone's passed on this one," I told the woman, who cackled and moved toward a knot of sightseers who were already making their getaway after lingering briefly at the entrance to the pier.

I headed for Venice to see if there were any scars from the gang face-off the day before. Just inland from the dramatic palisades, the land was as flat as anywhere in the basin. The flat open spaces were reminders that nearly every inch of the land had been farmed at one time. Part of the early vitriol spewed at LA was that its lively film industry had, as a larger setting, bean fields, mountains, beaches, and adobe desert—the air of rurality, together with the shallowness and shysterism of the heartless movie biz, must have made the new metropolis doubly infuriating. The lovely open spaces of LA have been paved and citified in just two generations; it is easy to forget that nasty old quotes refer to someplace that no longer exists. The screenwriters like Brecht and Faulkner who spewed such poison at LA must have been stung not only to be overpaid and underappreciated by philistines, but to drive by alfalfa fields and orange groves when they tried to get away from Hollywood—a reminder of how far into nowhere they had straggled in order to pander to Mammon.

In Venice itself, the beach is as long and gorgeously bare as at Santa Monica. The neighborhood was named for the concrete canals that its creator, cigarette magnate Abbott Kinney, in 1904 hoped would help to re-create Venice in America; most are now filled in. Venice was once an independent city but has been since 1925 part of the city of Los Angeles. It is almost too large to be filled by bathers, and in any case most visitors crowd onto its commercial boardwalk instead. This long strip is most famous for its daring roller blades, wearing only dental-floss bikinis or tiny, dramatically slit trunks, its body builders, and the unbroken row of shops and stalls selling ear piercing, roller skates, tattooings, T-shirts, baseball caps that say *X* or *meXican* or *Will Work for Sex,* and bales of erotic incense and oils: the scents of chocolate, patchouli, musk, vanilla, and love honey fill the boardwalk.

Fantasy has always been Venice's prime commodity, but in its days as an Italian theme park, the draw was architecture. One historian, looking back on the Venetian scene of 1908, recollected that "the pleasures it afforded were too innocent to match a landscape deliberately suggestive of the sinister delights of the Renaissance." There was an air of constant celebration ("of what I never was sure") amid the "intricate blend of Italian columns, porticos and balustrades, only slightly marred by the presence of guess-your-weight machines."

There is nothing remotely as tasteful as a guess-your-weight machine on the Venice boardwalk today. On the beach side, opposite the shops, you can get a massage, have your fortune told, commission an instant one-page novel for two dollars, or buy a hashish pipe. These merchants sit on crates, squat on their haunches, or preside over merchandise—earrings, T-shirts, sandals—set out on blankets. Venice-haters call this bohemian beach a slum, which it is not, though its bizarre mélange of the chic and the poor is a reminder that "slum" is also a verb.

The musclemen at the city Recreation Center (opposite the Sports and Musclewear Shop) are the main attraction, as they pose, flex, and strain at free weights. "Pay no attention to the pumping-iron showboats," John Waters urges visitors in his *Tour of L.A.* "Concentrate instead on their audience, and experience voyeurism of a new kind. Intently watching a voyeur as he voyeurs an exhibitionist is a thrill you probably won't get to experience at home."

It was here that the trouble had started the day before—twenty to thirty members of a South-Central gang had, according to the papers, got into a fistfight just before five o'-clock, then pulled out guns.

Today the invasion was all television news crews—cameraman, teased-blond reporter—interviewing boardwalk strollers. A KCAL news helicopter was skimming over the beach.

"Actually, they were facing off near the basketball courts," Zara the fortune-teller told me. "I seen everything." I did not ask her how much of it she had foreseen. "They were, like, throwing punches, and everyone called the police. Then a guy pulled out a gun. People ran all over. Then the police came in *on horses*—I thought I was seeing things. And in cars, and in riot gear, marching down the boardwalk. They cleared everyone out—there were thousands of people! The gangbangers, but everyone—the tourists, the people hanging out."

"Why everyone?"

"Because they used pepper spray, but it didn't work. I was telling a fortune, too. My friend told me it was because if they chased away the gangbangers, they'd just come back later, the gangsters, and start something else. So everybody closed up and lost their business. But it was the late afternoon anyway. It only took about a half hour. Well, we'll see if anyone comes back here next Sunday. It was like the cops had it planned."

Of course they had it planned—Venice had seen trouble before, though this was only the second time in history the boardwalk was forcibly closed. The first time had been almost exactly a year ago, when the city's drug gangs used the chaos of LA's riots as cover to attack Neighborhood Watch houses and other antidrug organizations. Some houses were ransacked and white residents were beaten up, but Venice mostly stayed cool. Of course, "riot" was a loaded word, and so was "uprising." In any case, the real marks of what some LA high school students wryly resorted to calling "the prom" were inland.

8

War and Peace

When I went back to Watts I went on the train. A commuter light rail system, the Blue Line, had started up operation in July 1990, running mostly along the former route of the old Pacific Electric Red Cars, in a slightly southeastern slant from downtown Los Angeles all the way to First Street in Long Beach, a block from the ocean. The twenty-two-mile run costs $1.10 and takes about fifty minutes.

People waited on the Pacific Station platform in Long Beach with excited but skeptical smiles, as if they never really expected the train to come. Even months after its opening it was still a novelty.

A group of enormous Samoan girls were occupying most of the benches, but there was an empty seat. One of them, wearing an Angels baseball cap, shouted to a girl who was standing on the platform reading a comic book.

"Hey, curly girl! Hey, curly girl! There's a seat! Come on over here!"

The girl glanced over and showed her a wan "no thanks" smile.

"Curly lady! You don't want the fuckin' seat?" She shrugged at her friends. "She don't want the fuckin' seat." There was no pushing when the train came, heralded by its melodious bells. It was like stepping into a church; and there were no crowds.

"Don't touch the windows!" a mother with four small children ordered her son, who was standing with his palms against the large pane as he watched Pacific Coast Highway slip past. I don't think she was afraid of smudging the brand-new glass; it was more likely part of the heady air of excitement and superstition that filled the cars in their early days, along with gawkers and thrill-seekers. This was a new LA innocence: no one knew how to ride a train. Touching a train window might give you an electric shock.

A certain vulnerability was almost palpable in the car, especially among the teenagers in their sagging pants and baseball caps. They were not at the wheel—they had no idea where the wheel was. None of us was in control. I had had a taste of this vulnerability facing a boulevard of traffic on foot, but here your movement was coerced. Even I, a subway rider since early childhood, sensed the feeling of being careless in LA—a gunman disarmed.

The train slid, humming, through north Long Beach and over the flat concrete bed of the Los Angeles River, along Willowbrook Avenue. Everyone was looking out the windows delightedly, as if none had never seen all these dry arroyos, car dealerships, and retirement homes before. Actually, most of the adults had never seen such a view without having their hands, feet, and gaze all busily at work driving a car. Now they were discovering that not only were their minds and limbs free but they could enjoy the view. They had nothing to do—they could relax, though no one was reading or doing a crossword. That would be wasting the view; you had to actively enjoy this innovative pleasure by paying attention. When the train glided to a halt at Artesia Boulevard, someone said, "This is Compton."

"This ain't Compton, it's still Long Beach. Artesia is Long Beach," said someone else.

"We're west of the river—it's Compton."

People looked around and then stared out the windows with light smiles. Everyone in the car seemed to be absorbing the same observation: complete strangers were talking to one another! This did not happen inching down the freeway. It was almost embarrassing—it really was like being in church. What was next, joining hands and singing? I was not reading the newspaper I had with me, and in fact had caught myself, in the empty stretches of the ride, with an impulse to step on the gas or turn on the radio. There was nothing to read but the silver plaque at the end wall of the car that read *City of Compton* and went on to sum up that city's history in a sentence or two of fine print. ("Its physical beauty and clean air are legend. It was the first city in the United States to declare official holidays for Martin Luther King Day and Cinco de Mayo.") Every car of the Blue Line system was named for one of LA's cities. I had already ridden in Rosemead, Compton, and El Segundo for short trips in the basin, but still lacked the knack for traveling without a dashboard.

"Well, I know we're west of Paramount, because we did go over the flood control," said the Samoan girl in the baseball hat importantly.

Wouldn't a teenager know? None of the adults knew the place from the ground, only from the borderless freeways that flowed all over the county within their beige sound barrier walls. Maybe the girl was a skateboarder. People knew the freeway and exit of their destination, and apart from that had no idea what was west of what, or near or far, except going by the time of day.

The next stop was at Compton Boulevard, in front of the Los Angeles County Courthouse and the Compton police station. The people getting off seemed reluctant, and the ones getting on were laughing with the giddiness of tourists clambering on board an amusement park ride. From this height—at Compton Boulevard, the train elevates above street level—you could see a flat expanse of little wooden houses to the west and a shopping mall with an empty parking lot to the east.

I had once tutored in Compton, seeking a change from troubled adults after Luis Frenes. While Project Read was geared toward adults starting at age sixteen, sometimes Ruth Stewart, the librarian who ran the program, agreed to "preemptive tutoring" for someone younger. She decided to do this for my next student, LaShawndraya Jaggers, not only because she lived in Compton, where the literacy program had a six-month waiting list to get a tutor. LaShawndraya's mother, a young African-American woman with neo-Egyptian braids on top of her head, had an elder daughter who was just fifteen, pregnant, defiant, and an active member of the Criplettes, the gang sorority affiliated with the Crips. One of my friends, the novelist and high school teacher Montserrat Fontes, had almost been pulled from her car on 103rd Street by some of these drug-dealing hussies.

"They had the car surrounded," Monsy recalled later. "I was afraid I'd have to go through the red light to get away from them. One of them said really menacingly, 'We're Criplettes,' and I was thinking, Shouldn't that be Cripettes maybe? I almost laughed and maybe they saw that on my face, but I gunned it and got out of there."

LaShawndraya's mother was so worried that the younger daughter, who was twelve years old and a slow learner, would follow in Shatorbia's footsteps that she took her out of the Compton junior high school she was attending and enrolled her in a Catholic school, St. Philip Neri. The school could do little for a girl who was four grade levels behind, but the mother was hoping that the nuns would be her allies in instilling discipline.

LaShawndraya was a child whose looks—baby fat and too much makeup—I associated with the Third World habits of fattening and dressing up prepubescent girls to marry them off. She had an insolent, undulating strut, like a stripper, but could lift her eyebrows at a stupid question like the haughtiest of old dowagers. Like many nonreaders who had come in on someone's initiative other than their own, she pretended to find the whole process of reading and writing a ridiculous waste of time. "She seems kind of hard," her mother had told Ruth, "but things have been rough for us." In a branch library near the Compton city line—where she entered, looked around at the wall of books, and cackled loudly—I got LaShawndraya talking about her parents.

"Your mother seems nice. She says you're smart. She's proud of you."

I explained that her mother had got us to bend the rules to provide free tutoring, and offered to pay in the event that the rules prevailed.

"She ain't got no money. My sister got money, what she ain't put up her nose. My daddy stopped working."

"For any particular reason?"

"He worked at some crazy car body shop in Willow-brook." This was an unincorporated neighborhood near Watts. "He got some crazy gangbanger work there. They had a drive-by, and my daddy caught the bullets. He's blind now."

We did "language experiences"—made a text for her to study by having her dictate one-page narrations of her father's condition, why she hated school, or her favorite shopping experiences. Then we picked out relevant vocabulary: "seeing-eye dog," "gangbanger," "Nordstrom," and "geography"—the subject she hated most. A brief look into why this was so provided a revelation: nonreaders had knowledge gaps everywhere. LaShawndraya did not know the capital city of California or the United States, how many states there were, or which ocean bordered Los Angeles. When asked to name any of these, she answered, "I don't know," like a queen being asked how to clean an oven.

"Are you happier at Philip Neri?"

"I don't know." She glared at me. "There's a lot too many Latinos, that's for sure."

"Most of the time Latinos are Catholics, that's probably why. They have a lot of kids. Do you get along with them?"

"Lots of them light-skinned ones get they ass kicked 'cause they look white." She chortled. "I get 'em mad when I call 'em Hispanics."

This was a raging debate that had just ended with the triumph of "Latino." Impassioned op-ed pieces in local papers pleaded for its adoption to replace "Hispanic," which was thought to refer too directly to Spanish, to Spain—to Europe. Why was Latino better? It was no better at encompassing the descendants of the native pre-Columbians whose Toltec profiles outnumbered Latin ones throughout LA. It was hard to believe that anyone took it seriously outside of the ethnic advocacy groups that had turned the whole subject of LA's diverse cultures into the city's biggest bore; even La-Shawndraya thought the Latino/Hispanic fuss was funny. She knew about it because it was discussed in her social studies class.

I asked her what her favorite book was.

"I don't know."

What was her favorite television show?

"Everything."

Did she have one special goal or wish?

"To get the hell out of Los Angeles, California."

This was all the more striking to me because she had *no idea* what else was out there. She may have got her wish sooner than expected, because after her sister was shot a few weeks later, her mother called the literacy program to cancel the tutoring, with thanks—they were "making a move." Two days later when I called to wish them well, their telephone was already disconnected.

This gave off the strong scent of LA's brittleness. To La-Shawndraya it was a nonplace. She knew nothing about its past—certainly had no pride or interest in it—or about her neighbors, and only wanted to leave. It would not have struck me as terribly unusual—after all, she was just twelve years old and having a hard time in school—had I not already seen specimens of what people think of as LA rootlessness. Actually, I sometimes got the feeling that Angelenos, both natives and transplants, were like rare plants that had had roots bred out of them. No wonder when they traveled they gushed about how "European" San Francisco was or fell apart at the beauty of Colorado or Vermont. At times like this LA seemed like a gigantic Las Vegas hotel, with requisite glitter, thousands of depressing rooms, and no long stays.

The train glided onward down Willowbrook Avenue, sounding a blast on its horn as a car tried to nose in front of the barrier at Rosecrans Avenue. This street, named for Union Civil War general William Rosecrans, was a good counterbalance to LeConte Avenue in West LA, incredibly named for a South Carolina professor, Joseph LeConte, who, with the onset of Reconstruction, absolutely refused to teach black students, and so moved out to UCLA. The car did not challenge the train, but remained dangerously close in the intersection. Angelenos were very slow learners about train etiquette—people actually tried to race the huge railway cars through intersections. This was more train innocence, but of a deadlier variety. In the Blue Line's first two years of operation, there were 148 accidents, and twelve people—nine drivers and three pedestrians—were killed. Eventually high-speed cameras would be installed at troublesome intersections to photograph people trying to cut around the trains, to fine them $271 and reduce collisions.

The Southern California Rapid Transit District must have known what it was dealing with, judging from the safety rules they plastered LA with before the rail line opened:

—*Never stand in the street when buses or other vehicles are passing or turning.*
—*Stand back from the curb or platform edge while waiting for your bus or train.*
—*Never run after a moving bus or train.*
—*If you or your child drop something under or near the bus, leave it and let the vehicle pull away.*
—*Don't get trapped on a railroad crossing.*
—*Don't climb over, under or between stopped rail cars.*

In January 1993, downtown Los Angeles blossomed with red-and-black banners reading VIAJE POR LA LINEA ROJA/RIDE

THE RED LINE. This was the east-west line gradually being established at the LA end of the Blue Line. It had been criticized for failing to connect downtown Los Angeles to the city's two major destinations, Hollywood and the airport, and for not serving the busiest artery in LA, the Wilshire Corridor that ran from downtown, through the business district, Beverly Hills, West LA, UCLA, Brentwood, and Santa Monica. Instead, the Red Line is projected to go west from downtown, then abruptly swing northward into the San Fernando Valley, and the Green Line would turn south before reaching the airport to serve the South Bay. The reason was simple: not only was Beverly Hills ambivalent about having the train go through, Wilshire was the fading central main artery of a decentralized city, and for much of its length was too downscale anyway. A large chunk of the county's tax base was in the affluent Valley, so the Red Line would obediently ferry its (far more numerous) commuters into downtown; the sleek white-and-red trains followed the money.

Watts came into view: the flat prairie of clapboard houses, the Rodia Towers, now enclosed in high steel fencing, the *White Men Can't Jump* basketball court, and a side view of Markham Junior High School, which was my destination. The train whooshed to a stop at the Blue Line's only stop that is an actual building instead of a platform: the original Pacific Electric's Watts railway station, standing since the turn of the century.

Killer Hutch, I had been told, was the person most worth meeting in Watts: a native Angeleno, born and bred in Imperial Court—one of South LA's gangiest public housing projects—and a major influence in the community, even if Killer called the slightly northerly Crenshaw District home now.

There are few names that can strike real fear into young people in a community that has seen every possible variety of abuse, harassment, neglect, and murder, but Killer Hutch, it seems, could bring the suggestion of tears into the eyes of young teenagers who had seen as much gore as army veterans. "I was scared when I found out I was going to be up against Killer Hutch all year," commented one young teenager in Watts, "but I decided I would wait and see what happened." I read that from a sheaf of testimonies written by seventh-graders at Markham Middle School in Watts; another said that "Killer Hutch might change my life; I don't know. I hope she does not kill me." This was followed by a small circular happy face.

When I asked about her reputation, Yvonne Hutchinson just laughed softly.

"That goes back some years. I was teaching a class, and an older boy who had wandered into the school stuck his head through the classroom door and said, 'Crip here.' I chased him right out of here, because I will have none of that. He ran, too. So I got the name Killer Hutch."

It is hard to believe that Hutchinson has taught at Markham for twenty-eight years, only because she does not look old enough. She is tall and slender, with an English teacher's cut-glass enunciation that has a hint of a soft African-American drawl and the discipline that makes children feel cherished. One day when I was visiting her homeroom, she asked a boy to shelve some books, and her voice rang out after him as he was on his way back to his seat.

"Would you kindly come back here and put those books right side up! I *cannot abide* to have a book upside down in this room!" When the boy realized that this was a serious request (this was the first day of school, and the look on his face expressed the amused fear that *this woman cannot be for real*), he replaced the books carefully, with a wary eye on Mrs. Hutchinson, who was absorbed passing out papers to the rest of the class, but rewarded him with a gentle "Thank you" that might have made someone five years older than he was fall in love on the spot.

I wanted to meet Yvonne Hutchinson because another LA public school teacher, my friend the novelist Montserrat Fontes, had recommended her to me as a dear friend and mentor, "back in the days," Monsy said, "when I used to have to smoke a whole joint in the car on my way to Markham just to get through the day." When I did first meet Yvonne, she was quick to deflect my interest away from her and to her class. "Most of these kids want to do the right thing," she pointed out. "I have some truly excellent students, but many of them don't have it easy." This was a few months after the spring 1992 riots in Los Angeles following the trial acquittal of the four police officers who had subdued and beaten Rodney Glenn King, and most Angelenos had Watts on the brain. This neighborhood would end up impoverished and dead, people seemed to think, and it deserved its fate. The only things on Watts's mind were drugs, gangs, and murder; and now arson and looting.

I had driven there the first time, struck by the visibility of the roots of the angry, rebellious, and yet consumerist violence that has torn southern Los Angeles apart twice in twenty-five years. You cannot miss it, no matter which way you drive to Markham, down Imperial Highway, Century Boulevard, Long Beach Boulevard, or Compton Avenue. Malevolent policing may have been the detonator of dormant violence, but the actual gunpowder was here, in south LA's Death Valley emptiness of diversions. Compared to the leisure-time overload of restaurants, movie theaters, video arcades, sports bars, bookstores, and parks that jam every thoroughfare in greater LA—Second Street in Long Beach, Ventura Boulevard in the Valley, Westwood Boulevard in West LA, Soto Street in East LA—the main boulevards in south LA are almost bare. Vacant city blocks are broken up only by barbershops with short names (AL'S) and churches with long names (GREATER EMMANUEL MISSIONARY APOSTOLIC CHURCH OF GOD IN CHRIST, INC.—no wonder these churches were such fertile ground for literacy students). What was there to do? Where was there to work? Any first-time visitor here could infer that drug-dealing gangs offered not only a job but a social life.

The interesting thing about the police was that there were none in sight. In Long Beach, police cars seem about as common as taxis—bearing in mind that taxis are not much used in southern California—but Los Angeles is severely underpoliced. With about 7,600 peace officers, the LAPD has about 2.1 officers per thousand citizens, less than half the ratio of New York City. It was even more troublesome given LA's staggering surface area. The result is that overworked police have no time for "community policing" and have a reputation for defensiveness and low morale. LA's small police force was already an issue in the mayoral campaign that was just beginning.

The proprietors of businesses that were open seemed to be advertising their lack of activity by sitting in rows in front of their doors, staring into the street. Nothing much happening at the Louisiana Motel or Guadalupe Novelties; not much demand for *Llantas Usadas Buenas*/Good Used Tires. There were, of course, acres of red and black gang graffiti, mostly illegible, except for the names sprayed in black and then obscured by an X. This was one gang notifying another of the death sentence pronounced on one of its members. There was SHORT-E—had he been executed yet? The paint was still new. It was probably too late for the very faded O-DOG. And there were nongang graffiti: FREE THE LA-4 (the men arrested for beating Reginald Denny during the riots) and, in bright red, REVOLUTIONARY COMMUNIST YOUTH BRIGADE with the afterthought VIVA GONZAGO beside a red flag.

Arrival by Blue Line is more scenic. From the Watts train stop, you walk down Grandee Avenue unable to spy out any graffiti. Of course, this was a year after my driving visit, and many of the gangs and graffiti artists were idle. The school is at the corner of Compton Avenue and 104th Street, in sight of the notorious Nickerson Gardens housing project and, through a frame of lavender jacaranda trees, the Watts Towers. Inside the school's office, there are signs displaying the black profile of a revolver inside a red ring with an oblique *verboten* stroke, with the legend *"Se prohiben las armas en el plantel/* No weapons on campus." Students running in an out, almost all wearing at least one item of bright purple clothing. I took this to be an alternative to the strongly discouraged red and blue of the Bloods and Crips gangs, whose truce had made this neighborhood quieter in the intervening year.

"Madrigal will guide you to Mrs. Hutchinson's classroom," a teenage girl at the office counter informed me. Actually, Madrigal and a suddenly materialized Hubert both escorted me through the grassy quadrangle that echoed with the goings-on in the schoolrooms, which sounded louder than a stock exchange. The school office was full of busy adults. I asked Madrigal whether she and Hubert were working there out of public-spiritedness or as punishment, or for course credit.

"To help out. They're short-handed sometimes."

There were two lines of four students each standing in the sun. Two women teachers sat in chairs facing them, shuffling papers.

"Who are they? Is this a break area?"

"It's the meditation garden," joked Hubert.

"Tardies. It's the eighth-grade quad," said Madrigal. "You have to stand there if you're late for a class. That's if it's the first time—you stand there for a period. The second time they telephone your home, and the third time you get suspended. Hubert got a call home just yesterday." She gave him a teenage look.

Both Madrigal and Hubert knew and liked Killer Hutch. "She's tough," said Madrigal. "She's the best." They were both in her eighth-grade English class, which was doing Shakespeare. "I'm Juliet—he's Mercutio."

I was going to talk to a class about a *National Geographic* assignment I had done on Cairo, under the impression that the study of Africa's largest city would be of interest in one of the New World's most famous African-American neighborhoods. Of course, I knew that Watts was now more than half Hispanic, and some of the accents that you heard among the children in the playground were distinctly Hindi, Korean, and Nahuatl. This was the melting pot, a low-rent neighborhood where poor newcomers started out. The knots of students, playing, talking, or chasing one another around, did not seem at all divided by ethnic group, though. Except for scattered teasing, the sexes seemed to ignore each other. That was the case in the journalism class, where all but one of the twelve students were girls. They had diligently read my article for homework, and were full of questions. How long did it take to write? How much had I been paid? Did the magazine try to change anything I had written? What did sneakers cost in Cairo? Were the Egyptians kind to Americans? Was Cairo safe? Were Egyptian boys cute?

Before the period was over, I turned the tables on them and started a reverse press conference. What if they were reporters? Would they rather write about a place they knew nothing about, like Cairo, or about a place they had experienced, like Los Angeles? They were divided almost evenly. I asked what, if anything, they liked best about living in LA.

"If anything!" was the first answer I got. The other girls laughed. "I want to move to Mississippi."

A black student in Los Angeles pining for the Deep South? I asked her why she liked Mississippi better.

"I haven't ever been to Mississippi, but my family comes from there. They say it is beautiful."

"What about you, Maria?"

"I don't mind LA, but I can't think of any best thing. School."

"Malika?"

"I want to move to Louisville, Kentucky. As soon as I'm old enough, I'm going there. I'll go to college there or something."

"Why there?"

"My grandparents live there—we come from there. Jesus, that place is pretty, and quiet. You can do whatever you want. Nobody gets in your face."

My final tally showed that more than half the class wanted to move out of LA; all the black students wanted to move to the South. No one could think of one good thing to say about LA—"this *dump*," as Malika described it. I pointed out that they were at a restless age, thirteen or fourteen, and might feel the same way about anywhere they were likely to live. They all nodded when Yolanda—who only marginally preferred LA to Oaxaca, Mexico—answered me very earnestly.

"For such a long time our parents never let us outside, except to go to school. We have to go right home, and stay indoors. So we study, or watch TV, or talk to our friends, or maybe my friends come over. You were afraid of getting killed—the streets here belonged to the gangbangers. Lots of people got killed just being in the wrong place. So now it's better. We can go out without the big gangs shooting at one another. But what are we going to do out there? There's nothing to do. There's no place to go. So we still stay in and study, or help our moms. If you have a boyfriend you can go driving around. But all we talk about is getting out."

Getting out would be the logical subject, I guessed, that the endless blocks of empty storefronts and squalid housing projects, high walls, and *Llantas Usadas Buenas* would inspire. To say nothing of the memory of the riots.

The bell rang and the girls vanished.

Actually, most of the damage of the riots one year before was not in Watts but in central LA: in Koreatown, where Korean businesses were targeted by arsonists, and in South-Central, the huge hundred-block long flatland—more than half the length of Manhattan—between downtown LA and Watts. Such distinctions were lost on the riot reporters who skimmed over this vast flatland in helicopters and, seeing black and brown rioters, dubbed the whole mess Watts; when fires were started near Wilshire Boulevard and Vermont Avenue, perilously close to the downtown financial district, the panicky blondes in the choppers reported "unrest in the Crenshaw district." Actually, that district was nearly a dozen miles away, to the southwest.

"They have no idea where Crenshaw is," said Monsy Fontes crossly. "Dorothy Lamour used to shop for dresses in the Crenshaw district!" She knew. Her family owned a restaurant on Third near La Cienega, where celebrities often dropped in for snacks, because it was near a recording studio. Her family had helped a furtive Bonnie Raitt cheat on her diet.

Most of the trouble came outside Watts, but the neighborhood stood out in the coverage, because it had hosted the city's last big riot, in 1965, and was located between South-Central to the north and Compton to the south. Of course, shooting and looting occurred as far north as Hollywood, but most of the serious violence and arson was in the central part of the city. Liquor stores, a favorite target for pillage, were hit especially hard, because so many in black and Latino neighborhoods were owned by Korean families who lived elsewhere and did not hire locally; a history of mutual murder existed even before the riots. The 40 percent of the city's population classified as Latino could not be classified as a bloc in the riots: the Mexican-American neighborhoods of East Los Angeles were serene, and the neighborhoods of new (and largely illegal) immigrants in Pico-Union were the most violent. When the violence died down, the city announced that Latinos accounted for 51 percent of the looters and 60 percent of business owners burned out.

I did not know about the rioting, or even about the acquittal verdicts that had set them off, until the evening of April 28, when I got a telephone call from my sister in Boston, who informed me that arsonists had set palm trees on fire along the Hollywood Freeway. It was not CNN; the local Boston station had gone live in LA.

I had no need to turn to the breathless, real-time television coverage on every local television station, only to look out the window. North across the Los Angeles Basin, the fires were visible from twenty miles away. The smoggy orange horizon was on fire in three or four places, with columns of black smoke bending skyward, turning into one dark horizontal, drifting off toward the high desert.

The next day was even more violent; every television station was like the twenty-four-hour Looting Channel. Two more solicitous telephone calls, ironically from the Middle East, taught me the shamed weariness of people living with horror they cannot control or explain. How many times had I called friends in Lebanon during its genocidal civil war, and felt that my concern was taken only as a reminder of how widespread their disgrace had become known? They always minimized it—"Well, there's electricity, and the airport is open, so those are good signs. We're fine." Now I heard myself telling worried Arabs, "There's a curfew tonight—yes, in Long Beach, too—so that should quiet things. Of course I'm fine. Don't worry."

At dusk, my north-facing desk in downtown Long Beach always seemed to have a long-distance hearth as the setting sun turned the glassy cluster of downtown LA skyscrapers orange, then fiery copper, rust, and an infernal crimson before leaving them ashy gray or invisible in the smog as dark closed in. On the first day of the riots, the same show was enhanced not only by the actual columns of smoke in LA, but by the incineration of the Department of Motor Vehicles in Long Beach. By chance, I had been inside that building only a few hours before, to pick up a vehicle registration card, and had read a cardboard sign that said, "The DMV will close at 3 P.M. instead of 5 today. We apologize for the inconvenience."

What kind of alarmists were running this place? I wondered. At that point, the office's patrons were trading gossip about the tragic events up in South-Central, and reassuring each other that it would be under control by tomorrow, scarcely expecting that this very building on quiet Pacific Avenue would be burned to the ground by then. A councilwoman later told her employees that the DMV had been set on fire by mysterious white men in black robes who had come down from Los Angeles—which no one believed—but anyone who had ever stood in its maddening quadrilingual lines knew that there must have been tens of thousands of suspects.

I had to go to the airport the next morning to pick up an old college friend, Louis, who was passing through town for two days. I thought he would be devastated by his insanely bad timing, but he was delighted.

"Punch your radio, hit *me*, give me your best shot," pleaded the African-American deejay on LA's Rhythm Radio, KJLH ("Kindness, Joy, Love, Happiness"). "Call us and let out those frustrations—punch your radio. But try to keep the peace."

The San Diego Freeway was very slow-moving, because it was doing double duty: most of the midtown exits of the Harbor Freeway, which runs through South-Central, had been closed by the police. I had not expected that—most businesses and city governments had given their employees the day off, or even two days, until the riots subsided, so there should have been light traffic. Then I saw why: at least half the cars and vans were crowded with whole families and piled up with luggage, trying to get out of Dodge. Century Boulevard, leading to the airport, was much more frantic, as it ran through Inglewood, a mostly black and Latino city which was, in the event, mostly quiet during the riots. When the traffic remained at a standstill for more than a minute or so, some drivers actually drove up on the sidewalk and sped into side streets, or tried to make U-turns. This sounded another Middle Eastern note: Beirut in its car-bomb period, when booby-trapped parked cars occasionally blew whole unsuspecting streets to glory. The Lebanese reacted in the same way: the sensation of being trapped in a city street brought on total desperation and nearly suicidal automotive stunts.

"I brought marshmallows!" said Louis brightly as he climbed into the car. It was already the fifth time that day I had heard a marshmallow-roasting joke. "Do we have to go right to Long Beach, or can we go look at the tragic effects of all this senseless violence? Is there time for us to be sick, ghoulish onlookers at these sobering events before the curfew takes effect?"

I headed back down Century. There was very little traffic heading toward South-Central, and the air was filled with sirens. Nearly every radio station was urging people to calm down and stay home, but Inglewood merchants were taking no chances: several stores had BLACK-OWNED BUSINESS scrawled on their windows, or, much more ominously, BLAK OWNED BUSINESS. In neighborhoods where the Bloods supplied the drugs, Crips were shot on sight, and even the letter C was eliminated by apple-polishing merchants.

The radio news mentioned two hundred fires. The huge postal facility in South-Central was on fire, and tomorrow, Friday, was the day the post office was supposed to deliver Social Security checks. Six branch libraries in Los Angeles had been vandalized, and two more, the John Muir and Junipero Serra branches, were burned down. A Pasadena evangelist in Hollywood was in a coma after being kicked in the head by Latinos—he had been trying to dissuade them from looting.

So far twenty people were dead in the rioting. All the hotels in Santa Barbara, a hundred miles to the northwest, were booked solid with wealthy LA refugees. In South-Central, gang members were shooting at the firemen who were fighting the arson fires. The bad news was interspersed with commercials—which sounded hilariously unnecessary in a city where armies of people were lustily invading the stores—and analysis.

"South-Central Los Angeles is the home of many economic ills," said a commentator on a public radio station. "Per capita retail sales in Los Angeles County are sixty-one hundred dollars every year, and yet in South-Central they amount to just eighteen hundred dollars."

"Well, they're fixing that in a hurry," marveled Louis, gazing out at the smoking storefronts and drenched sidewalks. He did not know that we were nowhere near South-Central, and getting farther away every second—we were speeding down Jefferson Boulevard in Culver City, heading back to the freeway. I had turned south as soon as I saw the word BLAK. With the exception of shopping centers in South-Central and Compton, most of the destruction had been in commercial areas that served smallish neighborhoods. And so the damage, which looked total on television, was partial or nonexistent in most of LA, and total in a few parts.

The curfew took effect at seven o'clock. Just one year earlier, the streets had been empty while everyone tuned in to the bombing of Baghdad; now everyone across LA was pouring cocktails and glued to the television, watching endless replays of the day's rioting, with intermittent live footage of police choppers zooming over the city's nearly empty streets. Then the National Guard came in, closing downtown streets with Humvees and striding across shopping-mall roofs, armed with enormous black guns.

The curfew ended two days later, extended one day past the weekend into the peaceful workweek, when the local television stations had resumed normal programming. "When I saw *The Price Is Right* come on," my tutoring student Luis assured me on the phone from Wilmington, "I knew everything was going to be okay." He had called to check on me. And how was he? Praising the Lord—Los Angeles was shown to be the devil's city.

The second wave of senseless tragedy came in the newspapers, where the riots were replayed for months. The first debate was over finding a name for what had happened— "riot," "uprising," "rebellion," "revolution," or "civil unrest," which, probably because of its blandness, was the winner. "Uprising" made a run for its money, though I was skeptical—I had seen one of the world's most publicized uprisings, the Palestinian *intifada*, firsthand, and in all the years it lasted, there had never been a single shop looted, only rock-throwing, and the deft assassination of perceived oppressors and collaborators. It took a New Yorker, Stanley Crouch, to explain this difference to Angelenos, telling a reporter that the rioters were "very well armed. . . . When the National Guard came in, they had the opportunity to become guerrilla warriors. [But] they went home and looked at their stolen televisions." Actually, many turned in their stolen televisions, or had them seized by the police. For some reason this was particularly the case in Long Beach, where nosy neighbors, incensed by their neighbors' new televisions and bicycles, were shattering all snitching records.

The Day of the Locust got quite a workout in some of the more literary coverage; the book ends with a mob scene at a movie premiere, which erupts into murder, rape, chaos, and general violence. It is a pretty merry affair ("they sang and danced joyously in the red light of the flames"). The whole mess is foreshadowed by the protagonist of Nathanael West's novel, Tod Hackett, who has been working on a painting entitled *The Burning of Los Angeles*. Long before the riot at the premiere, Hackett senses the festive and destructive sides of the city. "He wanted the city to have quite a gala air as it burned, to appear almost gay. And the people who set it on fire would be a holiday crowd."

West expertly detected the dormant violence in the Los Angeles of his day, but living in the well-upholstered eternal LA present of the 1920s, he did not notice that it was nothing new. Los Angeles had destroyed its Gabrielino Indians and lived by the lynch law. In 1871, a brawl among Chinese Angelenos led a white mob, three hundred strong, to lynch nineteen Chinese men and boys in downtown Los Angeles. The famous Zoot Suit riots of 1942 consisted of white citizens, soldiers, and sailors beating up hundreds of Latinos and other dark-skinned citizens; as the name those race riots acquired suggests, the Latinos' flashy suits further enraged the servicemen, who were severely impaired by a lethal mix of liquor, racism, and shore leave. The police diligently arrested the victims. LA has always been a violent, balkanized city. More recently it has become a victim of its own glamour as well, if only because local television news covers the film industry so relentlessly; gushing over movie stars is the local form of patriotism. One angry black man in South-Central complained to a reporter in 1992 about rich people glorified on television, with their "Rolls-Royces and gold telephones." He had undoubtedly been watching too many *Dynasty* reruns or very likely some of the more Mexican soaps, but his attitude was real: "It's like eating a big piece of meat in front of a dog: the first thing he's going to do is bite your ass! People are either going to *have,* or they're going to tear it up!"

"Destroying is a pleasure not to be despised," I was informed by Dr. Eugen Weber, one of UCLA's most venerable historians, and a veteran of World War II in Europe, when I happened to be visiting him a year after the riots. He had been a member of a British unit that had sacked defeated German villages. "And if you can steal, as well, I mean, hell! And I can see the comparison there, because we felt somehow sanctioned. We were in uniform. We were, on the whole, doing the right thing. These guys felt sort of the same. They felt sanctioned—it was a communal sanction. I have a feeling that the major difference between five hundred years ago and today—because people have *always* looted—is that today we justify it."

Dr. Weber's kindly accents—a blend of Eastern Europe and England—are known to almost every television viewer in Los Angeles because of his frequently rerun twenty-six-part educational series *The Western Tradition*. Television, he felt, played a crucial part in LA's dramatic troubles.

"I was coming home from UCLA that afternoon," he recalled of the first day of unrest, "and at about four or five o'clock I turned on the television. What I got was a lot of reporters standing in empty places, like before the courthouse or before the police center or whatever, and saying, 'Blah-blah-blah-blah, we expect trouble, there is none yet, but we know there will be, and we are going to be here for it, giving you an account of it.' I found that utterly fascinating. I mean, I've been at UCLA, and I have seen the interrelation between demonstrators and media. And it's very hard to tell if it's the chicken or the egg. Of course, if you're going to loot, you don't need television, of all things. And it's true that it's *fun*, running through the streets, throwing rocks."

It all reminded Dr. Weber of Lebanon, which he had visited before its civil war in the 1970s. He recalled that "except for the Palestinians, really, even the poor were not very poor. And then it just went *pfffff*. I imagine the only people who had a good time thereafter were the gangs. But there's nothing you can do about gangs—about barbarians. I suppose that's how the Roman Empire died."

LA's black gangs, which were reported to have organized a great deal of the looting, and which, in Venice, used the anarchy of the riots to settle scores with rival gangs and antigang citizens, declared a truce after the riots, on the grounds that their communities needed no more violence. (The agreement was based on the text of an Arab-Israeli armistice which, it was belatedly pointed out, had actually been written by the UN's Ralph Bunche, a native of Los Angeles— he was from Watts. None of the participants had any idea who the late Ralph Bunche was.) The Latino gangs had not rioted, and so established no truce, leading to the general assumption that there would therefore be no lasting gang peace.

The peace held, however, and I went to hear a performance of gang truce poets in South-Central—it was sponsored by the Los Angeles Cultural Affairs Department. The big boulevards of South-Central were where the gangs loved to cruise and "throw signs"—a thumb and crooked forefinger make the Crips' "C," for example—but the grimy thoroughfares hid some of LA's quietest and prettiest streets. The houses were larger than those in Watts, and had yards, trees, and driveways. The area was a mirror of the Valley, on the other side of the Santa Monica Mountains, except that the cars parked along the endless blocks of tract housing here were being hosed down and polished by black and Latino men instead of craggy blonds.

On Crenshaw Boulevard, the QuikQuote electric signboard at Baldwin Hills Crenshaw Mall—the kind of display that usually advertises sales, alternating with teabag wisdom such as "Do it nice or do it twice" or "Life is 2 B Spent Not 2 B Saved"—had a rotating menu of COLLECTION OF TRIFARI EARRINGS/MULTICULTURALISM IS THE WAVE OF THE FUTURE/ SELECTED REDUCED PETITE SPORTSWEAR/LET US ALL HAVE VISION. Across the street, the towering Crenshaw Plaza sign was still scorched—the plaza mall had been gutted in the riots.

Central LA is no Santa Monica, but it has its own forms of California Crazy. Every large boulevard was a smorgasbord of religious enterprises: Dianetics, the Nation of Islam, Saints City, and the Masjid (Mosque) of Bilal ibn Rabah. There was a huge anti-Catholic billboard with a smirking caricature of the pope in a towering miter and the inscription *"The Beast I saw was like a leopard.... To it the dragon gave its own power and throne, along with great authority." Rev. 13:2. For a free book, call 1-800-680-FACT.* A five-story-high wall on Crenshaw had a painting of an immense brown snowman with the legend "The Chocolate Snowman Land. Christmas Trees for the Rich [crossed out] Poor for All Girlfriend and You Bro the Rapper. Spend your $ Money in your 'Hood Where your love is understood. Praise the Lord." There is nothing else in sight but a parking lot.

"Come back in December," advised a man who was sitting against the wall smacking a hammer against the ground. "Get a Christmas tree. Pay what you can. God bless you."

The real oddity in central LA is the profusion of apartment buildings with Polynesian names: the El Tiki, Aloha Village, the Samoa, the Tahiti, and Bali Palms. They tend to be the most run-down properties of all, having been hurriedly thrown up fifty years ago. Their pastel colors are faded, and in the gardens outside their bottle-littered carports, which surely bloomed with tropical flowers once upon a time, only weeds and cactuses survive. The Polynesian theme had its roots in the 1940s, when thousands of male engineers and other wartime workers moved to southern California to work in aircraft plants. "Single-girl" secretaries lived alongside them in these apartment complexes with swimming pools in the middle—they were like theme motels. Tikis were popular, along with luaus and Hula Hoop parties. A few years later, many U.S. military men who did service in the South Pacific returned with Filipino, Japanese, and Korean wives. Some of LA's architectural mavens trace the styles back to an LA restaurant, Don the Beachcomber's, which promoted the Pacific paradise theme in the 1930s. It had tried to beguile Depressioneers with exotic drinks, soothing music, palm trees, tikis, ukuleles, and hula dances. The statehood of Hawaii in 1959 further spurred the tiki phenomenon.

"Peace L.A.: The Poetics of Gang Truce" was held in tiny but shady Leimert Park, in the heart of South-Central. Poetry readings had flourished in the city after the riots, even among celebrities. Some Hollywood nightclubs had open-mike poetry nights, and television actresses like Justine Bateman and Katie Sagal began reading their poems in coffeehouses. It was an amateur phenomenon, whether it involved TV performers or penitent gangbangers. "Peace L.A." got going two hours late. There was something deeply comforting in knowing that the gangs were not only at peace but completely disorganized. The gang members, while recognizable by their baggy jeans and slouching walk, were the smallest part of the program. They were briefly introduced, and made very bashful remarks about keeping the peace.

"We're all brothers," announced the principal ex-gangbanger. "You know what I'm sayin'? People think gangbangers are dogs. We're people like you. People think gangs are locked in Watts and South-Central. But you ever heard the expression 'Coming soon to a theater near you'?" He was vigorously applauded, nodded his head at the audience, and backed away from the microphone.

A diminutive Asian social worker read a poem about how she had been abused as a child. I did not see the point, but applauded along with everyone else, wondering how enthusiastic you should appear at having heard a description of sexual abuse.

"I do fail to see what her sex abuse has got to do with the community," said a lady in flowing African robes, echoing my own thoughts. It may have had nothing to do with the community, but it had something to do with the spirit of sharing pain and identifying, even appropriating, the pain of others. This was done both by sincere social reformers and idle cause-junkies, but the poet did not stick around long enough for me to figure out which she might be.

"That was actually a good poem," said a second woman in African robes. She was right—at least it had not been too graphic. There were perhaps thirty of us on folding chairs under the trees. The half-dozen who were not black were white but dressed all in black. Anyone who had small children had deposited them with a volunteer artist under a tree to help produce pro-truce posters. An old Royal typewriter was parked on a crate under a tree—the "Poetree"—for spontanteous poets.

"I came for the dancers," a young woman complained to her date. Then they came on: Le Ballet de Kouman Kele West African Dance Company. The three women—two skinny, one zaftig—wore bright African robes over black halters and purple-and-gold tops, and leaped and twirled in perfect harmony to the accompaniment, two men circling them with long drums; a small girl of about nine performed with them.

"Why are there synchronized traffic lights in South-Central?" asked the next speaker, a young male social worker. "I'm not saying it's a conspiracy, but those lights sure rush you through here. How can you stop for a hamburger?"

By just stopping, I thought. It wasn't red lights that made people think, "Oh, I might as well pull over and eat something until it turns green." But the speaker was sincere, and even shyer than the gang members.

"And, if you will, how come in Brentwood the streets are lit up at night? They're awful dark here. I'm not saying that's genocide. But hey. I have nothing against anyone in Brentwood. You know what I mean? And then, but what about all the good news that happens here? You never get to read about it! They only print bad news."

He did not know that good news is no news, but moved on to promote "Hands Across Watts," a program to persuade gang members to give up their lives of crime. This was a well-known program—it had sponsored the appearance of the mortified ex-gang members at the beginning of this program.

The already sparse crowd thinned out even more as three or four old dissidents, some from the Watts Prophets (a literary group formed after the 1965 riots), read some poetry and gave their views on Planned Parenthood ("When did Adolf Hitler become an American citizen?"—the old birth-control-is-genocide canard) and the old-fashioned gangs, who used nothing deadlier than switchblades, when they weren't actually fistfighting ("I'm not trying to put down drive-bys"). A Latino woman from a social program in the dreadful Pico-Union neighborhood—nearly destroyed in the riots—pleaded for "solidarity of our black and Chicano cultures against the establishment." Her audience at this point was half black and half establishment, and listening more to one another than to her. That may have been the point. She urged us to patronize Homeboy Tortillas, a business run by former gang members in downtown LA. I realized that I had once been there, without realizing that the Homeboy stall in the Grand Central Market represented a cause. You don't see peace happening.

The "Peace L.A." poetry reading was something of a letdown as an event; making peace interesting was one of the challenges citizens had to deal with. LA's riots had been as complex as a bomb: a chain reaction of anger, stoked-up consumerism, and the ability to make history, thanks to television cameras, which had been noticeably absent from the "Peace L.A." event in Leimert Park. I could imagine what a local conspiracy theorist might say: "They don't want to show us playing with kids and reading poetry; they show up when there's violence and TV ratings." The fact was that even this event, which had covered poetry, sex abuse, dancing, and social and commercial services, had avoided mentioning the riots by name. Surely this gathering included Angelenos who thought the riots had been wrong and those who thought the riots had been right, but one year later, both sides clearly wanted to forget.

9

Deathland and Its Suburbs

Neither consumer uprisings nor the love fests that follow them have the slightest effect on the lurking Pacific tectonic plate, which shortly after the riots twitched in its Triassic slumber and gave me a nasty whack on the head as the headboard of my bed smacked the wall. Remembering where I was (the red *4:58* on the digital clock did not give me a clue) was almost impossible, and the loud groaning and squeaking—the sounds of the building creaking and moaning for mercy—were no help either. When the quake happened, I was dreamily convinced that I was a hostage being rescued—I could hear the thumping footsteps of a dozen Navy SEALs across the roof. Surely the flashing explosions of white light at the window were concussion bombs. The walls were shaking from Green Berets rappelling down the side of the building— in a moment they would come bursting through the windows, which were already rattling in their frames. Or was it a mass landing of car thieves? The only other sounds in the opaque blackness were the screeching and honking of twenty car-alarm systems all the way down the street. I clutched my pillow, but the room was still pitching like a stateroom on the *Titanic*. Now I felt as though I were inside a *piñata*. Two rooms away, framed pictures were rapping against the wall. The brilliant but silent lightning still sporadically broke the darkness as the electric current in the streetlights arced, hissed, and popped like an evil alien.

When buildings shake, the body is faster than the mind. My brain may not have known what was happening, but my hand switched on the radio to find out how bad it was.

"Just a second here—no, we're fine. Whoa! Are you still feeling it? Well, Southlanders, we're getting a rude awakening this morning. Just stay calm. We will be getting a magnitude estimate from Caltech any minute now. In the meantime we ask you to stay off your phones . . ."

A siren sounded in the street.

The radio was still chattering breathlessly ("We are getting a report of a collapsed warehouse in the Inland Empire"), but I was already pulling on clothes and hurrying on rubbery legs past the aquarium, which had slopped water (but no fish, thank God) onto the floor, past the wall of trembling and tilted pictures, and out of the building.

The cars in the building's little lot were visibly trembling, and probably had been bouncing gently just a few moments before. One of my neighbors, bearded Marvin, was standing outside, leaning meditatively against his car, which had the radio turned up.

"—epicenter near Redlands or Landers. This was a strong one, folks, we do not know how strong, we are hearing six point five or higher, we have heard seven, that is unofficial. We have a listener from San Bernardino on the line, are you

there? Hello? Caller?" There was a stereophonic dial tone.
"It tripped the car alarm. I came out to turn it off and
decided I liked it better out here," Marvin said. Nothing
looked wrong with the building, and the energy-efficient orange streetlights had stopped arcing and were glowing nor-
mally. Marvin rubbed his beard and tugged up his sweat-
pants.

The sky was still dark but with streaks of gold and gray.
Other neighbors were hurrying out of the building, either to
reset their car alarms or to gather in small groups to giggle
and gasp. "Look where my cat scratched me," the treasurer
of the condo association told her neighbor. "She was *crazed*.
I locked her in. I would have brought her out but I'm sure
she'd have run away."

"My heart almost stopped," said Marvin's wife, Marilyn,
joining us by the car. She had apparently taken the time to
comb her hair before coming outside, but her clothes were as
spontaneous as everyone else's—wine-red silk pajama bottoms and a baseball jacket. The treasurer was wearing a night-
shirt and a man's smoking jacket. Except for the women's
lack of makeup, we looked like the type of crowds who line up
in front of all-night dance clubs in Hollywood. "When we go
back upstairs, let's start to pack," said Marilyn. Even at the
best of times she made half-joking remarks about going home
to New York, and the last two months had not been the best
of times. Marvin rolled his eyes, but fearfully.

In another minute there were a dozen of us shivering in the
dawn, watching a police helicopter skate over the dark sky-
scape of steam from the Wilmington refineries and the wheel-
ing sea gulls. Car alarms were whooping all over the neighborhood. Salvador and Kitty, whose car had a MARRIED AND
LOVING IT plate frame, were listening raptly to their own car

radio and looking very shaken. A group of girl and boy room-mates were laughing nervously. Dr. Nguyen and his room-mate, William, who had been diagnosed with AIDS-related lymphoma, came out to the sidewalk in pajamas and plaid bathrobes. I had seen little of Dr. Nguyen since the recent death of his mother, who had been my literacy student for several months. They looked back at the building as if expecting it to fall down. Would it? No; the Willmore had survived the massive Long Beach earthquake of 1933, and recently had had its seismic "retro-fit"—required of old buildings—to strengthen it further.

On the other hand, widespread destruction elsewhere in LA could make our lives miserable by wrecking aqueducts, freeways, power stations, and our workplaces. Among the special terrors of LA earthquakes are their unpredictability and frequency: a death-dealing quake might come in two years' time (as it would, in Northridge), or in two weeks, or at any moment, or all three. We folded our arms and waited.

"We're all doing the wrong thing," announced Nguyen wearily. "We should be standing in a doorway. Does anyone have double-A batteries?"

"We didn't lose power," said Marvin. "But we lost cable. We got nothing but snow on all the stations. At least I didn't smell any gas."

"We've been doing all the wrong things since it happened," confessed Marilyn. "We jumped out of bed and ran around, and called 911 to see what was going on. They say you're not supposed to use the phone. Don't ask me why."

"There are fewer lines, and they have to keep them open for emergencies," said William. "Earthquakes knock a lot of phones off the hook. Then there aren't enough dial tones to go around. Enough circuitry."

That was true. When the 7.1 Loma Prieta earthquake had struck Santa Cruz and San Francisco three years earlier, telephones went on the fritz even in Los Angeles, because hundreds of the Bay area's calls had to be rerouted through the southern part of the state.

"It seemed to last forever."

"I think it lasted a couple of minutes."

"Damn," said Salvador. *"Damn!"* He laughed nervously. "I can't believe this. *Damn!"*

What could anyone do? There was another burst of sirens. We could hear children crying and dogs barking from inside the building, some of whose windows were already turning golden with the sunrise.

The rolling had definitely stopped—everyone agreed that it had been a roller, not a rocker, which was a choppy up-and-down quake that generally felt harsher. Still, this had been scary.

"I'm not going to the beach today," Marilyn announced.

"Honey? Don't you guess the waves will be dangerous?"

"Let's see."

Everyone straggled back in. Some—William and the children especially—seemed to have enjoyed it. Earthquakes were at least rare enough to be a novelty, and had a way of making even the most important things—deadlines, promises, commitments, debts, errands—less important. All we had to do today was play hooky and worry about surviving— it gave a mixed feeling of dread and relief.

I had barely fallen asleep when the bed shook again, at first tentatively, and then insistently, again accompanied by the creaking of the ceiling. My heart sank even before I fully awoke, feeling slightly seasick. This was the result of two terrible fears, the only two fears every human carries out of the womb: fear of falling and fear of loud noises. Earthquakes pitilessly stoke both fears. This time I rolled out of bed and stood in a doorway in case the ceiling should fall, and when it didn't, I reached for the radio. "*Whoa!*" was the first word I heard. I turned the dial to an all-news station; yes, there had been a second earthquake. A shaker this time. Would there be a third? I knew I would not be able to sleep again. The phone rang. It was Nguyen.

"Did you feel the aftershock? I know I shouldn't use the phone but it's just for a second. Are you still up for the cemetery?"

It seemed appropriate.

I drove. The Harbor Freeway was nearly empty and far eerier than when it had been jammed after the riots just two months before. We learned, on the radio, that the earthquake we had survived, the Landers quake, had measured a very strong 7.6 magnitude on the Richter scale, meaning that it had released as much energy as twelve atomic bombs. The second shaker was no aftershock—it was, officially, the 6.6 Big Bear earthquake. All the callers-in to the radio stations agreed that the second, while not as strong, was scarier—"best supporting earthquake," as Nguyen put it. The surface of the desert near the epicenters of the quakes had shifted as much as five feet. In later news reports, it was announced that the city of San Bernardino had moved two inches to the northwest and Palm Springs had shifted four inches to the northeast. The entire Los Angeles Basin had been jolted half an inch.

"How is William?"

"Actually, he was doing well. He hadn't wanted to come with us anyway, but then he started to consider it for a minute. He was funny—when they said on the radio that this was the Lander's quake, he started calling it the Ann Landers quake, and said that she was trying to tell us something. You wait—when he hears about the Big Bear quake, he'll say it made him decide to have a big beer. Plus, it was like everyone was at equal risk all of a sudden. I swear to God, it crossed my mind that we might die together, and that almost felt like a miracle—a good and bad miracle. Didn't you feel vulnerable?"

"Yes." Three hours after the second quake struck, my heart was still pounding. I was tired from lost sleep but doubted that I would sleep that night.

William had not wanted to come because he preferred to avoid cemeteries while he was in the final stages of his illness. We were going to put a pot of begonias on Nguyen's mother's grave; although a relatively new Vietnamese immigrant to Long Beach, she had been captivated by Forest Lawn's television advertisements, which showed immense vistas of emerald-green grass—no graves in sight—and blond children feeding white swans that glided over glassy little ponds, and had decided that she wanted to be buried there. I did not know what her illness had been, but her tutor, Mrs. Archie, did. Mrs. Nguyen had progressed enough in her literacy tutoring to check out a workbook on wills and to write out hers. She died shortly after completing Skill Book 3, *Long Vowel Sounds*. Today, June 28, was her birthday.

The Vietnamese had once dominated Asian society in Long Beach, but now had mostly drifted off to Orange County, irritated by the pitiless gangs that had grown up within their community, and, according to Nguyen, by LA County's liberal politics. When they strolled through the nearly all-Asian Westminster Mall in Orange County, near Nguyen's dental practice, they all wore American-flag lapel pins, especially at Tet or Easter. Most were obsessively anti-Communist, staunch Republicans, and, not surprisingly, Vietnam veterans. They were surpassed in their patriotism only by the Cambodians, who managed 80 percent of Long Beach's doughnut shops; they saw doughnuts as the most American things they could sell.

We were passing through Koreatown. Looking off in the direction where arsonists had destroyed liquor stores and swap meets during the 1992 riots. I saw nothing but fastidiously neat vacant lots. Rebuilding had been slow, and some liquor stores were not being allowed to rebuild at all—the city was considering a plan to subsidize proprietors who would build laundromats where their old stores had been. The Los Angeles Planning Commission had put new restrictions on "controversial" businesses such as convenience stores that sold beer and wine or held liquor licenses, in addition to gun shops, swap meets, pawnshops, and, for some reason, auto parts stores. In the event that they would be allowed to rebuild, they would have to provide parking, face restrictions on hours of operation, keep the premises graffiti-free, and hire security guards: in short, go out of business.

The luxuriant sunshine on the peaceful empty lots on this day of shattered nerves was a bizarre reminder that LA might well perish not with a bang but a whimper. The perfectly blue sky and good air quality were much scarier than the columns of black smoke and grinning looters of 1992; today everyone had death in the back of his mind. That was partly because of the terror of having buildings shake around you, and the fact that even hours after the shakers, the earthquake coverage on the radio was unmercifully continuous. Many Angelenos had blamed twenty-four-hour riot coverage—"the Looting Channel"—for further encouraging riots. I had a superstitious notion that this earthquake coverage was also tempting fate and should just get off the subject.

"We cannot rule out a third temblor today. We may be talking about something building, about further pent-up energy being released. We want to emphasize, of course, that *no one knows*. No one knows *one way or the other*. We don't want to push your buttons out there, we know everyone is having a very stressful day—"

"Please push her button. This is all just hype. Turn to KRTH—they'll play oldies. I'm so tired of all this talk about temblors," said Nguyen. He played with the dial, but all the radio stations had earthquakes on the brain. There was no escaping the surging mental aftershocks. Since no one could rule out the possibility of a third earthquake that day, newspeople were nagging every seismologist they could get on the air for an even bigger story: are we going to get another one, and would it be the Big One? The Big One is the lurking Antichrist of southern California's geology, the 8.9 earthquake that would liquefy the seacoast and make tall buildings bob like beach balls before sinking. The freeways would snap, gas lines ignite, and bridges and buildings topple, until the whole city was in flames or sucked into a liquefacted swamp, like the mastodons at the La Brea Tar Pits.

Los Angeles could, in the meantime, congratulate itself on its tough earthquake building codes. All structures had to be able to withstand a 7.9 earthquake. In September 1985, a 7.8 earthquake had shaken much of Mexico City to the ground. The 7.5 roller we had just experienced this morning, which had killed one person, was, according to the logarithmic Richter scale, more than thirty-two times stronger than the one that had leveled buildings and killed nearly a thousand people in Long Beach in 1933.

Societies are supposed to be judged on the way they treat their poor, but the way they treat their dead really says much more about the spirit of the place. Boston's burial grounds are both austere and broodingly quaint, as you would expect the resting place of Mother Goose to be. London's great burial places often tend to be primly located inside cathedrals. The great Père Lachaise Cemetery in Paris is itself a deathly city of light, with all the grandeur and sexiness of Paris itself, and overrun with sprinting cats. But Los Angeles, the city of sunshine and youth, of surfers and plastic surgery (the Beverly Hills yellow pages lists six pages of plastic surgeons), has a virtual cult of death—the happiest cemeteries in the world.

The best way to appreciate LA's death theme parks is, of course, to have moved here from Arabia, where the world's most snarling puritans have banned headstones or any other memorial, as well as virtually all funeral rites. Their cemeteries look like vacant lots with regular mounds, strewn with trash and inhabited by bony dogs. There is no such thing as a marked grave. Perhaps it has something to do with the Nejdi Muslims' utter certainty of afterlife—the fanatical smugness.

LA is the opposite. There are all kinds of signs of religiosity in the working-class black, Latino, and Asian flatlands as you move north and west to the more affluent areas of LA. There are Catholic churches, storefront churches, Santero *botánicas*, statues, and bumper stickers like KNOW GOD, KNOW PEACE, NO GOD, NO PEACE. It may be a coincidence, but people in the flat basin also seem to age more or less as nature intended. This comes to a gradual end at about Wilshire; the heavily Jewish Fairfax district, LA's last reservoir of natural wrinkles, is an ocean of bus benches with mortuary ads ("At Time of Need, We're All You Need" or "Specializing in Burial in Israel"), and people who read them. The face-lifts kick in north of Santa Monica Boulevard, in the richer and more secular Westside, where tight faces are burnished with blusher and moisturizer. Leaving well enough alone is not the strong point of people who get tucks; it is an upgrade that seems to call for carrot-colored hair, rainbow eyelids, and brilliant lips. Repeat customers are immediately identifiable by a permanent half-smile and the total lack of a filtrum: the upper lip is a taut scroll, perfectly smooth and drawn slightly upward at the sides, and gives the impression of toothlessness.

It was the good health and insistent youth of Los Angeles that drew my attention to its cemeteries. Even if death could not be stamped out, at least youth could last right up to the last gasp. And what came after the last gasp truly made this city the Queen of Angels.

Tourists are welcomed at LA's glamorous cemeteries—the Forest Lawn Pictorial Map and Guide that Nguyen had showed me actually urged, "Please allow yourself at least two hours to visit all the attractions." Many of the other famous death sites, though, recall LA's many bad ends. The city's famous graves suggest the ghoulish fact that its famous names—Bugsy Siegel, Fatty Arbuckle, Sal Mineo, Dorothy Dandridge, John Belushi, Sharon Tate, Marilyn Monroe, and fifty more—were darkened by many combinations of scandal, suicide, tragedy, and murder. Even poor old Clara Blandick—Auntie Em of *The Wizard of Oz*—was a little-known Hollywood suicide. And Walt Disney's remains lie in the shadow of the rumor that he had put himself on ice for the ultimate sequel.

Shortly after moving here I had visited Holy Cross Cemetery and Hillside Memorial Park in Culver City. These are known for their lavish treatment of the dead, especially their celebrity dead. Holy Cross is officially one of the Catholic Cemeteries of the Archdiocese of Los Angeles. It subdivisions suggest a Catholic theme park: Mother of Mercy, Mother of Good Hope, Precious Blood, Mother of Sorrows, Holy Redeemer, Divine Saviour, Assumption, Holy Rosary, Good Shepherd, and more. The theme-park feeling is so strong that when you see a reference to the Ascension you wonder if it might be a ride. The gentle hills are capped by tall marble crucifixes, Madonnas, and a Pietà. There are memorials in Arabic and German, but after English most are in Spanish, and many are adorned with Virgins of Guadalupe. Pinwheels and metallic balloons sway atop Latino children's graves.

Holy Cross's famous remains are those of Bing Crosby, Sharon Tate, Rosalind Russell, Bela Lugosi, and Mario Lanza. All are plain. Hollywood guidebooks try to make the most of trivia: the fact that Lugosi was buried in his cape, the name of Sharon Tate's fetal son buried with her (Richard Paul), and suggestions that Lanza's death may have been a mob hit. However, the place seems tasteful and reverent. Most of the pious old Catholics seem to have lived to ripe old ages, but that changes in the Holy Rosary subdivision, new and heavily Latino, where it seems half the dead were twenty-two-year-olds, with graves dating from the early 1970s. There are mountain vistas behind the hills and statuary. It is scenic, multicultural, and except for the occasional jumbo jet thundering into nearby Los Angeles Airport, quiet.

There is a Star of David on the gate of Hillside Memorial, a few blocks to the south—it is the Jewish version of Holy Cross. Its subdivisions are Mount Sholom, Sunland Gardens, Hillside Slope, and Laurel Garden. Jack Benny, Eddie Cantor, and George Jessel are buried here, but it is chiefly known for its fabulous shrine to Al Jolson—the grandest tomb of any star in Hollywood. Legend has it that Hillside coaxed Jolson into planning his burial here rather than of his first choice, Forest Lawn, by giving him a free monument. They clearly decided to make the most of their coup—Jolson died in 1950, before Benny, Cantor, or Jessel, and their thinking may have been to make his memorial a landmark and a draw for other "pre-need" shoppers. The appalling result is easily visible from the San Diego Freeway: set near the top of the cemetery's dramatic hill, a black-marble, scrolled-top sarcophagus sits sheltered under a soaring cupola surmounting six tall columns and shaded by a few poplar trees. From the front of the monument, a six-story waterfall rushes over wide blue tile steps, where sea gulls from nearby Marina del Rey wade in the glassy shallows. Around the interior of the cupola runs the inscription THE MAN RAISED UP ON HIGH—THE SWEET SINGER OF ISRAEL. The inside of the dome is a color mosaic of Moses lurking in a nest of blue sky and foamy clouds, cradling a tablet of the Law, his cherry lips pouting amid a luxuriantly curly white beard.

Hollywood's second-greatest star grave is that of Douglas Fairbanks at Hollywood Memorial Cemetery, the archetypal Hollywood graveyard: it is in view of the Hollywood sign, and right next door to Paramount Studios. The tomb lies across from a marble entryway from which it is separated by a hundred-foot rectangular lily pond. The sarcophagus, engraved DOUGLAS FAIRBANKS 1883–1939, has a backdrop of marble columns and a portico with a portrait of Fairbanks in copper bas-relief. The sarcophagus is inscribed: *Good Night Sweet Prince, and Flights of Angels Sing Thee to Thy Rest.* Tyrone Power's grave nearby—it is a marble bench—displays three quotations from *Hamlet:* "*There is a special providence in the fate of sparrows . . .*" and "*If it be now, 'tis not to come,*" plus the "Good Night Sweet Prince" passage.

The grave of Mel Blanc, the voice of almost all Hollywood's cartoon characters, stands among glistening black headstones nearly all inscribed in Russian or Armenian. His displays a Star of David and the signoff "That's All Folks." Two child stars of the old *Our Gang* show, Carl "Alfalfa" Switzer and Darla Hood, are across the path—both died young, he at thirty-three and she at forty-eight.

Casual visitors to the cemetery have not escaped the notice of real mourners. Not far from Marion Davies's tomb is a tiny plot with well-kept flowers and a pocked white statue of the Virgin with a black scarf draped over her shoulders, against which a shingle is propped, reading *Go away you cheating croock and ofensive mokey and respect this nobles families sacred place.* It was undoubtedly prompted by the "ofensive mokeys" who visit the pink granite memorial immediately adjacent, inscribed *Jayne Mansfield, 1933–1967.*

Whimsy and boosterism are not absent, and even coexist in the rocket-shaped monument of Carl Morgan Bigsby. He was not an astronaut; the marble Atlas rocket, the stone reads, is "symbolic of his pioneering work in graphic arts" and was carved to the "exact scale of the original missile launched Dec. 18, 1958." The actual-size rocket, however, is put in the shade by the spectacle across the way.

The centerpiece of Hollywood Memorial is the Otis-Chandler compound, with four stone structures and a half-dozen trees, honoring the millionaire founders of the *Los Angeles Times:* Harry Chandler (1864–1944), Marian Otis Chandler (1866–1952), and Eliza S. Otis, wife of Harrison Gray Otis. There is a soaring obelisk, two altar-type displays, and three eagles, two of marble and one of copper. The fourth monument commemorates the deaths of the twenty men killed at the union bombing of the Times Mirror building on October 1, 1900. Entitled "Our Martyred Men" and capped with a statue named *The Angel of the Watch*, the monument supports a plaque that eulogizes the workers who now enjoy "eternal summer" in Los Angeles.

The "eternal summer" quote to the bombing victims neatly connects thoughts of death to the forgiving southern California climate. It certainly could be taken to mean heaven, hell, or Los Angeles.

We passed a Fatburger restaurant. The car wobbled slightly as we moved toward the San Fernando Road freeway exit.

"Don't tell me I have a flat," I said.

"Aftershock," said Nguyen.

We turned into the gated entrance of Forest Lawn. It is immediately clear to any visitor that Forest Lawn Glendale is the Buckingham Palace of Los Angeles cemeteries—actually, its iron gates, the largest in the world, are twice as wide and five feet higher than those at Buckingham Palace. They seem to lead into a stupendous golf course: from the towering gates on South Glendale Avenue, Forest Lawn swells like the Berkshire Hills. We coasted through, past a marble statue of Pharaoh's daughter, in the costume of an Attic Greek maiden, coming upon the infant Moses in a lily pond.

"It's like a sculpture garden," I told Nguyen, who laughed out loud.

"Fasten your seat belt," he said.

We followed the signs around to the right and came upon the Great Mausoleum, which seemed be a replica of an Oxford college. I said so.

" 'Replica' is the magic word here," conceded Nguyen.

"Here in LA or here in Forest Lawn?"

"Have a look at the 'The Builder's Creed,' " he said.

Forest Lawn was the model for the Happier Hunting Ground, the country club for the dead in Evelyn Waugh's *The Loved One;* its founder, Dr. Hubert Eaton, the Builder, was the model for Wilbur Kenworthy, the Dreamer of the novel. One wall of the Great Mausoleum is taken up by THE BUILDER'S CREED, a fifty-foot-high marble testament:

THE BUILDER'S CREED

I believe in a happy Eternal Life.

I believe those of us who are left behind should be glad in the certain belief that those gone before, who believed in Him, have entered into that happier Life. . . .

I therefore know the cemeteries of today are wrong, because they depict an end, not a beginning. They have consequently become unsightly stoneyards full of inartistic symbols and depressing customs. . . .

I therefore prayerfully resolve on this New Year's Day, 1917, that I shall endeavor to build Forest Lawn as different, as unlike other cemeteries as sunshine is unlike darkness. . . .

Forest Lawn shall become a place where lovers new and old shall love to stroll and watch the sunset's glow, planning for the future or reminiscing of the past; a place where artists study and sketch; where school teachers bring happy children to see the things they read of in books . . . where memorialization of Loved Ones in sculptured marble and pictorial glass shall be encouraged but controlled by acknowledged artists. . . .

The Builder

Waugh described this sculpture in *The Loved One* as "a singular and massive wall of marble [incised] in letters a foot high:

The Dream

Behold I dreamed a dream and I saw a New Earth sacred to
HAPPINESS. There amid all that Nature and Art could offer to
elevate the Soul of Man I saw the Happy Resting Place of
Countless Loved Ones. And I saw the Waiting Ones who still
stood at the brink of that narrow stream that now separated
them from those who had gone on before. Young and old,
they were happy too. . . .

"and below, in vast cursive facsimile, the signature:

WILBUR KENWORTHY,

THE DREAMER."

The actual words "The Builder" at Forest Lawn are, in
fact, written in "vast cursive facsimile," and there are a few
stranger-than-fiction touches that Waugh chose to leave out:
a caption on a marble slab, underneath, explaining the Creed
("On New Year's Day, 1917, a man stood on a hilltop . . ."),
and a marble statue of a very small girl, an even smaller boy,
and their little puppy on a wagon, gazing up at the Creed. In
the souvenir book *The Spirit of Forest Lawn,* the monolith is
photographed with a *real* boy and girl holding hands beside
the marble ones, tilting their blond locks upward toward the
Creed. And the theme of childlike innocence is carried on on
the other side of the mausoleum entrance, with a marble
statue of Jesus and six tots, entitled *". . . For Such Is the Kingdom of Heaven."*

"Look," I pointed out to Nguyen. There was a red button
to the left, with a sign: "Push button to hear the story of *For
Such Is the Kingdom of Heaven."*

"I've heard it," said Nguyen, with just a trace of pleading.
He wanted to get to the Court of Freedom subdivision,

where his mother was buried, and had promised only to show me a few of the attractions. "Let's get to the *Last Supper.*" The *Last Supper* stained-glass window is unveiled every half hour. A friendly guide admitted us to the Memorial Terrace entrance of the Great Mausoleum. "Was anything here damaged this morning?" I asked her. "Bless you, not a thing that I know of. But I sure felt it! My six-foot bookcase fell over, and that was a sight! I love your nails," she added to a woman who had come up behind us. "I live out in Sunland." This sounds like a cemetery subdivision but in fact is a Valley district of Los Angeles. "Hurry now, the window is shown in just one minute."

We hurried past a mammoth reproduction of Michelangelo's *Moses* and a wall of Last Suppers by various Old Masters—I counted nineteen—and through a stone corridor to the Memorial Court of Honor. It was built like a medieval chapel, with reproductions of Michelangelo's *Day and Night* on either side, and filled with ranks of folding chairs. A closed curtain covered the far wall, and underneath was a row of six engraved slabs with the inscription "Beneath the marble floor are crypts which money cannot buy . . . for those proclaimed 'immortals' by vote of the Council of Regents of the Memorial Court of Honor." Each of the immortals was eulogized in stone by someone more famous: Rudolf Friml by Richard Nixon, Jan Styka by Billy Graham, and Glenn Dumke by Ronald Reagan. Some of these were unknown to me in their mortal phase, let alone their immortality. I was peering at the others when the lights began to dim.

"Welcome to Forest Lawn," intoned a recorded voice that boomed through the gothic vaults of the Memorial Court of Honor.

Nguyen hissed at me to sit, and we sat through the pep

talk, which included a sales pitch and an invitation to visit Forest Lawn Hollywood Hills. Then, with a burst of music, came the parting of the curtain, revealing a huge stained-glass replica of Da Vinci's painting. In the lower right-hand corner was the stained-glass notation LEONARDO DA VINCI 1498/ FOREST LAWN 1931. The story of its recreation by an Italian glass artist and its shipment to Los Angeles was narrated to the accompaniment of the *New World* Symphony. The lights came up; after exactly one minute of solemn display, the curtains closed automatically. Sixty seconds are allowed for you to meditate upon the unseeability of Da Vinci's *Last Supper*. Even in bigger-than-life stained glass, the scene is so impossibly famous that it leaves an impression close to zero. Yet the painting clearly has an unusual grasp on the imagination of Los Angeles; not only is a replica displayed in almost every mortuary chapel, there is even a life-sized *Last Supper* at the Hollywood Wax Museum.

It becomes immediately clear, as you follow the gentle roadway that slopes over the rolling lawns, past the splendid grave of Aimee Semple McPherson, that the joke was on Waugh. His book poked fun at LA's philistine mania for replicas of culture, art, and spirituality, held together by commercialism, but it, his book, is a replica of something far bigger and more bizarre. LA accepts that gigantism and self-parody are normal modes of expression, not aberrations to write snide books about. The place may lack subtlety, like India, which, V. S. Naipaul observed, lacks subtlety in the most basic ways: "The poor are skinny, the rich are fat." LA mocks itself easily. What other city would have a hamburger chain called Fatburger? Foreigners, the English in particular, seem to congratulate themselves on discovering these LA oddities, but LA takes them for granted and enjoys them. Forest Lawn was far beyond parody, as a place paved with corpses should be, and on a day when everybody in town was painfully aware of his mortality, it actually provided comfort.

We drove through largely unused lawns, past Babyland, a small section with a statue of a plump toddler.

"This must be a section where they just bury young children," I said.

"No, that's Lullabyland. Go straight."

I thought he was joking, but actually the Builder had dedicated a particularly attractive slope with trees at the top to the graves of the very young. And I had thought Holy Cross was a theme park? This was Deathland itself, with suburbs—of which Lullabyland was one. The two paths that began toward the top and curved downward through the expanse of graves ended at a point just above the road. It was heart-shaped. "Have a look up there," Nguyen suggested. "I've seen it."

Many of the graves are engraved with nicknames. Some of them are funny, but only the hardest heart does not melt for the parents who had NITE NITE, JIMMIE CRICKET carved into their infant's headstone. The summit of Lullabyland is capped with a twenty-five-foot fairy castle decorated with butterflies. This is the continuation of a statue and bas-relief at eye level. It consists of a statue of a baby boy wistfully gazing at the bas-relief, which depicts ten cherubs in a daisy field, chasing the butterflies up into the clouds. The boy is reaching out into this other world, half in love with easeful death.

Child statuary is very big at Forest Lawn, even outside of Lullabyland. Perhaps it is intended to compensate for the fact that 99 percent of the actual graves are flat headstones—there are relatively few mourning Virgins or introspective angels, but children are everywhere. Even across from the Masonic section, where the plaques inform you that many of its features—an open Bible, fifteen steps leading up to it, light and dark marble—are properly Masonic, uncounted tons of marble have been carved into *Baby's Bath, Little Duck Mother, Little Pals, Look, Mommy!, Little Helper, First Lesson* (a toddler with a book and a doll, teaching the doll to read), and *Tender Flowers,* which is a cherub with a garland, adorning the Von Tacky family headstone. There is also a full-size replica of the *Little Mermaid* from Copenhagen Harbor, which was donated by Greer Garson in memory of her mother.

At last we reached the Court of Freedom, where Nguyen placed the flowers on his mother's grave. The subdivision is flanked by the patriotic Garden of Honor and a huge mosaic after the famous painting of the signing of the Declaration of Independence, accompanied by a numbered-silhouette key to the signatories. Strolling to the Garden of Honor—behind whose locked doors Sammy Davis, Jr., was buried—I noticed that most of the graves here, and virtually all of the newer ones, were Asian—many of the grave markers were inscribed with Korean and Cambodian characters; there was Japanese, too, and much of the Latin script spelled out Vietnamese. The only other visitor at the Court of Freedom was a stunning young Asian girl in a white dress and spike heels, meditating on a stone bench. Here was another example of red-blooded Asian-Americanism, I thought, and Nguyen concurred.

"Mother was very tempted by the Court of David and the Triumphant Faith Terraces"—according to my map, these were slightly to the west, our next stop—"but she loved the statue of George Washington better."

The heroic statue of Washington, which overlooks the Court of Freedom from the front of the severe, square Freedom Mausoleum—ironically, it has a very Soviet look—is one of only two in the world. This is Forest Lawnese for saying that it is a replica of the famous Washington statue that stands in front of the Subtreasury Building on Wall Street.

"Look here," said Nguyen, leading me into a small corner garden to the left of the mausoleum. It was empty except for a small statue of a cherub and a wall plaque reading *Walter Elias Disney*. "This is his grave. It was another big influence on Mom's wanting to be buried here."

"So he wasn't cryogenicized."

"Well, you don't see a sarcophagus."

Actually, he had probably been cremated, like most of the other loved ones whose graves were either the size of a shoebox or occupied a small garden or court without a tomb. The lilting notes of "Für Elise" could be heard among the trees crowding Disney's garden grave. I had been hearing music all morning—calliope, easy-listening violins, and solemn organ recitals—and just assumed that the workers mowing the laws and clipping the hedges had radios on. But when Nguyen saw me instinctively looking up into the trees for the source of the sound, he pointed it out, almost hidden by foliage: a black metal speaker bolted to the top of the high garden wall.

"Music is piped in all over the cemetery," he explained. This was yet another detail Waugh had poached for *The Loved One;* in the Happy Hunting Grounds, "music rose softly all round him, the subdued notes of the 'Hindu Love-song,' relayed from an organ through countless amplifiers concealed about the garden."

We drove on to the Court of David, a quadrangle with a snow-white, full-sized replica of Michelangelo's *David*, surrounded by bronze friezes set into the court's high stone walls that tell the story of how Michelangelo created the statue. When Jessica Mitford visited Forest Lawn in the 1950s to research her book *The American Way of Death*, she reported that a very un-Michelangelesque fig leaf had been forced upon the statue, "giving it a surprisingly indecent appearance," but it has been removed since then. You can press the nearby red button to hear the "Story of the Court of David," and as the disembodied voice intones the praises of the court—"the only place in the world where *all* of Michelangelo's great statues are gathered in faithful reproduction" (take that, St. Peter's)—you can contemplate the incongruously uncircumcised Jewish hero in his brilliantly sunny California courtyard. The next thing you know, the sparkling flow of historical narration has turned into a sales pitch: ". . . One phone call takes care of everything—mortuary, cemetery, mausoleum, crematory . . . low prices because of one management and low overhead, with savings passed on to you, . . ." The hearty but serious salesmanship is more interesting than the statue, perfect replica though it is. Like the *Last Supper* window, *David* is so colossally famous that there is nothing for your eye to discover; there is nothing new. A brother of mine who once took a train through France thought, gazing at a landscape that millions of travelers had seen, that "it was almost as if these hills and villages had been seen by so many people passing by that they have worn away from being looked at." *David,* too, had been almost obliterated by fame; being watched by his insistently perfect and celebrated features was the visual equivalent of nagging.

The classical conventionality radiates a lifelessness that gives you the feeling of sleepwalking through dreamily familiar territory; you have the certitude that a big marble Christ cannot be far off, and in fact, the Court of the Christus— Jesus and a waterfall in a Grimm's fantasy of evergreens—is next. The cumulative effect of the circuit through Forest Lawn is numbing, a womb of fragrantly mingled sun, Christianity, Greek antiquity, and Californian modernity, embodied in the ever-present red buttons. You feel almost crushed by all the condolence and serenity; the stupendous scale of the time, space, and expense invested in comforting and soothing you is surprisingly wearying. I had the feeling that the business of mourning and getting on with your life would seem simple to anyone leaving a loved one behind in Forest Lawn. You would have the distinct feeling that the deceased would be well cared for and entertained in your absence.

In fact, the beauty of Forest Lawn's genuine flowering hills and phony statuary is slathered on so unmercifully that you actually start to stagger a little as you head for the exact replica of the Church of the Recessional, so named because it is a copy of the Church of St. Margaret in Rottingdean where Kipling wrote his famous poem "Recessional." It is closed to the public, as it is used mostly for formal functions, but is located at the edge of the vast parking lot at whose far shore stands the Forest Lawn Museum and gift shop.

The museum is true to the cemetery's mania for replicas, with ersatz versions of the British crown jewels, Ghiberti's doors to the Baptistry in Florence, and the Sotteraneo, the room where Michelangelo hid from royalist troops in 1530 Florence; he had sketched all over the walls, and his sketches are faithfully reproduced. There is the head of a genuine Easter Island monolith, and genuine-looking portions of the *David*—the feet, a hand—which appeared to me to be studies. Or had Forest Lawn actually imported damaged pieces of the statue that quake-stricken Florentines no longer wanted? I knew of no quake that had ever struck Florence. On the pedestal of each fragment I saw a plaque reading "Fragment of David, Earthquake of 1971. Michelangelo Buonarroti."

"Oh, yes, that's our old *David,*" the museum guide told us. "It was destroyed in the Sylmar earthquake that hit Los Angeles in 1971. We just went ahead and cast a new one!"

Our last stop at Forest Lawn would be the Hall of the

Crucifixion-Resurrection, where the two great eponymous paintings were displayed every hour on the hour. We waited on the steps while a small crowd of visitors gathered, nearly all elderly men and women. One of the very diminutive women looked embalmed under her wide straw hat. I was thrilled to see an example of such defiance of time's passage in the middle of Deathland, even if she might have overdone it just a bit.

"Is this your first time to see the *Crucifixion?*" the embalmed-looking woman asked me. "It will bowl you over." She was smiling, but it was close enough to a sneer; the lack of loose skin gave her facial expressions very little "play." How many face-lifts had she undergone? She had the shrunken, parenthesized grin and prominent bony cheekbones of a mummy, features it seems to take two or three face-tightenings to achieve. The neck is always the giveaway—as creased as a turtle's, like her bare baggy arms.

"Do you come to see it often?"

"Oh, our church comes out this way for lunch from Alhambra, and we look in on it sometimes. I hope it wasn't damaged! It's a whole hell of a lot bigger than the *Resurrection*—nearly two hundred feet long."

"I guess you never run out of things to see at Forest Lawn," I suggested.

"Hell, no! Are you from out of town?" She smiled delightedly and moved closer, and I think if I had been wearing a jacket she would have toyed with one of the lapels. It made sense, I supposed. It was only to be expected that someone who had had so much plastic surgery had done it in order to be sociable. The oddity is that she found it so comforting here—I would not have expected that from someone who was obviously fighting Father Time tooth and nail. Perhaps the logic of plastic surgery lay in the backdrop of this parking lot, the sapphire California sky and perfect lawns: you want to look as good as your sun-drenched surroundings. This wasn't Boston, where gray wrinkles would blend right in, or one of the many cities of the world where they would be fastidiously veiled. Or was it just that the southern Californian sun forces you to show so much of yourself? This was, in every way, such an unembarrassed city.

Perhaps it was celebrity peer pressure, as many as one's famous coevals aged and yet seemed not to. The very idea brings the words "eternal summer" to mind—the fact that celebrities' faces virtually do not change: Lucille Ball, Phyllis Diller, Dinah Shore, John Davidson, Burt Reynolds, Elizabeth Taylor, Ronald Reagan, Liberace. At most they go from an eternal June to a slightly scorched August. It is a very LA phenomenon—people come here for plastic surgery, or have it because they live here.

I mentioned this to Nguyen out of the embalmed lady's hearing.

"We have one of the best doctor-patient ratios in the world, here in LA, but the figures are very misleading." He shrugged. "The trouble is that nearly a third are plastic and reconstructive surgeons. They feed on one another—so many advertise as being experts at 'correction of previous cosmetic surgery.' "

"No kidding? I would have thought only the best survive here."

"There are cheap doctors—plastic surgery isn't just for the rich. Everybody wants it. I had lunch at the Westside Pavilion the other day and I saw this girl with the worst nose job ever. They had *eliminated* her nose."

"Maybe they had removed her nose, because of a cancer or something."

"Oh, come on. This was a botch. You could tell she was very obsessed—one of these young LA girls, rich and skeletal.

Wasted from dieting. Her cheeks were hollow. She was wearing a very short miniskirt, and her thighs were tiny. She was going for this drop-dead thin Julia Roberts look. She actually looked ready to drop dead! I'll bet you she had anorexia, or is headed for it. But that nose! Or lack of it."

"Ten minutes," said one of the old men in jogging suits.

"So much of it is unnecessary. I mean, in Vietnam, I can see, they had a grave need for reconstructive surgery and prosthetics. To a much smaller extent here. But what you mostly have in LA is, you know, body sculpting. Calf implants—very big with men, especially gay men. For serious legs. Buttock tucks, liposuction, lipoplasty, and lipo-transfer. Scalp reductions and hair transplants, tummy tucks, chemical peels, collagen injections—especially for lip jobs. Dermabrasion. Eyelid work is big with Asians. Penile and hair implants, chin and cheekbone work, dimple jobs, ear jobs, breast enlargement, breast reduction. Jaw implants—William wanted one until he got his HIV test, and then that was the priority."

He gazed across the parking lot at the Church of the Recessional nestled among the oak trees, and let out a long breath.

"William wanted a jaw implant, with his looks?"

"He saw it in one of the gay Hollywood papers—they had a great ad with a picture of such a hot guy with a sexy jaw, with the old picture of him looking weak-chinned. There are more plastic surgery ads in those papers than anything else. Except for new books on handling grief and dying."

A godlike voice rumbled out of the sunny air.

"The next showing of the *Crucifixion* and the *Resurrection* will begin in five minutes."

"Come on, boys!" said the friendly embalmed lady, who thought she had us sized up. "This costs a dollar each. It's the only thing they need a donation for."

Calf implants? I suddenly thought. Of course. In what

other city were your legs showing so much of the time? Like the *Last Supper* stained-glass window, the *Crucifixion* is revealed by a parting curtain. According to the audio presentation that boomed through the dark auditorium, it was the world's largest religious oil painting, at nearly nine thousand square feet. It was painted by a Polish artist, Jan Styka, which explains why he was buried with the Immortals under the *Last Supper* window. The gigantic picture depicts the moment before the Crucifixion, and nearly everyone in the New Testament is placed somewhere in the crowds—according to the narration, even the shepherds who followed the star of Bethlehem are shown in the lower left corner, watching the scene on Calvary unfold from a distant rampart. To convey the Savior's anxiety at that moment, an amplified heartbeat booms through the auditorium along with the narration.

The *Resurrection* has a much larger cast. Set, like the first painting, on a hill outside Jerusalem, whose walls and Temple are visible, it portrays an illuminated Jesus with his arms outstretched; at least a million people are arriving on a vast carpet of cloud. You can pick out Pilgrims, Crusaders, Founding Fathers, monks, nuns, and people in Arab, Jewish, Chinese, and Native American garb—two thousand years of fashion. "There is King David in red," intoned the narrator, but I could not find him in the crowd.

"Forest Lawn *is* southern California," I concluded as we sped down Barham Boulevard to the Hollywood Freeway. Nguyen looked silently out the window—he had suffered through two earthquakes and a tour of Forest Lawn Glendale, which only served to remind him of his beloved William's near-deathly condition. To make matters worse, I had insisted on having a look at Forest Lawn Hollywood Hills on the way back—it was just ten minutes down the freeway, as the Forest Lawn staff constantly reminded you, and had been worth a short visit, even though Nguyen had seen it all before. "I was just glad that the Old North Church was closed," he admitted. "Being from Boston, you would have gone all through it."

The Hollywood Hills cemetery had full-size replicas not only of Boston's Old North Church, breathtakingly perfect except for the background of chaparral-covered Hollywood Hills, but of the Church of the Hills ("where Henry Wadsworth Longfellow worshiped as a boy"), a selection of Washington, Jefferson, and Lincoln statues, and the Liberty Bell. It had a heavily patriotic theme, but also boasted, perhaps as a counterweight, a very timely Mexican park, where the sign read: PLAZA OF MEXICAN HERITAGE. WALK COUNTERCLOCKWISE THROUGH THE HISTORY OF THE GREAT EARLY CIVILIZATIONS OF NORTH AMERICA. STAY ON WALK. AVOID THE CACTUS. I wanted to stroll through the history of the Olmecs, Zapotecs, Teotihuacans, Toltecs, and Maya, and many more, but Nguyen firmly vetoed the idea.

"I just wanted to place some flowers for my mother! Give me a break." Not only that, we had spent four hours rather than the recommended two in Glendale. Nguyen was so impatient by the time the viewing of the paintings was over that he pleaded with me not to visit the Wee Kirk o' the Heather, where Ronald Reagan and Jane Wyman had been married. Sixty thousand people had been married there—it was the cemetery's greatest evidence for its claim to be a place for the living and the dead. In recent days, though, for some reason a more popular if equally odd site for weddings was the Nixon Library in nearby Orange County. "Still, I was glad to see Bette Davis."

Her sarcophagus was in the Courts of Remembrance, with the inscription "She did it the hard way." Inside the nearby maze of wall crypts for the cremated, I had found Lucille Ball's resting place, beside her mother's ("OUR DEDE"). It was right after that that Nguyen grew upset at the sight of three Rastafarians photographing Liberace's sarcophagus and insisted on leaving.

"Forest Lawn *is* southern California," I repeated. It was even truer, I thought, of these sunny mourning theme parks than of the rigorous luxury of Beverly Hills. They epitomize the easy, temperate life of southern California that turned Huxley into a lotus eater. It is so overdone. The art is a replica, there is something colonial and secondhand in the way all of western civilization—from Moses to Michelangelo to George Washington to Hubert Eaton himself—is all about feeling good, about feeling very, very good. It is like the thin layer of tract housing by the mile that covers the adobe desert of Los Angeles. It is implanted and unnatural, and that is part of the fun, though there is no surprise or creativity or vitality in all the schlock art. Sometimes there comes a reminder, like the two earthquakes that had rattled us that morning, that none of this was meant to be, and suddenly our city's proud building codes seem like no more than a careful series of face-lifts and collagen injections to help us hang on for as long as possible against the inevitable.

"The art has no vitality."

"No *vitality?*" Nguyen gave me the obvious look.

I could not say what I thought. There was something decadent in the bloodlessly perfect replicas of art we had seen. I struggled to think against the easy metaphor of all the reverent copies of European art presiding over LA from a cemetery. Somewhere among the classical icebergs lay an argument for immigration or multiculturalism. My nerves, lulled by the otherworldly all afternoon, were still slightly raw from the instability of this world.

At least the weather was stable. Today the earth had bucked and buckled as if trying to throw us off its back, and our varied travels had taken us from the sea to the inland hills and through death and life, but it felt unthinkable that God or Mother Nature really had it in for us. For that, thunder, rain, and explosive lightning would have been needed. LA's angelic meteorology not only contradicted its geology, but also seemed to deny that time was passing. No wonder the sundial at the San Gabriel Mission had to remind those consulting it that every hour wounds, the last one kills. The seasons of the year pass subtly, almost unfelt, in southern California, unlike New England, where the march of the four very different seasons function almost like a set of Westminster chimes to remind you of the spiral of passing time. This sunny day was typical of LA's midsummer bright heat—it actually is called "earthquake weather."

The freeways are often full Sunday evenings, with people pouring back into town from weekends in Las Vegas, the inland valleys, the Ventura County and Orange County beach cities, and Palm Springs, but most of the lanes were still clear. Obviously people had not fled town as they had during the riots, or if they had, they were staying away. The riots, though, had left the city debauched and spiritless—there seemed to be a feeling that it would be a long time before people would have the energy to do it all again. The earthquake, on the other hand, had another bash at southern California only three hours after its first assault. The good news was that the temblors released a surge of earthquake awareness and planning. The bad news was that within a week or two it was all forgotten, and everyone's jitters were massaged away by the city's encroaching eternal present, until January 1994, when the freeway under these very wheels would be a shattered memory.

10

La Lucha Continua

Twenty-mile-long Sunset Boulevard zigzags from the grimy purlieus of Echo Park all the way to the Pacific Ocean. It is a bland commercial thoroughfare lined with guitar shops in Hollywood, but farther west, as you tool down the Sunset Strip in West Hollywood, you pass through the high balcony of West Los Angeles, looking down on the smoggy floor of the basin. It quickly becomes scenic in Beverly Hills, where the lawnscape of mansions and hedges is dominated by the pink heap of the Beverly Hills Hotel at Foothill Road. Sunset stays scenic all the way to the end, sweeping into Pacific Coast Highway at Pacific Palisades, where a sea breeze heralds the low-density sprawl of filling stations and gourmet grocery stores. Malibu is just north. Sunset's loveliest curves, however, undulate in the shady corridor through Bel Air that runs along the campus of the University of California at Los Angeles. A left at Westwood Plaza takes you into this grassy, red-brick academic galaxy. You are now in Westwood.

Westwood is in the heart of what Angelenos call the Westside, the jigsaw of wealthy, liberal, and mostly white neighborhoods bordered by Beverly Hills on the east, the ocean on the west, and the Santa Monica Mountains on the north— Los Angeles is the only city in the world to be bisected by a mountain range. The same native Angelenos who think San Francisco resembles Europe tend to think Westwood is like Back East. The reasons are that it is neither a suburb nor a slum, it is a concentrated commercial neighborhood not bisected by a freeway, it has at least three independently owned bookstores, and parking is nearly impossible. Westwood is a web of streets crammed with movie theaters and stores which give way to the grassy heights of the UCLA campus on the north; to the south, it is bounded by the mighty Wilshire, a raging six-lane throughway lined with the city's tallest skyscrapers outside of downtown Los Angeles. Some of the buildings contain cable television offices, oil companies, and foreign consulates, which allow Westwood the student demonstrations that give this corner of LA the feeling of a true college town. I had often been a spectator at demonstrations against the Saudi Arabian consulate in the building at the corner of Wilshire Boulevard and Westwood Boulevard; the demonstrators were friendly but anonymous behind their mirrored sunglasses, their heads swaddled in red-checked headcloths.

Westwood is the movie and shopping outlet for Bel Air, whose high gates and fanatically trim landscaping loom across Sunset Boulevard north of the UCLA campus. Westwood is dominated by the blondes and cheerleaders and affluent old Gentiles who are not found any closer to the east than Pasadena. It epitomizes the Los Angeles of the Wasp-dominated nineteenth century, whose great-grandchildren buy comic books and CDs and movie tickets. Shops in dingy south LA and rich Beverly Hills generally have highly visible security guards these days; Westwood is the happy medium, the comfortable middle-class bazaar where proprietors may worry about shoplifters but not shootouts.

Westwood's status as a civilized and educated bastion amid the Babel of Los Angeles was briefly shaken, however, in the uproar following its first gang shooting in 1988. A young moviegoer, Karen Toshima, was caught in the crossfire of a Crip-Blood gunfight and shot dead. Against Westwood type, she was Asian and from Long Beach, but the incident—the idea of bullets flying past Westwood's ice cream parlors and theaters—gave LA gang fighting a visibility it had never enjoyed before. It was one of the first times that the then-thriving drug war between the Crips and Bloods was fought outside the neighborhoods where the turf is actually defined (through graffiti) by local gang affiliation. After the shooting, coverage of gang activities skyrocketed. The fact that it was Westwood struck a nerve not only because the Westside—Venice excepted—had always felt immune from gang killings, but because this was a university enclave. UCLA has an enrollment of well over thirty thousand students, which meant that about sixty thousand anxious parents nationwide read about the murder.

Westwood absorbed another blow in 1991, when the premiere of *New Jack City* was followed by looting and vandalism. By then, the area's dwindling population of wealthy shoppers was overwhelmed by high school and college students, leading to a creeping invasion of T-shirt stores and yogurt and fast-food joints. One of the bookstores closed, along with several upscale stores and restaurants, but the neighborhood remained lively because of the surrounding university.

UCLA has the largest enrollment of all the University of

California's nine campuses, but, with 411 acres, the smallest area. It is small only by comparison—the Santa Cruz campus, for example, sits on two thousand wooded acres. Like most of the UCs, UCLA reflects California's many colors: about 40 percent white, over 30 percent Asian-Pacific, 16 percent Hispanic, and 6 percent African-American. It is the second-oldest UC, after Berkeley; its mascot, the bruin, is a tip of the hat to the older school's bear symbol. UCLA's other relationship with the upper half of the state is in the migration of college students: southern Californians tend to go north for their education, to Berkeley, San Francisco, and Stanford, and UCLA is heavily northern Californian.

Westwood grew along with UCLA, which, though founded in 1919, was part of the English-speaking ascendancy of Los Angeles' nineteenth century. The history of Mexico's Alta California, the huge state north of Baja California, ended in the 1840s when Mexico ceded the land to the United States, and was sealed by the stream of Yankee migrants and refugees which resulted only months later from the Gold Rush in 1848. As LA became more of a melting pot, Anglos migrated out of various parts of LA—out of Watts, Inglewood, and Boyle Heights in East LA, which had once been heavily Jewish—and they generally were drawn in this direction. Wars brought more exotic and more recent Europeans: Bertolt Brecht, Thomas Mann, Albert Einstein, and Vladimir Nabokov, who wrote screenplays in Mandeville Canyon Road in Brentwood.

Schoenberg Plaza at UCLA is named for one of LA's most brilliant European refugees: Arnold Schoenberg, composer of *Moses and Aaron* and inventor of atonal composition. I was a witness to one of those little shocks of LA's ethnic seismicity that temporarily named Schoenberg Plaza Plaza Aztlan.

East Los Angeles had been quiet during the riots, but the following year *la raza* swept into the headlines with a gala hunger strike, at the UCLA campus in Westwood. It had all begun with the establishment of UCLA's Chicano Studies program in 1973, which the university never upgraded to departmental status. The controversy lasted twenty years, and in 1992 and 1993, a movement of petitions and demonstrations began to force the issue, with the support of some Hispanic faculty and a new organization, the CSC (Conscious Students of Color). A refusal to establish the department, intended as definitive, came shortly after the death of Cesar Chavez, which led to a sit-in and mini-riot on the UCLA campus. After the destruction of the faculty lounge's windows and furniture, nearly a hundred students were arrested. That was when the hunger strike began, to protest the Chicano Studies program's status and the arrests. It was located at Schoenberg Plaza, renamed Aztlan—a mythical Aztecland of plenty—by its hungry occupiers.

In practical terms, it was just a bureaucratic wrinkle, but the fast grabbed headlines, and the "Plaza Aztlan" business quickly raised hackles. I had heard of Aztlan only by way of the proclamations posted by M.E.Ch.A., the Movimiento Estudiantil Chicana y Chicano de Aztlan—one of its posters in Westwood advertised a segregated "Raza Graduation" ceremony in Sunset Canyon for UCLA's Mexican-American graduating seniors. Finally a local Chicano journalist, Ruben Martinez, from the left-wing *LA Weekly,* cleared the air by voicing his pleasure at seeing "the transformation of UCLA's Schoenberg Plaza, named after a dead European composer, into Plaza Aztlan, heart of the mythical indigenous nation Chicano activists have long dreamed of." The piece did not run in the *LA Weekly,* which has a limited circulation in

Spanish-speaking LA, and none at all in South-Central, where it voluntarily does not distribute because of editorial fear that its upscale advertising would excite consumer envy and violence. It appeared in the *LA Times,* where it prompted an immediate response from Schoenberg's grandson—living in Westwood—who angrily pointed out that Arnold Schoenberg had himself been an immigrant and refugee from Nazism. "The world already has a Europe, a Korea, an Iran and Mexico," wrote E. Randol Schoenberg. "People come to Los Angeles to be somewhere else."

"Somewhere else" aptly described the appearance of the plaza at its mythical height, with about thirty pup tents erected in the brilliant dappled sunlight under the trees, adorned with portraits of Chavez, Sandino, Pancho Villa, and—a face justly absent from the annals of academic freedom—Ayatollah Khomeini. This touch must surely have been a sly expression of over-the-top anti-Americanism, to gall the university. No Iranian would have put it there; one of the few things LA's Iranians—Muslims, Jews, Armenians, Bahais—agreed upon was their hatred for the late ayatollah.

There was a sudden buzz of news—a settlement had been reached. Cameramen and television reporters began to venture out of their vans parked nearby to see what was up.

"There's going to be a press conference at eleven-thirty!" shouted a coed with long dark braids and wearing a long woolen poncho, though it was at least ninety degrees, as she moved down the plaza. She was handing out press statements to the students and tourists who had been gaping at the hunger strikers and the bedsheet banners draped across the Music Building. The largest read "The University Is Ours—Madres del Este de Los Angeles—Chicano Studies Now," and "EDUCACIÓN OR DEATH! VENCEREMOS," with a heroic portrait of Che Guevara.

"Excuse me! *Hey!*" a male student called to a newsman who had begun to open the door of one of the portable bathrooms installed beside the largest encampment. The newsman ignored him. *"Hey!* You! In the Music Building to the left! Can you read?"

The newsman followed the student's pointing finger to the door of the Port-a-Pottie, where a handwritten sign said, *Please do not use these rest rooms. They are for the use of hunger strikers and security guards.* He checked his watch—the press conference was just ten minutes away—and headed up the steps of the Music Building. Why the security? I speculated that it had something to do with sabotage—anyone could smuggle in an apple or Three Musketeers bar in an effort to cause a scandal. Suddenly I wondered whether the newsman might have been from a Spanish-speaking station—the Port-a-Pottie sign was thoughtlessly monolingual.

The English and Spanish orthography of the protest went far beyond the problems of choosing between "Chicano," "Latino," and "Hispanic." All spoken references to the sought-after department were to "Chicano and Chicana Studies," and written references were to "Chicano/a Studies," or the more chivalrously gender-deferential "Chicana/o Studies." But there were further complications—a flier boasted the support of "the majority of Chicana(o)/Latina(o) professors" on the UCLA faculty, and a brilliantly executed red-and-orange chalk drawing on a ten-foot stretch of the plaza walkway read XICANA/OS STUDIES NOW.

Beside the Mexican flag and fluttering slightly higher over the Chicano/a and Latino/a tent city was a black-and-red banner—the top half was black and bottom half crimson, with a gold medallion fastened between them. It was striking, but no one seemed to know what it stood for.

213

"They are the colors of the United Farm Workers," said Sam, a Latino student who was collecting signatures on a Chicano Studies petition from a small tent. "It's a Cesar Chavez flag." The farm-worker organizer, whom Robert Kennedy had called "a saint," had died only a few days before. UCLA's bilingual newspaper *La Gente* had included a free poster of him in its most recent issue (¡LA LUCHA CONTINUA!), and they were scattered all over the plaza. The fact UCLA chancellor Charles Young had refused to establish a Chicano Studies department just five days after Chavez's death had deeply offended the academic militants.

"But isn't the UFW flag red with a black eagle in the middle?" It was—a cartoon UFW flag fluttered behind the actual photograph head of Cesar Chavez on the poster.

"Or it could be the Nicaraguan flag."

What? I did not want to look like a flag trivia commissar, so I left Sam after signing his petition and asked a young woman who was holding a little replica of it; she did not speak English. I asked a girl in a Jurassic Park T-shirt with a Spartacus League pin.

"It is the flag symbolizing international strike," she said severely, then squinted at it again, and added, "It could be the flag for Sinaloa state. Anyway, that's the Mexican flag beside it."

La Gente had an editorial about Cesar Chavez ("*¡Que viva Cesar!*") on its masthead page, which listed not only the staff but the paper's thirty-five-strong Universal Council of Elders, which included Mother Earth, Che Guevara, Chico Mendez, Crazy Horse, Geronimo, Farabundo Martí, the prophet Abraham, Simón Bolívar, and Tupac Amaru. It is surely no accident that, wild cards like Abraham (and Mother Earth) apart, just about half the Council of Elders were indigenous to the Americas—a Netzahualcoyotl to balance every

Neruda. This would allow the Chicanas(os)/Latinas(os) some immunity against the dreaded charge of Eurocentrism, to which their promotion of the Spanish language, and overwhelmingly Iberian ethnicity, left them open. At eleven-thirty, there were shouts from the largest tent as the hunger strikers rolled out in triumph. They were preceded by dancers dressed in Aztec costume; one, a wizened old woman, lifted a large cream-colored conch shell to her lips and blew. It emitted a long, low note like a little foghorn, and got the caravan moving.

The Aztec costumes consisted of loinclothes, halters, leopard-print gaiters sewn with dozens of small shells and rattles, and high headdresses with vertical pheasant feathers. One short young man dressed in this outfit over a pair of blue Nike gym shorts wore a lilting spray of feathers that was slightly taller than he was. Pheasant plumes must have been in short supply, as the plump young woman beside him wore, instead, an array of pink ostrich feathers like a burlesque stripper's fan. The hunger strikers' support staff wore red armbands, and the actual fasters had tied red headbands across their foreheads. One male faster wore an orange one reading, in Arabic, *"la ilaha ila Allah"*—there is no god but God. It may have been a gift from the squat woman in the billowing Iranian chador which concealed everything but her nose and thick eyeglasses—like most of the demonstrators, she wore a red ribbon armband and joined in the clenched-fist salutes whenever a chant (*"Sí, se puede!"*) arose. I thought that she may have been connected to the pup tent adorned with the picture of the glowering ayatollah, but upon closer inspection she turned out to be a journalist—the press credentials pinned to her chador identified her as a correspondent for radio station KPFK-FM.

The hunger strikers were unmistakable in their wheelchairs, slightly gaunt but with beatific smiles. They were five women and two men, one in a serape, being pushed to the steps of the Music Building by a mixed group of students and celebrities that included Assemblyman Tom Hayden and Senator Art Torres, who had helped to mediate between the students and the administrators.

"Everyone, get out of the way, back up! Make way!" students shouted to the swelling crowd around the now-invisible hunger strikers. Two conchs were being blown, and a huge crowd was gathering from around the campus, attracted mostly by the presence of the television cameras and the seductive mooing of the conchs. The throngs grew thicker, still mostly Latino students but also white, black, and Asian. Some were high school students—girls wearing gold crosses and "skyscraper bangs"—who were perkier and laughed more shrilly, but most obstreperous of all were the news-media latecomers trying to squeeze through the throngs or to pass their tape recorders forward to the press conference table.

"Get back! Get behind the group!" shouted another organizer as he positioned the Aztec dancers behind the hunger strikers, who were ensconced at the foot of the Music Building steps. "We need a big crowd behind them for solidarity!"

"Did we get it?" the students were asking one another.

"We got most of it."

"We got two years without budget cuts. That's pretty good, because they're shutting undergraduate nursing."

"Sigma Nu is next!"

"I heard the Jewish Defense League was going to come in and bust us up."

Not much Spanish was being spoken, at least until an unseen strike staffer took the microphone; even then only snatches of his introduction floated through the talkative crowd.

"Una victoria por la comunidad . . . una victoria por todas las comunidades . . . viva la raza!"

When the strikers took the mike, their weakened voices were too soft to be heard, so I strolled away to get a look at the tent city before it was dismantled. The tents, like the buildings, were adorned with huge portraits: Malcolm X, Zapata, Chavez, Villa, and Sandino. Between the small tents were numerous altars, most with painted plaster statues of the Virgin of Guadalupe as centerpieces, surrounded with candles, maracas, small keepsakes such as photographs and keys, and tin coffee cans filled with sand and bristling with skinny sticks of incense. The altar in the north part of the plaza, where the strikers' large tent stood, was overwhelmed by a pine coffin with an attached letter, purportedly from a distraught Latino father rather incoherently scolding the state for giving his daughter a poor education. "This coffin is what you have given me," the letter ran.

The trees on the south side of the plaza were strung with banners that listed the hunger strikers: "STARVING FOR A DE-PARTMENT: Dr. Jorge Mancillas, Pastel y Marcos Aguilar, Cindy Montanez, Maria Lara, Balvina Collazco, Norma Montanez, Arturo Diaz, Juaquin Ochoa y [crossed out]." Someone had dropped out. "CULTURAL AND ACADEMIC EQUALITY IS A RIGHT NOT A PRIVELEGE [sic]—CHICANO/A STUDIES DEPARTMENT NOW," "END INSTITUTIONAL RACISM," "M.U.J.E.R.: Mujeres Unidas par Justicia Educación y Revolución," and "500 Years of Oppression."

A green chalkboard listed the hunger strikers' demands: "1. Chicano Studies Department, 2. Drop *all* charges (no academic sanctions), 3. Full funding for *all* ethnic and gender studies!" The second demand referred to the eighty or so students charged with vandalizing the faculty lounge—the general understanding was that felony charges would not be pressed, but academic suspensions or fines were still likely. The third referred to the larger context of demands listed in *La Gente,* for "more financial aid, campus safety, ethnic studies, undocumented students' rights, lesbian, gay, and bisexual civil rights, the end of fee hikes, and more!"

A Latino ice cream vendor pedaled by on his "La Mexicana" brand bicycle-driven freezer ("Paletas de Frutas Naturales"), wearing a Passionist Fathers retreat T-shirt and ringing his handlebar-mounted bell, but there were few takers while the press conference, twenty deep in spectators, remained in progress.

I strolled down one of the walkways, punctuated with staircases and grassy clearings, that run down the steep campus, making the university's elevation feel like the Hanging Gardens of Babylon. There was a copy of the free campus newspaper, the *Daily Bruin,* with a front-page story that explained the Sigma Nu controversy someone had been shouting about. The Campus and Student Life office was studying an offensive party given by that fraternity, whose theme had been "Boston Tea Party." Partygoers had been invited to dress as colonists, frontiersmen, and "colonists disguised as Native Americans." An offended student had videotaped the scene. The *Bruin* reported that "according to university policy on theme-based social activities, university-affiliated social events must not 'reinforce group stereotypes.'" And yet the students had not been dressed as Native Americans, but as colonists dressed as Native Americans. I wondered whether the frat rats would have the insight to argue that they were celebrating a grass-roots protest of oppressed citizen against the exploitative, consumerist, imperialist, multinational East India Company. Only fifty yards away there were protesting UCLA students dressed as befeathered Native Americans and being applauded as well as videotaped. Wasn't there a symmetry, an irony, possibly even a solution, in there somewhere?

The cement clearings were full of tables brokering summer apartment swaps and sublets, and distributing candidate literature for the imminent Los Angeles mayoral election. There was a crowd around the Michael Woo table—he was a liberal Democrat in tune with change-oriented undergraduate ambitions—but the two Riordan representatives, despite their lack of visitors, already seemed confident of victory. One young blond man actually seemed to be sleeping, his somnolent face tilted back against his clasped hands, and the other, who was black, was drowsily rereading campaign booklets. I took samples of both candidates' literature, though I thought I knew what the outcome would be. The nastiness of the campaign would assure a low turnout, helpful to Riordan, who had also dared to say what Woo could not. Most Angelenos had hated the riots and felt threatened by them, and Riordan, knowing that, was emphasizing law and order. Woo was more comfortable blaming the system, and was currying the favor of ethnic minorities. It was a miscalculation: he was ignoring the fact that while a tiny majority of the rioters were Latino, so were most of the victims. The multicultural tack failed because Latinos did not need Woo's help to be Latino; they did need his help to fight crime.

"The *LA Times* has endorsed Woo, even though it's not a partisan election. And so did Clinton," Henry, the lucid campaign worker, complained, gratefully chucking aside the pamphlet *Tough Enough to Turn LA Around.* He ran through the litany of Riordan positions: LA needed to be turned around; only business, not taxes, would create jobs; Woo had been a terrible councilman in Hollywood ("Have you *seen* Hollywood?" he asked), and his racial politics were ludicrous. "Woo tiptoes around the riots when he talks to people of color. He calls them the uprising, but among whites he says 'riots.' What goes unsaid is that he figures, don't bad-mouth looters in front of looters. Riordan talks to all the people of LA like citizens. And," he added before I could ask, "*many* Africans are voting for him."

I did have a question for him, though not the one he was anticipating, but before I could ask, an explosion of applause and ululations from Schoenberg Plaza announced the end of the press conference. I hurried up the steps to see the former hunger strikers being wheeled away, flanked by the conch-blowers in their Mesoamerican finery. The speaker system erupted in a torrent of *ranchera* music; in contrast to the combative fight songs it had been playing before the press conference, now it broadcast old tunes like "Rancho Grande" and "The Mexican Hat Dance."

Tom Hayden and Art Torres stood around under the trees giving interviews. The university had compromised on Chicano studies: no department, but the founding of the in-terdisciplinary Cesar Chavez Center for Chicana and Chicano Studies. The problem of the ninety-nine students charged with causing thirty to fifty thousand dollars' worth of damage would be settled out of court. Budgets for the Chavez Center and all ethnic and gender studies would be spared cuts for two years. The hunger strike would officially end at seven o'clock. Some of the fasters had eaten a little chocolate, but the fast would be broken that evening with tortillas and salsa. That part made me hungry—I had not had lunch.

"I'm so glad we got this! *Felicidades!*" Cheerleader types were hugging one another ecstatically. "I feel *great!*" "*Sí, se puede! Sí, se puede!*" shouted young men in baseball hats over the *ranchera* music, giving the clenched-fist salute to the Mexican flag and the red-and-black one. The promise not to cut the new ethnic and gender programs for two years was a greater victory than many of the students knew. UCLA was in such bad financial shape that it was considering closing its schools of public health, social welfare, and urban planning and architecture. These schools "provide the most direct service to the people of Los Angeles, especially to minority groups," argued Dr. Roger Detels, the dean emeritus of the School of Public Health at the time, but a few weeks later the university did "disestablish" the schools, along with the graduate school of information sciences. Shortly after that, three highly successful athletic programs— men's swimming and men's and women's gymnastics—were eliminated. The programs had produced dozens of Olympians and several gold medalists, so the closures caused widespread gloom at the sports-crazed school. The information brochure for entering freshmen made it very clear that "cheering on the Bruins is a central part of campus life."

The costumed dancers quit the hunger strikers' tent in single file, marching placidly across the plaza to the tents that held their street clothes. There had been a distinct mistake in the ostentatious Olmec fashions that had accompanied the demonstrations—ethnic costumes are supposed to be festive or humorous. These dancers had taken themselves very seriously. Americans love to dress up as Scots, Puritans, Cherokees, African villagers, and German Oktoberfest revelers, but it is usually done with a smile, which, ironically, usually disarms the poison of nationalism. Someone preaching German racial superiority would never dream of wearing a Tyrolean hat and *Lederhosen*. Reaching back to the couture of the hideously cruel era of pre-Columbian Mexico, scarcely less cruel that what followed its discovery by Europeans, seemed only silly when treated with the scowling seriousness of these folkloric performers. An Aztec demanding gender rights was just as ludicrous as a Puritan demanding religious tolerance. The signs reading 500 YEARS OF OPPRESSION and reminding onlookers that "this is our land" had a distinctly dark undertone, and the pre-Columbian business only made me wonder why the push for bilingual education wasn't centered on Nahuatl and English rather than Spanish and English. We-were-here-first-ism is obnoxious; if they were to argue that Spanish is more widely understood, then the English-only argument would clobber it. Mostly it is obnoxious because of the unspoken we-were-here-last majority of LA's melting pot.

The Chicano LA celebrated by the demonstrators and hunger strikers was the product not so much of the city's very old Mexican roots as of its very modern Mexican migrations, which began in the decade preceding the founding of UCLA as a result of the Mexican civil war of 1910. It sent Latinos to LA en masse as refugees. The migration was so sustained, and the community so Americanized, that 500,000 Mexican-Americans served in World War II, more than any other ethnic minority. They were just 6 percent of LA's population in the 1940s, but suffered 10 percent of the casualties because they were put in the front lines; they were said to have fought valiantly. This made the Zoot Suit riots all the more ironic. The Zoot Suiters—the dance-hall Lotharios in baggy suits who had been savagely beaten by xenophobic U.S. servicemen on leave in 1945—were seen, through drunken or racist eyes, as draft dodgers.

In fifty years, Angelenos of Mexican and South American descent had gone from 6 to 40 percent of LA's population, because of political and economic refugees from Nicaragua, Guatemala, El Salvador, and South America as well as Mexico. By the time the Immigration Reform and Control Act of 1986 came into force, the United States granted permanent residence to more than 2.6 million formerly illegal immigrants; most were in California, and about half of the total in LA. A million of these immigrants will be eligible for citizenship in 1996; nearly all are from Mexico and of voting age. And yet the result is really underwhelming. The school system lives with its multilingual classes. There was no tremendous Catholic movement accompanying it, with defections going in reverse from the Roman Church to Protestant sects or Mormonism.

Chicano LA's center of gravity is East Los Angeles, the constellation of neighborhoods—principally Boyle Heights, Lincoln Heights, and El Sereno—dominated by decades of Mexican migration. The general area of East LA stretches through the other cities of eastern LA County, as far as the Puente Hills near the Orange County border. Unlike the theme-park Mexico-America of Olvera Street, East LA is virtually indistinguishable from any other of LA's suburb-in-the-city neighborhoods. The blight of colorful urban murals, once almost exclusive to East LA, has spread everywhere. The main difference is the predominance of Spanish signs and the astonishingly staid landmarks: its main strip, Soto Street, and Garfield High School, where Jaime Escalante became the country's most famous calculus teacher, immortalized in the movie *Stand and Deliver*. A further difference is the overwhelming traditionalism evidenced by the multitude of children, especially girls in frilly dresses, grandmothers in black, and chockablock businesses and churches.

The long roots and maturity of LA's Latino community can be seen in its visible clashes with other groups besides the one that activists call "Anglo," and the complex interactions of the Latino communities from various countries. Two years before this hunger strike, a Los Angeles County health worker, Gloria Lozano, had been awarded nearly a quarter of a million dollars in damages after racial harassment from black coworkers, whose efforts to "get rid of the Mexican" included banging on her desk, making racial slurs, laughing at her, and telling her that she "could not go to heaven" because she was Catholic. A few months later, the first all-Chicano city council of the LA suburb of Bell Gardens had caused a scandal by throwing furniture in a meeting and making anti-Semitic remarks; it started over a minor hiring decision. Chicano citizens showed up at the following week's meeting to shriek "Shame!" at them and voice their regret at having voted for racial rather than political reasons. In the city of Los Angeles, there was a divide between the well-established Chicano citizens of East LA and the poor and illegal Guatemalans, Nicaraguans, and Salvadorans of south LA.

"It took a year for the flames to spread to the Westside," UCLA professor Vilma Ortiz had told a pro–Chicano Studies rally during the hunger strike. "Now we are making this university burn. . . . More than eighty students were arrested for seeking an education because they know that education is power." This was a rather forlorn effort to link the LA riots to the Chicano Studies fuss. UCLA protesters were relatively upper-crust, and the Chicano Studies effort was an overwhelmingly Mexican-oriented effort. The Central Americans who had rioted enthusiastically were left out of the UCLA strike.

Another sign of the acknowledged status of LA's Latinos was the highly corporate Cinco de Mayo celebrations downtown. Disney provided a mariachi band, and free concerts and merchandise were donated by Coca-Cola, Marlboro and Viceroy cigarettes, Budweiser beer, diaper manufacturers, and the Metro Red Line, with the wealthy sponsors generally in inverse proportion to the crowds who had dozens of children and stood in line under the hot sun for hours to get a free Pamper or paddle ball. Thirty-six square blocks of downtown Los Angeles were closed off for the gigantic event, which is a relatively minor Mexican holiday, the anniversary of the day Mexican forces ended the French siege of Puebla in 1862. But just as it became a rallying point for the country's ultimate independence, it has become a rallying point for Mexican Los Angeles, in part because May is a more opportune time for a holiday in LA than Mexico's actual Independence Day, which falls on September 16, just when school goes back into session. The larger reason was that Tom Bradley, LA's mayor of twenty years, had made the popularization of Cinco de Mayo his bridge to the Chicano community. The city of Los Angeles actively promotes Mexican celebrations to further ethnic pride, and the Spanish language enjoys special status in the LA school system, where it is the mother tongue of 64 percent of the students, who technically must not be taught to read English until they are literate in Spanish.

Los Angeles has adopted other Mexican holidays, religious and secular. The Franciscan practice of a mass blessing of animals on the Saturday before Easter is held annually on Olvera Street, and mariachi bands serenade the pet owners who line up for blocks with their cats, turtles, and boa constrictors to have them blessed and flecked with holy water by the archbishop of Los Angeles. The practice of blessing pets has even been adopted by Episcopal churches in Hollywood and Santa

Monica, as a feature even quainter than brass-rubbing. Another Olvera Street event is Las Posadas, a Christmas-season reenactment of Mary and Joseph's entry into Bethlehem. Both of these events are hugely popular with non-Latinos, but nothing compares with Cinco de Mayo. Los Angeles was always trying to graft holidays onto its calendar. Was it to impress, empower, placate, curry favor, or synthesize a new ecumenical culture? It was probably for the healthiest motives of all, to commercialize wildly and let the good times roll.

"Don't forget! Seven o'clock!" shouted a student with a load of fliers pressed to her chest. She handed me one—it was actually a three-page photocopy of a faxed *UCLA News* summarizing the outcome of the negotiations. The headline announced a Center for Interdisciplinary Instruction; the word "department" was nowhere to be found.

"Will it become a department?" I asked.

"I don't know, but June seventh will go down in history anyway," she declared. "Seven o'clock! Eat with us—tortillas and salsa! Bring *horchata!*"

She was probably right that it would go down in history: East LA had planted its flag in the west, on television. My guess was that Plaza Aztlan would be an annual event, a fleeting Brigadoon embodiment of a dreamland.

My hope was that the new center would at least do its job, but I had my doubts. My experiences of college campuses— usually as a visiting translator of Third World literature—had shown me that in certain cases the multiculturalism phenomenon was the opposite of broadening. At times it resembled a dogmatic tribal nationalism that actually ruled out a multicultural understanding of humanity. Student-dictated curricula of African literature, for example, were strong on Alice Walker, Toni Morrison, and Ishmael Reed, because no one had ever heard of Naguib Mahfouz, Camara Laye, or Wole Soyinka. The Asian push was on to read Amy Tan and Maxine Hong Kingston, since Lady Murasaki, Tsao Hsueh-Chin, and Shusako Endo were unknown. America's unparalleled collection of cultures makes it easy to jettison the rest of the world, along with the past, in favor of the only country, America; the only, time, the present; and, here, the only city, LA.

The whole fuss was easy to criticize, of course. Now that the hunger strike had more or less served its purpose by locking in a paper compromise, it looked staged and overblown— it had been a publicity-crazed life-or-death stunt on an issue that was anything but life-or-death—a matter not only of bureaucracy but of academic bureaucracy. The speeches had gone on too long. The portraits of Pancho Villa and Khomeini were illustrations of what the strike had not been about. Hayden and Torres were basking in glory with visible bliss—they had acquired a load of saintliness on the cheap. The same was true of the fasters, whose wan smiles at their near-martyrdom blazed with self-pity and self-love. Shouldn't the high school girl who had fasted, Norma Montanez, have been talked out of it? Her mother had not stopped her—why had the professors not tried? One-issue nationalism was perfectly idiotic to anyone who knew the Third World—all nationalism was destructive, even the low-stakes academic variety. And yet the atmosphere was gay.

"Someone said Cindy's keeping her new name!" shrieked one girl to another. "I love that! I'm pumped! She's going to be called Chilictlixatl Montanez for good, or just plain Chilictlixatl."

This was Norma's older sister. One of the girls obligingly helped me spell her name.

"Her full name?"

"No," I said, "just plain Chilictlixatl."

"It means 'heart of the white butterfly,' " she noted carefully.

I had the sudden stray thought that our multicultural society would be far easier to handle if we weren't so mad on name changes. The entertainment industry LA represented was especially to blame. If we had grown up listening to Henry Deutschendorf instead of John Denver, Natasha Gurdin instead of Natalie Wood, Ramón Estevez instead of Martin Sheen, and Cherilyn Sarkisian instead of Cher, perhaps things would be different. There was a backlash: after an era when Margarita Carmen Dolores Cansino had to become Rita Hayworth, you had teenage girls going from Cindy to Chilictlixatl.

In the days to come, one UCLA history professor, Robert Dallek, called on the hunger strikers to consider the ways in which other ethnic minorities in the United States had gained access to "regard and influence. . . . The Irish in Boston, for example, even though they were a despised minority, did not seek consolation in Irish studies. Those fortunate enough to have the opportunity of higher education seized it and made their way in a society that is ever receptive to talented and ambitious people."

This casual but penetrating comparison had special resonance for a Boston-born Angeleno. I tried to imagine the spectacle of Harvard Yard or Boston Common crowded with tents, posters of Ossian, Saint Mel, Charles Stewart Parnell, Bobby Sands, and Bernard Shaw; a public-address system blaring the anti-English folksongs of Hamish Imlach; numbing lectures about the historic oppressors of Ireland, whose descendants now ruled Boston and named its universities' dormitories; altars of shamrocks, clay pipes, shillelaghs, and

statues of Saint Patrick; the Mothers of South Boston string-
ing banners from the oppressive English oaks outside University Hall, which sitters-in would have renamed Cuchulain
Hall. It was unthinkable, and embarrassment would prevent
it from ever happening. The show-biz shamelessness of the
scene was imaginable only in LA, where starvation, fabulous
costumes, lawns, altars, and TV cameras had been sewn up
into an event.

Janitors began to sweep up leaflets and otherwise restore
Schoenberg Plaza, and it became clear that the fasters were
not going to show themselves again until evening. On my
way out, I stopped again to chat with Henry, the Riordan
campaign worker, to get his view of the Chicano Studies affair.

"I guess I support it," he said and stopped there. "As long
as they know they're Americans, not Mexicans."

That reminded me what I had wanted to ask him about
earlier—black Republicans rarely used the word "African" to
describe themselves.

"It's short, and you can't say it's inaccurate."

"Look at it this way," I said. "My ancestors came from
France, but I don't call myself French. I speak French, I've
been to France, and I share the religion of most French people. None of that makes me French. The French wouldn't
accept me as French. And I don't want to be French."

"I accept that," he said readily. "You know exactly where
your ancestors come from. You know the language and have
the religion. You don't need ethnic terms. You can just let it
go. If you just knew that your ancestors came from somewhere in Europe, and had no knowledge beyond that about
their language or religion, you might connect in a more, you
know, general, but intense, way, especially if people thought

Europeans were just nobodies. You'd want to connect with what all of Europe was about. Maybe it isn't so clear or easy for me. Hey, are you going to vote for Riordan?" He laughed and added, "You couldn't have had this conversation with one of them," without specifying who, and gave me a campaign button to get rid of me, because some women in shorts had begun to browse through his materials.

It was unlikely that there were many Riordan supporters among the strikers or their supporters, but there was an irony in Henry's support of him. Riordan was a newcomer to politics but an old hand of the hierarchy of Los Angeles; not the city or the county, but the archdiocese. He was a close ally of the liberal, Spanish-speaking, and very pro-Chicanismo archbishop, Roger Mahony. A close interest in the very Latino future of the church and a commitment to very traditional values in LA led both these ethnic Celts to work together; as the diocese's financial adviser, Riordan ended years of deficit and put it $24 million in the black. He had also presented Mahony with a $400,000 jet-powered helicopter as a gift.

So the most Eurocentric leaders were adapting, even Riordan, who frequently described himself as Irish and bristled at being called Anglo ("My father would turn in his grave if he heard that"). The religious and linguistic legacies of the Spanish Empire are among the stabler themes in the city history, so perhaps not a bad thing to rally around after all. They tie together Aztec-leaning sentimentality with traditional thinking on religion and family, and represent both the traditional and the radical in LA's history.

The thought reminded me that I was hungry, and I made my way down to a restaurant on Westwood Boulevard.

"You should reconsider going in here. We may be doing some leaflets here. We're looking into boycotting this business," said a blond student with a navy-blue paisley bandanna tied around his head as he intercepted me outside the Mexican restaurant. "We're talking to the owner now."

"What's the problem?"

"Well, it's basically a matter of interpretation. We found her fliers under car windshields—she was trying get some business out of the Chicano Studies publicity by offering two-for-one tacos to show support. Except, it looks kind of rude, because this whole thing was about a hunger strike."

A young woman whom I recognized from the Schoenberg Plaza sit-in approached us and was listening attentively. She was one of the students who had been so pleased that Chilictlixatl was considering keeping her name.

"Are they still serving two for one?" she asked, and pushed past the bandanna boy when he nodded, but before he could speak.

11

A Complete Set

The steep canyon roads of Los Angeles—Topanga, Coldwater, Laurel, Dixie, and the rest—flow through the Santa Monica Mountains to the San Fernando Valley as tributaries to Ventura Boulevard, the unparalleled market street which links LA's wealthy hill and valley communities and carries traffic between the bases of the frozen monuments to the city's seismic architecture: the Simi Hills to the west, the Santa Susana Mountains, the little Verdugo Mountains, and the enormous San Gabriels behind them to the north. Between the ramparts of these mile-high stone walls lies the San Fernando Valley, from which all the mountain ranges are invisible in LA's thickest smog, especially rich in carbon monoxide and carbon dioxide. Unlike the noxious nitrogen oxide that draws a horizontal brown bar across the base of the San Gabriels in the Los Angeles Basin, these two colorless and odorless pollutants seem to paint the mountainous horizon completely out of existence from wherever you stand in the Valley.

I was driving to Burbank along Ventura Boulevard headed east, wondering whether people in hot climates speak more slowly. I had asked a gift shop dealer for directions to the Burbank Studios, and though he knew exactly how to get there, it seemed to take him a full minute to say, "Basically, go straight to where Ventura becomes Cahuenga, and cross the freeway bridge on Barham, up to Hollywood Way, and you're there."

He ran Shiraz Imports—I had asked directions there because I thought I might find some rare Iranian goods. It was crammed with china statues of seventeenth-century Frenchmen in powdered wigs and swallowtail coats and Marie Antoinettes with colossal bustles and hairdos. There were candelabra, miniature spoons, gilt mirrors, hourglasses, tea services, fishbowls, snuff boxes, vases with Watteau scenes, statues of Greek gods and goddesses.

"Is any of this Persian?"

"Persian *taste*," he said.

It was an amazing street, flat, endless, and straight, and very low, but not just a tourist strip. There were lots of supermarkets—the Hughes Market at the corner of Coldwater Canyon had an orchard of fir trees in its parking lot. High above Ventura, behind the commercial throughway, were big hot hills, bare or covered with dry scrub, topped with walled villas or housing developments commanding the heights like fortified medieval cities.

And there was a high billboard: VALENCIA, THE CITY FOR THE 90s, NORTH ON I-5—EXIT VALENCIA BLVD. This was the sort of billboard that had built Los Angeles, and now they were showing the way out. Not very far out, though—you could live in Valencia, which was in nearby Ventura County, and work in the Valley.

I passed a baby-blue car wash with towers surmounted by

three-dimensional asterisks, like a rack of sparklers or magic wands—it was architecture that made fun of architecture. I was reminded that a few years before there had been a battle to landmark a populuxe car wash in the Valley. It stood in the way of some other development and the owner wanted to demolish it, but the goofy charm of the 1950s look—the whole decade had shaped the Valley more than any other— led its defenders to put up a huge battle, which they lost. And here was a pink car wash with the same Car Wash Moderne design, whose staff, all young men, wore short-sleeved white shirts and bow ties, an even bigger blast of the 1950s.

The splendiferous car washes were a reminder of the landmarks that Ventura Boulevard did not have—there were no statues, no monuments, no churches, no synagogues, no museums, no train stations, no civic or government buildings; there were no squares, no bridges, and no rivers. Not even any department stores. There was nothing big, except the mountains, of course, and they were invisible in the smog.

Ventura Boulevard is different from the rest of LA in its spectacular prosperity. In six miles I had seen only two or three empty storefronts. There were restaurants, real estate offices, dry cleaners, greeting card stores, more supermarkets and car washes, clothing stores, butchers, some nightclubs (the Cabaret Tehran), and a hall for the Jehovah's Witnesses/ Testigos de Jehova. I noticed a great deal of foreign-language signposting, in Arabic, Armenian, Persian, and Spanish (a stern anti-fireworks banner warned that *Todas las clases de fuegos artificiales están prohibidas*—it was nearly the Fourth of July), but no single one predominated. There were relatively few pedestrians, and a single prostitute. She looked quite elegant with her short blond hair and beachy shorts and T-shirt ("Go Dodger Blue"), and you would never have known her line of work had she not been hitchhiking, her thumb high, facing the sidewalk rather than the street.

Despite the steady stream of slow traffic, the Valley was a quiet place, and this did not change after I crossed the Hollywood Freeway and arrived in Burbank. Its over-the-hill location had been one of the keys to its prosperity; movie studios value quiet as much as cemeteries. That is why so many of both are on the San Fernando Valley side of the Hollywood Hills, where the sounds of planes, trains, taxis, and police sirens used to intrude less than in the loud, expensive, fully urbanized basin. Until World War II the Valley was almost completely rural; its miles of flatness were perfect for potato and strawberry fields, dotted with scattered villages like San Fernando, Van Nuys, and Burbank, which as recently as 1947 had a one-room jail. In the 1950s it became LA's bedroom community of choice, and was quickly paved and populated. The disconnected suburbia reputation long outlived its open spaces. It went from being a Caucasian backwater—the Valley Girl craze of the 1980s was the crest of that wave—to the heavily Latino and Iranian conurbation of the 1990s. While "LA" applies to many places that are not part of Los Angeles, most of the Valley is part and parcel of the city of Los Angeles but is rigid in its use of aliases, using the names of its postal districts: Sherman Oaks, Van Nuys, Sylmar, North Hollywood.

Lunch hour in Burbank gives the impression that the city is patrolled by the Movie Police. Along Hollywood Way and Alameda Avenue, which borders Disney, NBC, and Warner Brothers, male security guards—white, black, Asian, and Latino, of all ages—stroll alone and in pairs. They may only be on their way to buy a burrito or some sun block, but their short haircuts, navy-blue uniforms, mirror sunglasses, and thumbs in their beltloops give you the distinct impression that the movie industry is keeping a sharp eye on any behavior that might be interpreted as anti-entertainment. Actually, it is not the people outside who are being patrolled, but the studio walls themselves, which protect movie stars, executives, and the industrial secrets of the business.

The Valley has the air of being a company town much more than Hollywood, where the record industry is more visible even than the movies, and the rest of the economy has diversified into upscale restaurateuring, books, interior design, and highly visible prostitution. In Burbank—not beautiful, no downtown—nearly all of the restaurants are the forty-five-minute-in-and-out lunch-special kind that cater to crowds of busy security guards and women in big sunglasses and unstructured suits who carry out files or scripts to examine over plates of *capellini checca*.

There is very little graffiti in this Valley town, but a great deal of its literate equivalent, protest fliers posted to the telephone poles and plywood barriers shielding the sidewalks from the din of new construction sites. The barriers are, by some LA tradition, always decorated with brightly painted lineups of the Hollywood pantheon: Marilyn Monroe, Humphrey Bogart, Lucille Ball, Clark Gable, Charlie Chaplin, and James Stewart. The fliers all address the issue of gender inequality in movie pay. One showed a still from the film *Frankie and Johnnie*, of Michelle Pfeiffer joshing Al Pacino over the counter of a diner, with "$3 million" printed over Michelle's head and "$6 million" printed over Al's. Underneath, the legend is REEL ROLES FOR REAL WOMEN! *Only 9 percent of all roles in film, in 1992, went to women over 40!*

Burbank is home to four movie and television production studios, with Universal Studios next door in Universal City.

Many of them offer tours to the public. The opposite ends of the tour spectrum are Universal and Disney. Universal Studios Hollywood, which is really a movie theme park, earns more money annually than Universal's movies. Universal Studios offers an expensive all-day extravaganza with rides, reenactments, spectacles, and merchandizing. You are always being left off waiting for the next segment, which always seems to be in about forty-five minutes, while you have nothing else to do with your time but buy food or souvenirs in a glossy little logo village designed for that purpose. A tram ride through the back lot takes in famous movie sites. You see the Red Sea part, the facade of the Bates mansion from *Psycho*, and the adobe village which serves for Mexican shootouts and Biblical epics; you get frightened by sudden appearances by King Kong and Jaws from their movies. You watch stunts and explosions taken from prime-time television. It is a very long and hot day. Universal regards the tour as a competitor to Disneyland, and added, in 1993, a controversial feature called CityWalk, which architectural critics, urban planners, and sociologists hated—one derided it as "Los Angeles in a coffin." After floods, riots, and earthquakes, Angeleno nerves were so shattered that even an amusement park mall caused pain.

Actually, CityWalk is an immaculate two-block market street in Cahuenga Pass, beside Universal City. There are no spectacles, games, or rides, and nothing to do but shop and eat. There is a branch of Gladstone's 4 Fish, a Malibu seafood restaurant, and of Sausage Kingdom ("Home of the Haut Dog") in Venice Beach, where you can have Portuguese fig and pinenut haut dogs. A branch of the UCLA Extension School provides a whiff of Westwood, and a towering replica of the Hollywood Athletic Club is under construction. The sidewalk is painted with stars like the ones on Hollywood

Boulevard's Walk of Fame. There is even an imported beach—Lighthouse Beach is an open-air restaurant with dozens of tables and chairs set in six inches of sand. Down the block, a combination pool and fountain replicates the wet part of the beach: waves rush up a terrazzo slope and are sucked back, with sound effects provided.

CityWalk was described by one of its promoters as "a place for people to be, to eat, to shop, to mingle," and actually it does link Universal Studios, at one end, with the eighteen-screen Universal Cineplex, at the other, which has separate parking. CityWalk's controversial appeal is that it seems to be nothing but a closed, unpeopled, eerily sanitized street: at last, a 100 percent synthetic Los Angeles where no one lives, there are no cars, you have to pay to get in, the only things to do are get a tan and spend money, and everything was built yesterday and could be different tomorrow. Unquestionably CityWalk was dreamed up to please the tourists who discover that Hollywood Boulevard is squalid and Sunset too long and spread out—that, in fact, almost all of Los Angeles is too "real." It is not the capital of illusion but a sweaty, smoggy, and sometimes dangerous city. The answer was to try to turn everyday life into a theme park, a Stepford City. And yet the artificiality of CityWalk, plain as it is, can appal; none of the bikers, beggars, hustlers, or crackheads that lurch down Hollywood Boulevard give you as much of a *frisson* as the sight of street musicians singing and playing guitars on the curb—*without a guitar case opened to receive donations!*

Disney Studios in Burbank is the opposite of Universal: it offers no tours and wants no part of visitors, whose time it doubtless thinks would be better spent at Disneyland in Anaheim. Disneyland is for rides and spectacles, and Disney Studios is an entertainment factory. It is probably no coincidence that the roof of the massive corporate headquarters is supported by the Seven Dwarfs, bulb-nosed and potbellied, but distinctly the only animated Disney creations with a strong work ethic. William A. Gordon, author of *The Ultimate Hollywood Tour Book,* reports that Disney's notoriously tough management is so hard on employees that some of its workers call it "Mouschwitz." (He suggests an alternative, "Duckau.")

The happy medium is Warner Brothers, whose "VIP tour" sticks to the nuts and bolts of moviemaking. It is for movie buffs, and you need a reservation. The lot is used for movie and television production; it is nestled against the northern foothills of Hollywood on the south and bordered by a tiny bend of the Los Angeles River.

American television rules the world, of course; it is what makes foreign friend's and foes think they are experts on American values, politics, and life-styles. It is one of the United States' most unfailingly lucrative exports—no other country in the world is so successfully market-oriented in its television as America is.

I was personally very aware of the clout of TV abroad, in the Third World; I knew that *Dallas* was monstrously popular in France. U.S. journalists visiting the Middle East always wrote about bedouin watching Lou Grant or ayatollahs' families secretly watching tapes of *Dynasty*. I knew a radically devout and uncompromisingly anti-American Shiite Muslim in Saudi Arabia who used to watch *The Brady Bunch* dubbed in Arabic and murmur, "It is so beautiful, it is like the most beautiful dream. . . ." Even so I was taken aback by the television fervor of Mr. Cracknell.

"I've got one word for you—Hammer! Right? Hammer!" Our greeter at Warner Brothers pumped Mr. Cracknell's hand as soon as he heard his soft Sussex accent. "The greatest mystery movies ever made, right in England."

"Oh, yes," said Mr. Cracknell, but he was not the kind of English old-timer that our greeter thought. We had parked our cars simultaneously in the guest park near Hollywood Way, and gotten talking. He was driving a Geo Metro rental, he wore socks with his sandals, his sunglasses were pushed back on his bald head, and he carried a camera; yes, he said, as a matter of fact he was from Europe. He lived in retirement just outside London. Widower.

"First time?"

"Oh, my dear no. I have made many previous visits to Los Angeles. I feel quite acclimatized here." He pronounced "Los Angeles" to rhyme with "cheese." And he obviously was acclimatized—he had English cordiality but in a very un-English way had volunteered his job and marital status, and where he lived.

His name was Archie. He had been on tours of Paramount Studios and Universal Studios and had sniffed out the sites of the MGM and Roach Studios—*Our Gang*—in Culver City.

"I am a great admirer of early television. I don't suppose you remember *The Life of Riley* or *Ozzie and Harriet.*"

He held the door open for me, and we paid for the tour. Warner Brothers offers one of the more expensive ones, Twenty-five dollars for about two hours. It was at this point that our greeter tried to interest him in talking about Hammer films. When we sat down waiting for the rest of the group, beside a Coca-Cola machine—Coca-Cola owns Columbia, which owns Lorimar, which owns Warner Brothers—I told him that I did have foggy recollections of the shows he had mentioned.

"In fact, you can go and have a look at the house where

Ozzie and Harriet Nelson lived for about twenty years. Have you had a tour of the stars' homes in Beverly Hills?"

"Oh, yes, of course," he hastily assured me. "I've seen the Nelsons' home—on Camino Palermo. It's in the Hollywood Hills. They lived there for more than twenty-five years. Their boys attended the Hollywood High School. Of course, it is not open to the public. Their house, I mean." He pursed his lips. "I *have* looked in on the school. You can hear the class-room noise from out in the street. One supposes it does not graduate too many Carol Burnetts or Lana Turners these days."

It mostly graduates the children of Russian and Iranian im-migrants, and has a terrible gang problem. Even the Koreans in Hollywood have gangs: KK, or Korean Killers, who are out to squash the devout, quiet, shopkeeper reputation that has stuck to LA Koreans.

Two young Germans with shoulder bags and sandals came in and got into a conversation with the woman signing them up. You had to turn in your camera; no photography was allowed on the backlot. They shuffled in, looking at the movie posters in the waiting room, took in Mr. Cracknell and me, and then sat next to an American couple, who quickly drew them into conversation and soon mentioned that they had visited Germany and loved it. It was these Germans' first visit to the United States and it would be their last.

"The Americans are the biggest bastards when you apply for visas," I heard one of them explain.

"Culver City was another great disappointment to me," Archie confided. "I wanted to see the Hal Roach Studios, where the *Our Gang* comedies were filmed. I remember every one of those pictures. I can see that sunlight now on those outdoor scenes. Well, the studio is gone. It was on

Washington Boulevard, once upon a time. Car lot now."

"You might want to check out Hollywood Memorial Cemetery to see where some of the *Our Gang* cast members are buried," I suggested.

It had never crossed his mind to go to a cemetery. He did not look very enthusiastic about it, but I gave him the cross streets of some of the cemeteries, and pointed out that Forest Lawn was only fifteen minutes away.

Our guide showed up, a dark-haired Valley Boy in the studio guide uniform, black Reeboks and trousers and a black Warner Brothers logo shirt. His right earlobe was pierced twice, but he wore no earrings. We were a group of six: Mary Rose and her husband, Dana, from San Francisco; the two young Germans, both named Hans; Mr. Cracknell; and me. Emmanuel, the guide, introduced himself and learned our names and origins. I expected him to make a joke about having two Hanses along—maybe telling the two Hanses to stand on their two feet—but he did not.

"We have lots of foreign visitors here, and you will have an excellent time," he assured them when we had been squeezed into a little open-sided tour vehicle with wheels the size of very big doughnuts. "I'll keep, maybe, my references to American television shows to a minimum, because you might not be quite as familiar with those?"

"I have seen most of them, actually, or read books about them," announced Mr. Cracknell, who wanted everyone to call him Archie.

"Really?" asked Emmanuel in such a Valley voice—*rully?*—that Mary Rose nudged Dana.

"We have always seen masses of American television in the UK, and I lived in New York City, as well, in the sixties. My first vacation from New York was out this way. I had the good fortune to see Dino's Lodge on Sunset Boulevard, when it was still there. It was used in nearly every episode of my favorite television show, *77 Sunset Strip*. It was torn down some years back, and I do think that was a very great shame."

"For sure," said Emmanuel a little uncertainly, and resumed his speech as we climbed out of the motorized cart to stand under the blank marquee of a theater facade. Everyone peeked inside to see the empty space and light cables, and Emmanuel pointed out the *Daily Planet* logo on the door of the shell of an office building across the little street. We had alit in one of the deserted back lots that look like a deserted city, except that one street is Georgian and runs into a Wild West intersection that leads to an idealized suburbia or replica of New York's Little Italy.

"If they knocked the walls of this place down, all this would blend right into LA," said Mary Rose, the San Francisco wife. "The neighborhood of our hotel is just like this. It's all Spanishy and then it gets real corporate, and then there's a motel like an Arab castle."

"I wish I had my camera," said one of the Germans testily.

The rest of the buildings were false fronts, too, and I was glad that no one made remarks drawing comparisons of LA and its citizens to the wild assortment of false fronts, facades, empty shells, and Potemkin beauty parlors. These job sites of the entertainment industry left LA very vulnerable to metaphors about skin-deep culture.

"Filming for a new television series called *Lois and Clark* has been going on here," Emmanuel said. "It's based on the Superman story. This is the *Daily Planet* building! See the trapdoor in the sidewalk in front? We made it look like a subway entrance for the show, which airs this fall. It will star Teri Hatcher from the movie *Tango and Cash*—did you all see

Tango and Cash? Excellent!—and Dean Cain from *Beverly Hills 90210*. Later on we'll be seeing the soundstage where the interiors for the show are shot."

We strolled down the street. The rest of the tour would be on foot—we had been told to wear comfortable shoes.

"There generally is rather a lot of salesmanship in these tours," said Archie. "Universal is the big offender, of course. They want to do a bit of merchandising—put you in the know a bit. You are quite naturally not going to miss a television episode filmed where you actually walked!"

"Okay, you guys, I'm going to walk backwards, to face you guys? Let me know if a truck comes up behind me? Okay, this is the Batman courthouse from the old television series with Adam West and Burt Ward." He pointed with his right hand over his left shoulder. "That's where Chief O'Hara's office was. The Batmobile often came screeching up to that curb. Of course, it's basically a shell. The interiors were filmed on a soundstage. I'll bet some of you recognize the beautiful little location behind me!"

Opposite the courthouse was a spacious town square with a bandstand and flower beds, with a street of turn-of-the-century mansions shaded by shapely elms.

"Anyone? Anyone?"

"*The Dukes of Hazzard*, of course," said Archie. "It's extraordinary! But I know I've seen it in many films."

"You got it, this set was used extensively in *The Dukes of Hazzard*, and in *Mayberry, R.F.D*. It's basically an ideal little village center. The city street behind it has been used in literally hundreds of movies—it can be dressed up or dressed down as a big city or a small town, or even a foreign city. We've got some hitching posts lined up there, and they can be replaced with parking meters. Pollyanna, anyone?"

Emmanuel twirled around to indicate a white clapboard house at the corner of the shady street.

"That is Pollyanna's house. Notice that all the houses on this street are different styles—they can be used for street scenes or individually for very different types of movies. Look at this old thing!" He led us past a spooky old gray wreck, like an abandoned version of Pollyanna's house.

"What has that been in?" asked one of the Germans.

"God, I'm drawing a blank on that, but, basically in horror movies?" Emmanuel nodded.

Everyone stared slightly because of his pronunciation: whore movies.

"Ah, *horror* movies," I clarified, giving it almost three syllables, and everyone relaxed slightly.

We followed Emmanuel through the behind-the-scenes areas: props, a soundstage, and the rows of trailers that actors used on sets.

"I wonder why they film so much inside, with all this beautiful sunshine," said one of the Germans.

"Whoops! Don't want too much sunshine—not always, anyway!" said Emmanuel, still gamely walking backward through the narrow streets between electrical and furniture workshops. "*My Fair Lady* with Audrey Hepburn and Rex Harrison was filmed here, all on soundstages. Every single shot was in studio—not one outdoor set was used."

"But when Jeremy Brett sings 'On the Street Where You Live,' " protested Archie.

"Soundstage. Gotcha!"

"Then there's the Ascot race."

"That is the one segment of film shot outdoors, but not here—that was a clip of actual Ascot footage used as an establishing shot, to set the scene. The rest of the race scenes were shot on soundstages. We couldn't have London covered with California sunshine, even in a musical comedy! We're heading for the garage now."

"Brilliant," said Archie.

The Germans trailed behind slightly. I heard them mutter the word "camera," and I gathered that they were still resentful about the no-camera policy. There was no clear reason for it to be in effect. What harm was there in photographing a back lot that had already been seen in a hundred episodes of *Batman*? Perhaps it was because the tour was available even when filming was in progress, and possibly no photography was allowed then. On the other hand, it was a great gimmick. Anywhere you were not allowed to take a camera had the cachet of being a place you were very privileged to be.

We strolled through the long rectangular sheds like airplane hangars that covered most of the huge lot. Some, Emmanuel was saying, contained soundstages; others, paint shops, wood shops, and storage. These made you reflect that it is a tribute to the magic of the movies that people will come halfway around the world to hike through a largely empty industrial space and tiptoe around as if in a museum, to peek at still lives like "Pollyanna House Facade" and *"Mayberry, R.F.D.* Flowerbed," or to listen to a guide's recitation—like Emmanuel's now to the rapt San Franciscans—about the intricacies of ADR, or automatic dialogue replacement, the process of re-recording muddled live dialogue in a sound studio.

Driving down Ventura Boulevard, I had been struck by the absence of statues, cathedrals, or any of the other public monuments that cities put up to advertise their civic or religious heritage. More than any other part of Los Angeles, the Valley is relentlessly commercial, utilitarian, and private. And yet here were a group of travelers paying their respects to an even duller collection of settings because of what they had once been—briefly, at that. The history they commemorated was not even real, but pretend. No, I corrected that thought: these visitors were not walking slowly, meditatively, and happily down this alley because Eliza Doolittle had been here, but because Audrey Hepburn had. It was the same little leap of faith or the imagination that sent people to look at Torrance High School because it was used in exterior shots as West Beverly High on the TV series *Beverly Hills 90210,* or the house on Lonzo Street in suburban Tujunga where *E.T.* was filmed. These ecumenical shrines force you to use your imagination, but not for very long; you stare at them for long enough to feel you have really been there, and the rest of the fun is in telling people you have seen it. No wonder some studios had introduced rides.

"This is the garage," Emmanuel announced.

The garage, like the furniture and prop departments we had looked in on, was bustling with activity. Some men seemed to be nonchalantly buzz-sawing a car in half.

"This is where we keep cars used in television shows and movies," said Emmanuel. He went on to explain that cars tended to be rented or leased, since it was too expensive to garage too many of them at once. Anyway, many of the vehicles used in movies and television episodes are needed for only a short time. "Here are some of the exceptions!"

There was a row of cars, some covered with tarpaulins, along the wall, and two tarpaulin-swathed hulks behind a high chain-link enclosure at the far end. Some of the cars had current registrations.

"Any of you recognize this one?" Emmanuel flung the tarp off a long maroon Hudson from at least the early 1950s but in perfect condition, shining like a maroon mirror despite its age.

"*Driving Miss Daisy,*" said the Germans in unison. The car had an old black California license plate, 615 TDX.

"That Dodge is from *The Dukes of Hazzard,* said Mary Rose.

"Right," Emmanuel congratulated her. "Are you ready for this?" He led us across to the chain-link fence and we peeked through as he reached inside it and threw aside one of the tarpaulins.

"Two Batmobiles!" said Mary Rose's husband.

"From the 1990 Warner Brothers picture directed by Tim Burton," said Emmanuel.

The two glossy black Batmobiles were a sea of curves and fins, and the expanse of rumpled black tarpaulins gave the impression that the two bizarre vehicles were in bed together in decadent black sheets. Emmanuel draped them again.

"What happened to the original Batmobile, from the television series?"

"There were more than a dozen of the old Batmobiles used for the series. Unfortunately we don't have any of them here on the lot. They all belong to a single collector."

"He bought all of them?" asked a German.

"He bought them all. He's a very special collector."

"Sounds like a nutter," murmured Archie.

We moved along to the lighting warehouse, where shelves groaned under thousands of lamps and gigantic chandeliers hung from the rafters.

"None of them are catalogued," Emmanuel informed us. "When someone's making a picture, they just come in and shop around and take what they want. They check it out, just like getting a book from the library. Of course, not too many library books cost a thousand dollars to rent!"

We browsed briefly down the aisle, mostly looking up at the Victorian chandeliers. They were gigantic, and very polished, but it still felt like a glorified Goodwill store, or a warehouse—perhaps that of the evil magician of the Aladdin story who peddled "new lamps for old." Most of our group plainly were giving this stop the lowest mark until Emmanuel announced, "Now for our treasures!"

He led the way around a bank of shelves glittering with candelabra and crystal-drop lampshades and pointed up to two large bronze Moroccan-style hanging lamps.

"Casablanca," said one of the Hanses reverently.

Everyone gazed up at these fat bronze globes that stood out from the glassy junk that hung around them. They were pointed like Christmas ornaments at the bottom, with tops like bronze turnips and triple chains linking the crown to the rounded sides scored with S-shaped slits like delicate stained-glass windows, and hundreds of pointillistic Moorish perforations. Planned or not, this was the holy moment of the tour, and Archie, who had exuded the air of a pilgrim throughout the whole tour, now looked even more prayerful than usual.

"These are the lamps from Rick's Bar in *Casablanca,* Warner Brothers, 1942, with Humphrey Bogart, Ingrid Bergman, Paul Henreid, Sydney Greenstreet, and Peter Lorre. Jack L. Warner, executive producer. They are not rented out for moviemaking any more."

"It's incredible," said Mary Rose. "I can just see Ingrid Bergman coming into Rick's Bar under those lamps."

" 'I am shocked—shocked!—to find that gambling is going on in here!' " Archie mimicked Claude Rains.

" 'Play *"La Marseillaise"*!' " Dana commanded.

"My favorite line is 'Round up the usual suspects,' " smiled Emmanuel. "Although these chandeliers are not used in filmmaking, there is some talk of using them in a little restaurant here on the lot. It isn't built yet—it might be a café modeled on the one from *Casablanca,* for studio staff and visitors like yourselves to have coffee or sandwiches."

"Was *Casablanca* filmed on this lot?" I asked.

Emmanuel rolled his eyes ever so briefly to show that he knew this one by heart.

"Basically, movies are shot on so many soundstages that no one can remember where each little thing happened. *Casablanca* was shot on Stage Five and Stage Nine. I think Nine was Rick's Bar. What about the airport scene? Some movie buffs say it was shot at Glendale Airport, some say it was Van Nuys. Both are here in the Valley. Actually, the airport scene was shot at Van Nuys Airport, which during the war was called Marshall Airfield. That is, Conrad Veidt's arrival, the scene with Major Strasser's coming in to take charge in *Casablanca,* was shot on the tarmac there."

"And the ending scene with Rick and Ilsa, when Captain Renault says, 'Round up the usual suspects,' " Mary Rose reminded him.

"That was done on a soundstage," said Emmanuel, with just a trace of singsong and another roll of the eyes. "It was shot on Stage One, with midgets in the background to give the impression of distance and depth."

" 'I came to Casablanca for the waters,' " said Archie.

"I hope they build that café," said Mary Rose's husband.

" 'What's your nationality?' 'I'm a drunkard,' " recited one of the Hanses.

"I don't know. They don't make changes very fast around here," explained Emmanuel. "Like, there's been talk of some kind of amusements here, like a park, basically, with rides, but basically we're more interested in a technical tour for movie and television lovers."

"I think that would be a distinct loss, frankly, to lose what you have got here," said Archie.

Emmanuel began to lead us away, but no one followed him. I had the thought that the fabulous lamps should be installed in the café as soon as possible, so that there could be some satisfying little ritual of pilgrimage that involved having a meal and spending money under them. As it was, given the inability to take pictures, a spiritual void remained unfilled. We needed to do something else: drop a coin in a grate, light a candle, make a wish, buy something, or genuflect. The fact that this greatest of Hollywood romances and all its Moroccan and Parisian ambience had been created in these massive corrugated-steel sheds took a great deal of time to think about.

We wandered reluctantly out into the sun and hiked to another long, high shed.

The interior newsroom soundstage of *Lois and Clark* should have been a thrill, but came as letdown after the two legendary lamps. Everyone looked casually around this one set we were allowed to explore, but seemed lost in memories of French Morocco. The tour wound down quickly, with a stop at the gift shop—Mary Rose bought a videocassette of *Casablanca*—and that was that.

"I wouldn't have minded seeing a star," said Mary Rose's husband. Maybe that was why he had been so quiet. Did he feel let down?

"You have some cool stars who live in San Francisco, including Robin Williams and Whoopi Goldberg," Emmanuel said, and the husband shrugged.

"Well, they'll have to do, because we're going back tonight," said Mary Rose.

We were back in the square from which we had set out,

with the theater facade, and obediently boarded the little touring cart parked at the curb. In no time we were back at the VIP tour office, and by the time everyone had retrieved his camera the conversation had turned to Los Angeles—how awful it was. They automatically excluded me and Mr. Cracknell, who in any case was preoccupied, futilely quizzing Emmanuel about the career of Inge Stevens.

"I can't believe this air. I can feel my throat getting hot."

"This is such an inhuman city. I could never live here," said one of the Germans.

"Well, it's not really a city at all. It's like a collection of cities. It has no heart—in all senses of the word."

"You sense a kind of shallowness."

"I'd like to get out of here before I feel the earth move," said Mary Rose.

Everyone had just spent a lovely afternoon spying on the back room of a major Hollywood studio, and yet could make remarks like these. The riots and earthquakes had them scared, though they had not gone near any riot zones. A San Franciscan was afraid of the earth moving here? And the shallowness of LA was deeply troubling—this from a German who had spent the whole afternoon in a snit because he didn't have his camera to photograph a Batmobile.

"I wanted to see the Watts Towers," Mary Rose said.

"You should have," I said. "I'm sure you would have liked them."

"Well, we were mostly interested in movie-related sites."

"A scene from *White Men Can't Jump* was filmed there," I pointed out, but Mary Rose made a face.

"I don't think they like people who look like us down there," she said meaningfully.

"We wanted to see the Olympiad village from the 1984

games, but no one knows where it is. It seems the sites were scattered," said one of the Germans.

"That was before I lived here, but I think that's true. The fencing and some of the swimming events were in Long Beach. But most of the big events were at the USC Coliseum. Did you go there?"

"It's a very dangerous area," he said, frowning.

"But that's where the Museum of Natural History is, and the Museum of Science and Technology. You should really see it." They shook their heads. "So what will you go to see next?"

"San Francisco," they said together, and this got them into a new huddle with Mary Rose and her husband.

At least Archie was not leaving LA in a hurry. He actually had a notepad with his day's itinerary. He was off to West Hollywood to drive up Mount Lee to get above the Hollywood sign. As we strolled to the parking lot with a wave to Mary Rose, Dana, and the Hanses, he looked appreciatively around at the tall palms outside the studio walls and enumerated his business.

"I shall try to photograph Madonna's house for my granddaughter. They say it's painted orange—shouldn't be too hard to spot, do you think? Then I'm going to find Blue Jay Way. George Harrison named a Beatles song after it. I have the directions. And I'm joining an old New York friend in Santa Monica for cocktails and dinner."

"It's almost rush hour," I warned him. "You might find it pretty slow."

"The Ventura Freeway shouldn't be too bad, though I will get a move on."

Clearly Archie had no problem cruising around LA. I admired him for taking the place in stride. As he doubled up to back into his little car, I asked him whether he would be going to one of Santa Monica's famous English pubs.

"Oh, my dear no. I should think my friend would take me somewhere posher than that," he said, starting the car and switching on the radio. "He's trying to get me to move here."

I wished him luck and unlocked my car. "I suppose it's easy to get residence if you're retired?"

"I'm American. From my New York days," he said with an ambiguous smile, then cocked an ear to KFWB FM. "Sigalert on the Ventura westbound. Oh, blast. Cheers!"

12

The Flextrain

"**G**oodbye, LA," sang the white-haired woman with feeling as she boarded the white-and-plum-colored train on Platform 8 of Union Station.

"You can say that again," added two of the three women she was with, who cackled at having said the same thing as they helped one another up the stairs to the train car. And they all did seem delighted to be leaving, though none looked as though she was going very far; all they had in their net and straw bags was novels and knitting. Then again, well-dressed southern California women wearing straw hats and Ferragamo shoes and pearls and without face-lifts would not be carrying their own luggage; it probably had been stowed before they even got to the platform.

This was not an Amtrak train but Metrolink, LA's new metropolitan rail system. It is chiefly a commuter system, but this was not very much of a commuter run. At this time of day, in the midday sun, no more than five or six of the dozens of passengers boarding the high double-decker train were wearing a suit or carrying a briefcase. Most passengers were dressed in flashy summer clothes and talking excitedly, like tourists or people leaving for good. But what tourist would be going to the inland desert city of Riverside? I saw the mixed group as a snapshot of people on their way out for good, or LA exiles heading back home to the Inland Empire, once a desert region, then a vast orchard of oranges and grapes, and now the latest affordable bolthole for families moving out of the city.

Two men with camera bags walked down the platform and boarded. Two black families boarded, four adults with six children. The adults had shoulder bags. Like the women, they climbed the steps to the train's upper deck, following their children, who had raced up the carpeted stairs without looking back.

This did not surprise me. I knew that in the ten years between 1980 and 1990, when the black population of south LA dropped 20 percent, the black population of Riverside—the destination of this train—had doubled to nearly 60,000. San Bernardino County to the north, an equal distance from LA, had seen its black population grow from about 46,000 to nearly 110,000. The black population of Moreno Valley, just east of Riverside, tripled in three years to more than 50,000. The exodus from Los Angeles was multivarious, and the Inland Empire was the fastest-growing black area in the western United States.

Four Korean men boarded. I had seen them in front of Union Station, holding napkins and munching on bars of *calabaza* and *chilacayote,* the pumpkin and watermelon candy sold across the way on Olvera Street. I had bought a little block of cactus candy, *biznaya,* and a *bandera de coco,* a coconut bar in the colors of the Mexican flag. Despite being near the four-level interchange of the Harbor and Hollywood freeways, this part of downtown LA was human in scale, and nothing like the titanic skyscraper-darkened downtown a few blocks to the west. The interior of the old Spanish colonial railway terminus was an adobe, wood, and leather cathedral of travel, with its mixture of Streamline Moderne, Art Deco, Southwestern, Moorish, and Beaux Arts styles. Across Alameda Street was the Old Plaza, the Queen of Angels Church, and Olvera Street. At midday, Olvera and the shady plaza adjacent are full of tourists and downtown workers eating lunch in the checkered shade and listening to mariachi bands. It is as if the train station were put into this setting just to make you sorry to be leaving LA.

Union Station is the centerpiece of $15.5 billion in public investment to link all of greater LA—now spilling over five counties—by rail. Optimism in the whole project was boosted by the success of the Metro Blue Line. In its first three years, Blue Line ridership tripled, from 13,000 per day in 1990 to 38,500 in 1993. When the downtown's first Red Line segment opened in 1993, it added 4,000 riders per day. The whole train system had been the scene of just three muggings in all that time, though 32,000 tickets had been issued for fare evasion. The $1.10 fare is on the honors system: there are no turnstiles or ticket-takers, but the citation is $104. Scofflaws may have raised more than $3 million for the Sheriff's Department.

Metrolink and Metrorail now connect downtown Los Angeles with two eastern desert cities, Riverside and San Bernardino, with two almost parallel lines that also parallel heavily used freeways, the 10 and the 60. To the northwest, the plum-and-white trains serve Glendale and Burbank; a fork there leads north to Santa Clarita and west to Moorpark in Ventura County. Success with the Blue Line from Long Beach encouraged Metrolink to believe that it would reach its goal of 250,000 riders per day even before the target year, 2010. Part of the reason the goal should be reached is the growth of LA's far-flung suburbs. In the late 1980s, Santa Clarita and Ontario, on the Riverside line, took turns being the fastest-growing cities in the country. Santa Clarita had always been a popular bedroom community, but grew so quickly that when it incorporated as LA's newest city in December 1987, it had the largest population of any newly incorporated city in American history: 147,000 people. Their linkage by train was a blast from the past—before the automobile, all of Los Angeles had been served by cable cars, streetcars, trolleys, and trains, especially the Big Red Cars. It was happening again, only on a much larger scale.

The conductor let out a blast on his whistle, and I boarded the train almost as it began to roll. It pulled out with a sense of purpose. Like the city's Blue and Red Line trains, Metrolink did not go clackety-clack, not even softly. It glided, very slowly at first, away from the platform and into a northeastern curve. I went to the upper level, where most of the passengers were sitting.

"It feels like the Orient Express," said one of the foursome of women. I had no way of knowing but thought not. Perhaps the international character of the passengers made her think so, but instead of acting mysterious everyone was full of Californian good humor, smiling and chatting and pointing out the window at the LA County Central Jail Facility sliding by on the right: a dozen sleek, stocky stories that might have been an unmarked Hilton, except for its oblique gun-slit windows. Except for the primly dressed group of women, everyone was wearing the southern California uniform of shorts, sneakers, and T-shirt. The Koreans were riffling through the Metrolink timetable folder and speaking Korean with some English words thrown in, mostly the names of destinations. "Pedley," one man said, and the youngest man added, "Penultimate Pedley!"

"Well, we finally got a move on," said the white-haired woman.

As we left downtown Los Angeles, a low red-brick public housing project sprang into view on the left. The word DOG- TOWN had been spray-painted hundreds of times over its roofs and walls and the concrete barrier separating it from the train tracks. Behind the project were gentle green hills: Mount Washington and Elysian Park, in which nestled Chavez Ravine, the home of Dodger Stadium. In the foreground, the project's neighbor was a huge yard filled with truck-sized square bales of compacted paper waste for recycling. Off to the right towered the white stone County-USC Medical Center, as high and stylized as a designer Alp. The train straightened out moving southeast, picking up speed through LA's backyard: cold-storage buildings for produce, furniture warehouses, and truck fleet yards.

A white eight-legged water tower to the right was labeled "City of Vernon" in blue paint. It somehow gave the distinct impression of having once stood amid farmlands, but now looked out over railyards and low warehousing and factories. On the outskirts of tiny Vernon were rows of little white adobe houses with blue trim. The walls had only scattered graffiti (STONERS X LOCOS), but before I could spot any more the end of that little suburbia came with a gigantic lot of Entenmann's-Orowheat bread trucks.

I had no sense of leaving Los Angeles, not after having left the Los Angeles River behind or even now, crossing the Rio Hondo in Montebello, dark emerald and flat in its concrete bed. Even though the huge scale of Los Angeles is apparent throughout the city, you cannot go very far north, west, or south without coming up against its natural boundaries: mountains or ocean. Heading east, the city never ends, and instead of the ocean there are fifty-nine varieties of stagnant water. The gutters of these grimy edge towns had big puddles: LA's Biblical seven years of drought had recently ended with torrential rains in the city and mountains. It was good news for LA's major source of drinking water. The eastern Sierra snowpack had gone from half of normal to 140 percent above normal. But the precipitation that buried the Sierra mountaintops in thirty-five feet of snow had filled Montebello with green puddles. We passed another riverbed, the San Gabriel, jungly with slimy vegetation. And as we approached the Puente Hills, the small square backyard pools were green with algae. Only the tall buildings of the city disappear, not development—there is barely an unbuilt patch. And there was a lot of truck traffic. The trees here were higher than the houses, and the transcontinental freight trucks were higher than the trees.

"And she said, 'I gave myself to the Lord when I was five years old,' " one of the women was saying. "And *on* and *on* and *on* till I practically threw up!"

"I didn't get that part, but I surely will remember her as the UCLA graduate who doesn't even know what a linking verb is!" said one of her traveling companions. From the time the train had left Union Station, all four of them had been making needling remarks about LA. I had tuned them out when we passed the DOGTOWN-covered housing project, which drew the predictable comments about how people didn't value what they got for free, and "this town"—that always meant LA—was full of people getting something for nothing. None of the women's remarks had earned any response from the other three, so I assumed they had heard it all from one another many times before. I gathered that three were Los Angeles natives—one had mentioned that she was afraid to go back to the neighborhood where she was born, and two had chimed in to second the motion—and the fourth I guessed to be a Southerner. Between japes at the tackiness of Los Angeles, she was vainly trying to recount a lovely *loonch* she had once enjoyed at the *Hat* (Hyatt, I supposed) on Sunset.

"But I wouldn't go back to that area, either," she finally concluded.

Clearly LA had become, for many people, just another New York, a large-scale experiment that was going badly wrong, someplace to desert and talk about behind its back. Even before the riots, the polluted air, bad traffic, and expensive houses were driving people out. Net migration into LA from other parts of the United States went from about 200,000 persons per year in 1990 to zero in 1991, with a net loss of 50,000 per year in 1992. More than half of the 750,000 jobs California had lost since 1990—at least 400,000—had been Los Angeles County's loss. A thousand manufacturing firms had left since 1980. The orange groves are long gone, the real estate bubble has burst, the two generations of high-tech war industries have ended, and more movies are made outside of Hollywood than in it. The LA press was constantly selling the idea that you had to be out of your mind to stay here or move here. The population of the city of Los Angeles itself was actually falling.

"Our first stop will be the City of Industry. City of Industry," the speaker crackled.

I glanced through the Metrolink and subway brochures I had picked up in Union Station. In typically friendly LA fashion, the men at the information window don't merely hand you brochures and free Metrolink refrigerator magnets, they gladly escort you to the ticket machine and help you buy your ticket. Also in typical LA fashion, the bilingualism of the brochures is Spanish-friendly to the point of being totally unhelpful. They had translated the street names. Did they really think that using names like Calle 1 and Calle 2 would help Spanish-speaking travelers identify signs reading First Street and Second Street?

We had still not reached open country. Except for a glimpse of a lost-looking couple in cowboy hats on horseback, we had seen nothing but smog-shrouded mountains to the north. For miles, both sides of the tracks had been choked with large commercial buildings displaying uninformative light-industry names like Zezex or CompuFan or AccuDrive. Beyond these businesses was the hump of an occasional hill, either in its natural state or in the process of being leveled. One was half flattened with six bulldozers parked on the flat half.

No one got off at City of Industry, and the stop was so brief that by the time I noticed the sprawling Brea Canyon Business Park, and the fact that one of its industrial storefront premises was occupied by a church, the train's brakes sneezed and we were rolling again.

We left Los Angeles County behind a few minutes later, and almost immediately encountered an endless vista of parked cars.

This was the Ontario airport. The town was christened by

two nineteenth-century Canadian pioneers, William and George Chaffey, for their native province. This was the latest urban center of greater Los Angeles—another of LA's "multiple urban cores," with a six-city population of nearly half a million people. It took our train nearly a full minute to slide past the airport, which is something of a monument and omen. Ontario is a little LA in the making thanks to this airport, which already handles more air traffic than Orange County Airport and is scheduled to expand to the size of San Francisco International by 2003.

The sprawl of Los Angeles is a fact of life in southern California, but it is probably the key to its future, too. Unlike conventional cities, LA applies no stigma to living far from the center. The weather is just as lovely in San Dimas or Whittier as in Beverly Hills. Sprawl doesn't carry you out into the boondocks—it carries you up the coast, into the mountains, or into the desert. The city has always grown like a griddle of sloppy pancakes. After pulling together its contiguous neighborhoods, annexing Hollywood, dribbling southward for a seaport, and swallowing Venice and the Valley, Los Angeles achieved its final shape: a Rorschach blot. Population growth came around the edges, within commuter striking distance. In the 1950s and 1960s, the rural San Fernando Valley to the north was the quietest refuge for Angelenos disillusioned by the city's hill and basin growth, and it was the most affordable place for young families starting out as pioneer suburbanites. When all LA was full, southerly Orange County became the next province of the Empire of Los Angeles. This was growth in terms of demography, not annexation, but for all practical purposes, every blob of the spreading blot was part of LA. Now the movement is headed east, where there are no limits but the Arizona border.

"East Ontario, East Ontario," the conductor announced as we rolled past the last of the Ontario airport's packed parking lots.

This really did look like the Inland Empire. East Ontario was a lonely prairie up to the foothills of the San Gabriels, imperial in its emptiness, which advertised only possibility. The train we were riding, I reflected, was tantamount to the arrival of the forty-four original *pobladores* who had straggled into the tiny village of Yangna in 1781 and begotten Los Angeles. Perhaps the Steer 'n Stein restaurant in this mini-mall near the train tracks—it was the only business I could see—would be the centerpiece of the Inland Empire's Olvera Street of the twenty-third century.

It is only a half hour's drive north from this shimmering flatland to the Cajon Pass, where the Mojave Freeway squeezes between the San Gabriel and San Bernardino mountain ranges to reveal the Mojave Desert, which is very likely LA's next commuter suburb, or at least a commuter moon in Riverside's orbit.

No one got off the train. I reminded myself that these were not commuters, and that our destination was, after all, Riverside.

"Ooooh-akh!" One of the Koreans let out an almost operatic yawn that ended in a bark. He folded his arms and squinted at the back page of the newspaper the fellow across from him was reading, which displayed a large photograph of a merchant standing in front of a liquor store. He then turned to his seatmate and spoke to him in a tone that suggested the imparting of valuable advice. I caught the word *sa-i-gu*. This was one of the few Korean words slowly entering the LA lexicon: it meant April 29, the first of the three days of the famous riots; Korean generally reference memorable days by their date. He must have been saying, "You won't be sorry we moved out here. April 29 rolls around next year, too!"

The depot at Pedley—it actually was the penultimate stop on the Riverside line—was still under construction. There were the signs of a little town to the south, but the other side of the tracks was adorned only by one grassy slope and one small white clapboard house. The unfinished Metro lot contained parking for about 250 cars and was dotted with old-fashioned Belle Epoque lampposts with lights like drooping daffodils. Someone must already have determined that when Riverside became the LA of the Inland Empire, with its international (Ontario has one daily flight to Mexico) airport at a respectable distance, Pedley would be the Charming Suburb. The Santa Ana River flows just to the south of it, through a golf course. Developers had probably already discussed how future Pedleyites would be saying, "Yes, we're just a step from the airport, and a minute from Riverside, and"—I checked my watch—"exactly one hour from downtown Los Angeles."

No one got off at Pedley either. The parking lot was mostly empty, and no one was waiting for the train. The only people in sight were construction workers in hard hats and T-shirts with trowels, leveling new concrete on the sidewalk with cake-icing movements.

"Next stop Riverside, our final stop," intoned the conductor.

"Go wash your hands," one of the fathers told his daughter, and began to collect some of the candy wrappers and crayons that the children had been playing with. He lifted himself off the seat for a second to retrieve a crayon from under his thigh. Here was a reminder that the movement to the Inland Empire from LA was no white flight: I had read that 43 percent of its new residents were black, Latino, and Asian. It was the settling of the Valley or Orange County all over again, only in a multicultural fashion. Perhaps by the time the Mojave was covered with driveways and lawn sprinklers, it would be mostly black and Latino; perhaps they would be bad-mouthing the Inland Empire and congratulating themselves for having got out of Pedley and bought early in Mojave.

This was the certain future of LA: it would just keep growing, and few people would ever completely leave. Like Hollywood, it would always be a state of mind as much as a place. Even if the spell stopped working on Americans, its effect on foreigners would last far longer. Almost any schoolchild in LA can tell you that in 1992, 200,000 legal and more than 100,000 illegal immigrants settled in California. These accounted for 85 to 90 percent of California's population growth for the year. Fewer than half of LA's 641,000 schoolchildren speak English fluently. Top languages other than English are Spanish, Chinese, Tagalog, Korean, Japanese, Vietnamese, French, German, Arabic, and Italian. For myself, I had the rosy vision of a city breeding a generation of translators and interpreters, but there was the other view, with its grain of truth, that feared balkanization, Babel, nationalism, and other tragic Old World conditions.

Coming on top of the riots, these facts were great rhetoric fodder. Completing the trifecta of pessimism is some of LA's silly social engineering, including the idiotic school district rule that all children entering public school illiterate (as almost all kindergartners do) must be taught in their own language, not English. LA's pessimists failed to realize that such rules were unenforceable, and subverted by parents who were desperate for their families to learn English. My tutoring had taught me that, and more. I knew in the truest but most casual way that 99 percent of the city had not rioted, that foreigners moving to LA wanted to be Americans and often just did not know how.

It was when the riots were followed by the double earthquakes that it crossed my mind to leave Los Angeles. Like the riots themselves, my half-serious interest in getting out was motivated by spite. I temporarily thought that LA should suffer without me, but the militant bitterness and gloating of Angelenos who were planning their moves to Las Vegas or Seattle (where people never wanted to lay their eyes on another fleeing Californian) got on my nerves and made me change my mind. LA had opened its doors to me, and I was at home. It always felt like a new place, with its resentment of East Coast superciliousness—which exists to a considerable extent only in the golden Californian imagination. The mix of old nationalities in this young city was one of its best features—its nagging obsession with their origins, instead of their destination, was one of its worst features, but not an offensive one. The main trouble was LA's failing to ask itself why so many tribes had gathered here; the answer was that westward-moving liberal civilization that had chased gold and the sun to this coast. I had spent my life in great cities that boasted of being crossroads of the world. LA is something better, a destination par excellence, the place that is as far as you can go.

The rioters' stamina and lack of embarrassment gave me pause more than anything else. It advertised their contempt for the city and themselves, and a certain measure of helplessness: if they could not live here, they could not live anywhere, and they knew that better than anyone. Some riot victims may have moved out of LA as time went by, but it is reasonably safe to assume that it has never occurred to the looters to leave.

The antidote to my spiteful if short-lived impulse to leave LA was the self-righteous Third World response to the civil disturbances—even to the earthquakes, seen in some Middle Eastern quarters as a further scourge of God. Thanks to the translating I did to earn my living, I knew that Egypt, Iran, Nigeria, and Lebanon had had riots or demonstrations around the same time as the LA riots. Some were for almost the same reasons. In Mashhad, Iran, thousands of Afghani refugees rioted the same week as the LA riots to protest economic and ethnic discrimination—three hundred people were killed, six times as many as in Los Angeles. No one said that Iran was going to hell in a handbasket, because the dishonest Iranian government did not broadcast the events. Los Angeles was the opposite, one of the world's most watched and least known places, frantic to understand and to market even its bad news. In this it was the opposite of a Third World city. Who knew which sort of place was the city of the future—what mattered to me was that LA was the city of *my* future.

The earthquakes, though, had a way of standing the world on its head. Landers and Big Bear had produced short-lived terror, but the Northridge earthquake brought terror, death, hardship, changed lives, and a true fear of the future. LA has always lived on optimism, and is a total stranger to that most Old World of sentiments, resignation. The 6.6 smasher of freeways and hospitals went much farther than the riots in revealing a twisted mess of denial, shortsightedness, and fear; it introduced parts of the city to profound insecurity and pessimism. For me, it was like watching a careful and sensitive translation collapse into a heap of Scrabble tiles.

It was understandable, of course. Charles Darwin had written of "the perfect horror of earthquakes" after experiencing one in Valdivia, Chile, in 1835. "A bad earthquake at once destroys our oldest associations," he wrote in *The Voyage of the Beagle*. "The earth, the very emblem of solidity, has moved beneath our feet like a thin crust over a fluid;—one second of time has created in the mind a strange idea of insecurity, which hours of reflection would not have produced."

And yet here we all were. The city was once again being repaired and prepared, and the gentle weather seemed to promise that God had not meant it after all. The rails under this Metrolink train were part of the way out of LA's seismic tribulations: when freeways collapsed, the train system took on much of the commuter burden, and new lines were immediately extended to Lancaster and Palmdale, an aerospace suburb located just yards from the San Andreas Fault.

The sight of actual suburbs with bright green lawns derailed my train of thought. This approach to Riverside was no longer grape and orange country, but still looked lush. As the train slowed, it became clear that most of the securely walled neighborhoods consisted of tract housing. However, the houses, mostly white with arches and red tile roofs, looked roomy and expensive. There were parks every few streets, and a tall brown peak looming behind, probably mile-high Cajon Mountain.

No one was waiting for the train when it pulled into Riverside, but this was the end of the line, and everyone piled out. The men in suits jogged down the steps, already fishing for their car keys, heading for the vast parking lot and fanning out to their cars. The rest of us stood by the small gateway to the platform, which was nothing but a long sidewalk level with the tracks. There was no station. There was no movement to unload luggage from the train. The children ran around playing tag, and everyone else stretched or yawned, admiring the fresh paint of the massive train. Two of the four women pulled cameras out of their straw bags, but no one took a picture.

"Doesn't look like much," the Southern woman said.

To the north, the Jurupa Mountains were barely visible in the Empire's furnace-hot smog. Riverside had once been a spa famous for its orange groves and clean, dry desert air, but in the 1950s its worsening air pollution started killing orange crops. As in Los Angeles, the air stayed bad only because of the growing population. Emissions themselves were getting better: in 1966, each southern California car emitted 100 pounds of hydrocarbons; in 1976 the figure was 30, and in 1991 it was 13.2. There was virtually no lead in the air now. It was nitrogen dioxide and ozone—and dust—that were blocking the Jurupas. Unlike the rest of the Metrolink passengers waiting for their rides, I would head back into LA to breathe air that, though it used to be worse, is still the worst in America.

"All aboard for Los Angeles in ten minutes!" called the conductor, checking the tickets of some teenagers with suitcases who had turned up for the LA run. Now there was some picture-taking, smiles and posing. Here was an optimistic if glib LA metaphor: a little throng of young and old shading their eyes with their hands and chatting companionably with one another on the platform where the train to Los Angeles was about to chuff away. Some of the Korean and African-American family members were even holding hands, though not with each other. The Koreans turned around and re-boarded the train. I had only taken the train out here to see what Metrolink was like, but why had they changed their minds? They weren't even day-trippers; we had spent barely twenty minutes in Riverside.

"This is the last train out of here. The flextrain," the conductor explained when I commented that some passengers weren't spending very long in Riverside. "The trains run from about five o'clock in the morning until seven-thirty at night, but if you ride between eight-thirty in the morning and three-thirty in the afternoon, you get twenty-five percent off your ticket."

That could not have been to encourage staggered working hours, except for people who had very short workdays, or who were taking it one-way. Perhaps some of the passengers were like me, just taking a quick two-way ride for fun, as on the old Balloon Route that had provided trips to Santa Monica decades ago. There must have been a certain adventure, for people living in Riverside, in taking the choo-choo train in and out of beautiful Union Station, with just enough time to buy some *dulce de tamarindo* and listen to the mariachis. I was already looking forward to the curves, arches, and warmth of the station, where I would have a martini at the bar before riding the red and blue cars back to the fresh air of Long Beach.

I boarded the LA train, went to the upper deck, and found a seat near the top of the stairs in time to look out the window and see that not some but all of those on the platform were heading back to the massive cars. We were all flextrain tourists, excited by a one-hour train ride to nowhere, where we could stretch our legs for twenty minutes. The white-haired woman was the last to board, and asked the conductor, "Can we get a move on?" as she puffed past him up the stairs.